GOOD INTENTIONS

ALERT
PRESS

Montréal, Québec, Canada
2014

GOOD INTENTIONS

Norms and Practices of Imperial Humanitarianism

The New Imperialism, Volume 4

Edited by
Maximilian C. Forte

ALERT PRESS

Montréal, Québec, Canada
2014

Library and Archives Canada Cataloguing in Publication

Good intentions : norms and practices of imperial humanitarianism /
edited by Maximilian C. Forte.
(The new imperialism ; volume 4)
Includes bibliographical references and index.

ISBN 978-0-9868021-5-7 (bound).--ISBN 978-0-9868021-4-0 (pbk.)
1. Humanitarian intervention. 2. Imperialism. I. Forte, Maximilian C.,
1967-, editor II. Series: New imperialism (Montréal, Québec) ; v. 4
JZ6369.G66 2014   341.5'84   C2014-905200-6

Front cover image: According to the official caption, this is US Navy Hospital Corpsman 2nd Class Porfirio Nino, from Maritime Civil Affairs Team 104, who practices speaking Kinyarwanda, one of the official languages of Rwanda, during a civil observation mission in Bunyamanza, Rwanda, August 7, 2009. (DoD photo by Senior Chief Mass Communication Specialist Jon E. McMillan, US Navy. Public domain.) This particular photograph was also used as the lead image for a 2011 presentation by AFRICOM titled, "United States Africa Command: The First Three Years". On the image the following words were superimposed: "'Umuntu Ngumuntu Ngamantu' I am a person through other people. My humanity is tied to yours.~ Zulu proverb"

Back cover image: According to the official caption, these are US Airmen assigned to the 23rd Equipment Maintenance Squadron, 75th Aircraft Maintenance Unit "downloading" an A-10C Thunderbolt II aircraft during an operational readiness exercise at Moody Air Force Base, Georgia, August 4, 2009. (DoD photo by Airman 1st Class Joshua Green, US Air Force. Public domain.)

© 2014 Alert Press
1455 de Maisonneuve Blvd., W.,
Montreal, Quebec, Canada, H3G-1M8
www.alertpress.net

Printed in Canada

CONTENTS

FIGURES

PREFACE

How do "good intentions" pave the road for empire? There is some confusion, especially in North America, that reflects the dominant ideological charter for interventionism abroad and increased moral regulation at home (that is, politics masked as morality), with one result being increased militarization in order to forever be at the ready to intervene. The confusion is deliberate by those doing the work of mystification, feigned by those who spin multiple simultaneous contradictions in order to distract and distort, and innocent on the part of those who trust experts and authorities. The confusion in question has multiple facets that take the form of various myths and inaccuracies: a) that the intentions are good, and thus they justify all actions taken, while expressions of anti-interventionism are to be judged as born of malice and ill-will; b) that the motivations have little to do with protecting or enhancing corporate power and neoliberal socio-economic restructuring; c) that our violence is civilized, while the violence of others is barbaric; d) that our political systems are democracies, while regimes rule others; e) that there really is no imperialism, and if there is then it is both eternal and a fundamental part of an unchanging human nature; f) that we must never stand idly by while others suffer (except, I would interject, for when it is suitable to our leaders, especially when we commit atrocities); g) that there is no basic, underlying political uniformity within our dominant political and media institutions; h) that we practice good governance, both transparent and accountable, without pandering to private interests; and, i) that we encourage and tolerate a broad range of views, and do not narrow down discourse to a select few allowable perspectives. These myths and a few more form part of the orthodoxy of what is now a post-liberal society.

It is thus with honour and pleasure that I present the salutary works of advanced research students who have dedicated themselves to questioning these dominant "truths," and who are also willing to share their work to better inform a wider public. The chapters presented here, in what is already the fourth volume in this series, stemmed from a seminar on the New Imperialism, offered in 2014 in the Department of Sociology and Anthropology at Concordia University in Montreal. Chapters went through several stages of planning, drafting and revision, and reflect theoretical, analytical, and empirical mastery of their respective subjects. Taken together, the chapters have multiple, valuable considerations and revelations to offer the reader.

Whether it is iatrogenic violence, voluntourism, the misappropriation of gay rights, or NGOs serving as the Trojan Horses of US dominance and neoliberal social reengineering, contributors to this volume expose and analyze the many ways in which the new imperialism involves partitioning the world into tutors and wards, saviours and victims. Underlying the seduction of imperial elite-lore are established modes of socialization and enculturation, ranging from the elaborate and persistent demonization of chief opponents of US empire to the lionization of military actors commonly rendered as heroes. Also scrutinized in this volume are the domestic social and political costs, reaching as far as the displacement of urban populations to make way for the expansion of the informatic industries of empire, paving the way for the unprecedented dominance of corporations in our daily lives.

A final question lingers in the background throughout this volume. How much longer will we continue to buy into projects proclaiming "good intentions"?

Imperial Abduction Lore and Humanitarian Seduction

✮ ✮ ✮ ✮ ✮

Maximilian C. Forte

> "I am serious about making sure we have the best relationship with the NGOs who are such a force multiplier for us, such an important part of our combat team". — US Secretary of State Colin L. Powell (2001)

> "The countries that cooperate with us get at least a free pass. Whereas other countries that don't cooperate, we ream them as best we can". — A senior US official specializing on Africa (quoted in Whitlock 2013/4/13)

Two of the most enduring beliefs, among at least the political elites and a substantial portion of the wider population in North America, are that military intervention abroad and all sorts of other less forceful interventions, are: (a) for the good of other societies, whose lives and whose very nature as human beings will experience progress as a result of our intervention; and, (b) that the security of the intervening society will thus be enhanced, while its global leadership will also be secured. These constitute *beliefs* akin to any other beliefs that anthropologists and sociologists have studied in the value systems of other, discrete populations: as beliefs they maintain contradictions without resolving them, and as beliefs they can thrive in the absence of serious questioning, and in the absence of empirical support. One main difference about these beliefs, however, is that situated as we are in North America, we do not require the minimalistic year-long ritual of "fieldwork" abroad in order to discover them: we are all already immersed in this value system, and have been all of our lives. So let us proceed to extricate ourselves and question what we have received.

We proceed not only by "studying up," but also studying horizontally in social terms (the society as we experience it directly), and introspectively (reflecting on the meanings of various codes we have been taught by parents, schools, the media, and what we then hold as if they had always been our very own). We can become aware of our own very deeply planted *faith* in the value and necessity of our interventions abroad when we find ourselves in situations where such beliefs are openly questioned, contested, or refuted. This is especially the case when we are faced with seemingly hard-line rejections of western interventionism: then, we invariably always ask, and we feel impelled to ask, "But aren't there times when we *should* intervene?" This is always the immediate default question, and one that not coincidentally also preserves our belief in our own special role in history, as the special people with the right answers, as special forces who have either the right or the duty to impose our solutions from the top down. We will even rewrite history to mandate the only allowed "positive" answers, so we tell each other that we intervened in World War II to put a stop to the Holocaust, and that our alleged "non-intervention" allowed Rwanda's "genocide" to happen (instead, see Philpot, 2014).

We believe that our right to safety or security is an absolute imperative. The ultimate default question/belief, behind or beyond this one, concerns our very nature as human beings — is it not an essential part of human nature to engage in war? Deconstructing such an ostensibly straightforward question takes time (and many others have done so), especially since the question elides violence with war, and war with empire, and renders both war and empire as "natural" and thus normal. At the same time this position assumes a single human nature that is everywhere the same, and always has been. It is interesting to witness that when our "culture" of interventionism suffers setbacks, we always beat a hasty retreat back to "nature".

Much of the same pattern of elision and naturalization occurs when it is assumed that either war and/or empire are essential to the maintenance of our ultimate security, and all human beings, we believe, assert their security through violence — never through cooperation, collaboration, solidarity or reciprocity. Under the constraints of what is ideologically amiable to the power elites, we thus toil at reimagining our most distant human ancestors as prototypical warrior capitalists. What makes all of this possible is *belief* — not that beliefs unilaterally determine the imperial system.

The Humanitarian Syndrome of Western Interventionism

The dominant ideology of US-led globalization since September 11, 2001, is one that configures society as existing in a state of emergency — one that constructs exceptional circumstances, where exceptional rules and exceptional self-representations prevail. A defining feature of this post-9/11 orientation is therefore one that frames perceptions or constructions of global disorder in terms of emergency and threats to security. As in the case of the pre-9/11 "neocon" classic, Robert Kaplan's "The Coming Anarchy" (1994/2), the ideological expressions of the state of exception as a normative framework for constructing practical action, gained not just currency but authority. In this framework, other people — especially in Africa — are problems. They are an immediate "threat" to themselves, and an eventual threat to "us". As Kaplan (1994/2) put it:

> "West Africa is becoming the symbol of worldwide demographic, environmental, and societal stress, in which criminal anarchy emerges as the real 'strategic' danger....West Africa provides an appropriate introduction to the issues, often extremely unpleasant to discuss, that will soon confront our civilization".

The "crisis" in West Africa, the causes of which Kaplan essentially sees as inherent to West Africa itself, is not just a mortal threat to West Africans, it is a security threat. Repeatedly Kaplan frames these issues in his essay in terms of "national security," the "core foreign-policy challenge" and the "strategic impact" of these African problems for the US. Here again we see the power of belief in holding at bay any acknowledgment of self-contradiction: if problems for the US can come from abroad, why is the same not true for West Africa? How is Kaplan's West African crisis *sui generis*, while any eventual crisis for the US is always of exogenous provenance? It is a very *useful* belief if anything: it preserves American exceptionalism by positing the innate inferiority of other societies. Moreover, it casts Americans as innocent and self-sufficient, and foreigners as menacing and dependent.

It follows logically that if these others are the problem — and a problem for us ultimately — *then we must be the solution.* Constructing other people's situations as problems, and the West as the source of solutions, has meant (a) the fusion of the military and humanitarian into a single form of governance (Fassin & Pandolfi, 2010, p. 10), and (b) a situation where we in the West renew our former colonial right to intervene against militarily and economically weaker states, now dubbed "failed states" (Helman & Ratner, 1992–1993; Gordon, 1997). In this process, both the sovereignty and self-determination of the formerly colonized, limited as they have been by the persistent realities of neocolonialism, have been challenged, eroded and deliberately undermined. The ideal way to justify this new wave of western interventions since the end of the Cold War has been "humanitarianism". Ideal, because this mode of justification can, (a) simultaneously pay some respect to international law (by revitalizing international law's colonial roots and making renewed use of the trusteeship model); (b) immobilize potential critics at home, lest they be accused of not wanting to "help" others and "save lives"; and, (c) using the language of salvation and freedom out of necessary recognition that the residue of the world's anti-colonial struggles of the 1960s would not tolerate an outright return to blunt statements of the West's "civilizing mission" (Mooers, 2006, p. 2).

Consequently, the narrative and practice of "humanitarianism" can serve as a new (possibly preemptive) counterinsurgency, on both the domestic and global levels, that seek to neutralize critiques, limit the range of acceptable options, build new civilian-military coalitions, overthrow noncompliant governments, and thus delay the decline of western hegemony. Humanitarianism may thus be very much a sign of a *late imperialism*.

While humanitarian notions of some sort have been expressed by almost every modern empire, off and on throughout the course of a given empire's existence, one should note however that the last two global hegemons, the UK and the US, both heightened the "humanitarian" ethos in the final decades of their imperial dominance. *Why?* There are a number of possible reasons. One is to shift the cost burden to a wider array of partners recruited by the politics of humanitarianism, partners both local and international, whether sovereign or among the collaborator class of the colonized, in order to preserve the expanse of empire while trying to manage its increasingly unaffordable costs. Also trying to ward off rising challengers is common to both the UK and US examples. "Everyone to the frontlines" might be the rallying call at this stage of increasing desperation—and one way to rope in everyone is to appeal to intimate values and emtions. Another is the attempt to minimize the costs of resistance by attempting to "win hearts and minds"—"we," after all, are undertaking all this trouble and expense just for "your" welfare. Such a narrative is possibly more successful at home than anywhere else: witness the countless right-wing media pundits in the US who speak as if they sincerely believe that US military forces launch expeditions primarily to help others—invasion as a form of charity. Another reason for the humanitarian turn may be the legacy factor, a last-ditch effort to rewrite history to preserve at least the symbolic capital of exceptionalism, to be converted into political capital as post-imperial leadership entitlements (as with the UK, sitting on the UN Security Council, and Queen Elizabeth II formally leading the Commonwealth of Nations).

Of great assistance in spreading the burden of "humanitarian intervention," while simultaneously working to roll back the state, is the ever-expanding complex of non-governmental organizations (NGOs), whose number worldwide is perhaps several million. Western NGOs, and especially those in receipt of government funding and whose work abroad meets with the approval of the US and/or the EU, have been instrumental in promoting top-down solutions that strengthen "civil society" at the expense of states in Africa, Asia, Latin America, and the Caribbean.

Outsourcing Empire, Privatizing State Functions: NGOs

First, we need to get a sense of the size and scope of the spread of just those NGOs that work on an international plane, or INGOs, many of which are officially associated with, though not part of, the UN. Estimates of the number of INGOs (such as Care, Oxfam, Médecins Sans Frontières) vary greatly depending on the source, the definition of INGOs used, and the methods used to locate and count them. In broad terms, INGOs numbered roughly 28,000 by the mid-1990s, which represented a 500% increase from the 1970s; other estimates suggest that by the early years of this century they numbered 40,000, while some put the number at around 30,000, which is still nearly double the number of INGOs in 1990, and some figures are lower at 20,000 by 2005 (Anheier & Themudo, 2005, p. 106; Bloodgood & Schmitz, 2012, p. 10; Boli, 2006, p. 334; Makoba, 2002, p. 54). While the sources differ in their estimates, all of them agree that there has been a substantial rise in the number of INGOs over the past two decades.

Second, there is also evidence that INGOs and local NGOs are taking on a much larger role in international development assistance than ever before. The UK's Overseas Development Institute reported in 1996 that, by then, between 10% and 15% of all aid to developing countries was channeled through NGOs, accounting for a total amount of $6 billion US. Other sources report that "about a fifth of all reported official and private aid to developing countries has been provided or managed by NGOs and public-private partnerships" (International Development Association [IDA], 2007, p. 31). It has also been reported that, "from 1970 to 1985 total development aid disbursed by international NGOs increased ten-fold," while in 1992 INGOs, "channeled over $7.6 billion of aid to developing countries".[1] In 2004, INGOs "employed the full time equivalent of 140,000 staff — probably larger than the total staff of all bilateral and multilateral donors combined — and generated revenues for US$13 billion from philanthropy (36%), government contributions (35%) and fees (29%)" (IDA, 2007, p. 31). The budgets of the larger INGOs "have surpassed those of some Organisation for Economic Co-operation and Development (OECD) donor countries" (Morton, n.d., p. 325). For its part, the US government "gave more than twice the amount of aid assistance in 2000 ($4 billion) through nongovernmental organizations than was given directly to foreign governments (est. $1.9 billion)" (Kinney, 2006, p. 3).

The military is one arm of the imperialist order, and the other arm is made up of NGOs (though often these two arms are interlocked, as even Colin Powell says in the introductory quote in this chapter). The political-economic program of neoliberalism is, as Hanieh (2006, p. 168) argues, the economic logic of the current imperialist drive. This agenda involves, among other policies, cutbacks to state services and social spending by governments in order to open up local economies to private and nongovernmental interests. Indeed, the meteoric rise of NGOs, and the great increase in their numbers, came at a particular time in history: "the conservative governments of

Ronald Reagan and Margaret Thatcher made support for the voluntary sector a central part of their strategies to reduce government social spending" (Salamon, 1994). By more or less direct means, sometimes diffuse and other times well-coordinated, the interests of the US and its allies can thus be pursued under the cover of humanitarian "aid," "charity," and "development assistance".

In his extensive critique of neoliberalism, David Harvey (2005) credits the explosive growth of the NGO sector under neoliberalism with the rise of, "the belief that opposition mobilized outside the state apparatus and within some separate entity called 'civil society' is the powerhouse of oppositional politics and social transformation" (p. 78). Yet many of these NGOs are commanded by unelected and elite actors, who are accountable primarily to their chief sources of funds, which may include governments and usually includes corporate donors and private foundations. The broader point of importance is that this rise of NGOs under neoliberalism is also the period in which the concept of "civil society" has become central not just to the formulation of oppositional politics, as Harvey (2005, p. 78) argues, but also central to the modes of covert intervention and destabilization openly adopted by the US around the world. More on this just below, but first we need to pause and focus on this emergence of "civil society" as a topic in the new imperialism.

The "Civil Society" of the New Imperialism: Neoliberal Solutions to Problems Created by Neoliberalism

There has been a growing popularization of "civil society," that James Ferguson, an anthropologist, even calls a "fad". Part of the growing popularity of this concept is tied to some social scientists' attraction to democratization, social movements and NGOs, and even some anthropologists have been inspired to recoup *the local* under the heading of "civil society" (Ferguson, 2007, p. 383). The very notion of "civil society" comes from 18th-century European liberal thought of the Enlightenment, as something that stood between the state and the family. "Civil society" has been universalized, with "little regard for historical context or critical genealogy":

> "this new conception (of 'civil society' as the road to democracy) not only met the political needs of the Eastern European struggle against communist statism, it also found a ready export market—both in the First World (where it was appropriated by conservative Reagan/Thatcher projects for 'rolling back the state') and in the Third World...". (Ferguson, 2007, p. 384)

Today "civil society" has been reconceived as the road to democratization and freedom, and is explicitly promoted as such by the US State Department. Whether from the western left or right which have both appropriated the concern for "civil society," Ferguson argues that the concept helps to legitimate a profoundly anti-democratic politics (2007, p. 385).

The African state, once held high as the chief engine of development, is now treated as the enemy of development and nation-building (especially by western elites), constructed as too bureaucratic, stagnant and corrupt. Now "civil society" is celebrated as the hero of liberatory change, and the aim is to get the state to become more aligned with civil society (Ferguson, 2007, p. 387). Not only that, the aim is to *standardize* state practices, so as to lessen or remove barriers to foreign penetration and to increase predictability of political outcomes and investment decisions (see Obama, 2013/7/1).

In practice, most writers conceive of contemporary "civil society" as composed of small, voluntary, grassroots organizations (which opens the door, conceptually, to the focus on NGOs). As Ferguson notes, civil society is largely made up of *international organizations*:

> "For indeed, the local voluntary organizations in Africa, so beloved of 'civil society' theorists, very often, upon inspection, turn out to be integrally linked with national

and transnational-level entities. One might think, for instance, of the myriad South African 'community organizations' that are bankrolled by USAID or European church groups; or of the profusion of 'local' Christian development NGOs in Zimbabwe, which may be conceived equally well as the most local, 'grassroots' expressions of civil society, or as parts of the vast international bureaucratic organizations that organize and sustain their deletion. When such organizations begin to take over the most basic functions and powers of the state, it becomes only too clear that 'NGOs' are not as 'NG' as they might wish us to believe. Indeed, the World Bank baldly refers to what they call BONGOs (Bank-organized NGOs) and now even GONGOs (Government-organized NGOs)". (Ferguson, 2007, p. 391).

That NGOs serve the purpose of privatizing state functions, is also demonstrated by Schuller (2009) with reference to Haiti. NGOs provide legitimacy to neoliberal globalization by filling in the "gaps" in the state's social services created by structural adjustment programs (Schuller, 2009, p. 85) – a neoliberal solution to a problem first created by neoliberalism itself. Moreover, in providing high-paying jobs to an educated middle class, NGOs serve to reproduce the global inequalities created by, and required by, neoliberal globalization (Schuller, 2009, p. 85). NGOs also work as "buffers between elites and impoverished masses" and can thus erect or reinforce "institutional barriers against local participation and priority setting" (Schuller, 2009, p. 85).

Thanks to neoliberal structural adjustment, INGOs and other international organizations (such as the UN, IMF, and World Bank) are "eroding the power of African states (and usurping their sovereignty)," and are busy making "end runs around these states" by "directly sponsoring their own programs or interventions via NGOs in a wide range of areas" (Ferguson, 2007, p. 391). INGOs and some local NGOs thus also serve the purposes of neoliberal interventionism.

Trojan Horses: NGOs, Human Rights, and Intervention to "Save" the "Needy"

David Harvey argues that "the rise of advocacy groups and NGOs has, like rights discourses more generally, accompanied the neoliberal turn and increased spectacularly since 1980 or so" (2005, p. 177). NGOs have been called forth, and have been abundantly provisioned as we saw above, in a situation where neoliberal programs have forced the withdrawal of the state away from social welfare. As Harvey puts it, "this amounts to privatization by NGO" (2005, p. 177). NGOs function as the Trojan Horses of global neoliberalism. Following Chandler (2002, p. 89), those NGOs that are oriented toward human rights issues and humanitarian assistance find support "in the growing consensus of support for Western involvement in the internal affairs of the developing world since the 1970s". Moreover, as Horace Campbell explained,

> "During the nineties military journals such as Parameters honed the discussion of the planning for the increased engagement of international NGO's and by the end of the 20th century the big international NGO's [like] Care, Catholic Relief Services, Save The Children, World Vision, and Medicins Sans Frontieres (MSF) were acting like major international corporations doing subcontracting work for the US military". (Campbell (2014/5/2)[2]

Private military contractors in the US, many of them part of Fortune 500 companies, are indispensable to the US military—and in some cases there are "clear linkages between the 'development 'agencies and Wall Street" as perhaps best exemplified by Casals & Associates, Inc., a subsidiary of Dyncorp, a private military contractor that was itself purchased by Cerberus Capital Management for $1.5 billion in 2010, and which received financing commitments from Bank of America Merrill Lynch, Citigroup, Barclays, and Deutsche Bank (Campbell (2014/5/2). Casals declares that its work is about "international development," "democracy and governance," and various humanitarian aid initiatives, in over 25 countries, in some instances working in partnership with USAID and the State Department's Office of Transition Initiatives (Campbell (2014/5/2).

In order for NGOs to intervene and take on a more prominent role, something else is required for their work to be carried out, in addition to gaining visibility, attracting funding and support from powerful institutions, and being well placed to capitalize on the opportunities created by neoliberal structural adjustment. They require a "need" for their work. In other words, to have humanitarian action, one must have a needy subject. As Andria Timmer (2010) explains, NGOs overemphasize poverty and stories of discrimination, in order to construct a "needy subject" — a population constructed as a "problem" in need of a "solution". The needs identified by NGOs may not correspond to the actual needs of the people in question, but need, nonetheless, is the dominant discourse by which those people come to be defined as a "humanitarian project". To attract funding, and to gain visibility by claiming that its work is *necessary*, a NGO must have "tales that inspire pathos and encourage people to act" (Timmer, 2010, p. 268). However, in constantly producing images of poverty, despair, hopelessness, and helplessness, NGOs reinforce "an Orientialist dialectic," especially when these images are loaded with markers of ethnic otherness (Timmer, 2010, p. 269). Entire peoples then come to be known through their poverty, particularly by audiences in the global North who only see particular peoples "through the lens of aid and need" (Timmer, 2010, p. 269). In the process what is also (re)created is the anthropological myth of the *helpless* object, one devoid of any agency at all, one cast as a void, as a barely animate object through which we define our special subjecthood. By constructing the needy as the effectively empty, we thus monopolize not only agency but we also corner the market on "humanity".

Humanitarian Imperialism as the Globalization of Residential Schooling

In Canada, there have been official government apologies for the abuses committed during the residential schooling era (which lasted until 1996), plus monetary compensation, and a truth and reconciliation commission that was constituted and recently finished its work. Nonetheless the fundamental ethos of residential schooling has not only been preserved, it has been amplified into a template containing the basic operating instructions for how to approach peoples around the world who are understood to be inferior. Such inferiority can be understood, for example, in the way that other people's governments, no matter how indisputably democratic or legitimate they may be, are consistently treated as if they were disposable.

Residential schooling in Canada and its counterpart systems in Australia and the US, all intended to "save" Native children, to "educate" and thus "improve" them, is reflective of a classic settler state ideology of the late 1800s, which emphasized evolutionary progress through assimilation. It is not an unfamiliar ideology either, for those familiar with the thinking behind "modernization" theory and the basic thrust of international developmentalism. What is interesting to note is that it is only out of these same settler states that ideas of the "responsibility to protect" (R2P) emerged and were propagated at the UN in recent years. The main actors who articulated and advocated for R2P have been primarily Canadian and Australian.

The globalization of residential schooling means that certain basic working principles now constitute a template that is applied to a broader set of international relations, as well as revamped forms of counterinsurgency in foreign military occupations. This template consists of the following elements:

(a) the binary between racially and/or culturally differentiated tutors and wards;

(b) a process of abduction, understood broadly, and exemplified by such phenomena as the international traffic in non-western babies in the adoption industry, to the re-implementation of the trusteeship system, to the neoliberal destruction of state-regulated economies and the military occupation of other nations—thus the seizure of individuals and nation-states, rendering them more or less captive to agendas imposed by western powers; and,

(c) what is still essentially a civilizing mission cloaked as "humanitarianism," the defence of "human rights," or "democracy promotion"—that is, ideological narratives and their corresponding practices whose aim is sill that of "saving the natives from themselves" and to prepare them for life in the white man's world (the "international community," or "the community of civilized nations"), so that they may lead productive lives as law-abiding, well mannered servants of the global capitalist economy.

What "abduction" can also mean is that in order for "us" (the interventionists) to presume to "care" for little known and even less understood strangers, these "others" must be seen as living in a state of some sort of neglect and unfulfilled need. That other thus becomes like an object that is first "seized" so that it can be set free. That other is an object set low within a hierarchy, one that resembles old cultural evolutionist schemes where Europeans were always at the top, and Africans locked far down below in a Paleolithic time zone awaiting redemption. Western "humanitarianism" thus works within an imperialist ideological framework: that object—for example an Africa once again imagined as a zone of ultimately helpless destitution—needs *our* "protection" (we are the prime actors, they are the terrain upon which we act). This requires that we do at least two things that one would expect of imperialists. First, we need to construct images of "Africa" as a dark place of gaunt, hungry, pleading quasi-humans, where we effectively open the door to ourselves, and usher ourselves in as their self-appointed saviours. This is not the same thing as abduction in the form of kidnapping (not yet anyway): it is more of a virtual abduction, an imaginary capture that places "Africa" on a lower scale of welfare and self-fulfillment, and implies our "duty" to rescue them by "raising" them "up" to where we are. Second, we can work to ensure that the material conditions of *need* are effectively reproduced: we can do that with "aid," with "investment" (an odd word, because in practice it means taking away), with "trade" (where the preconditions are that Africans privatize themselves[3]), and with direct military intervention to bomb back down to size any upstart that threatens to guard his dignity (Libya). These too constitute capture. And then there is actual capture: seizing children, indicting "war criminals," or inviting students to come on over and "learn" like we do so that they can become "educated" — or stay there, and let our students teach you.

Two of the most widely read proponents of this application of a neocolonial form of residential schooling, more properly known in international law as "trusteeship" and "conservatorship," were Gerald B. Helman and Steven R. Ratner, both of whom served in the US State Department in different capacities at different points in their career. In what is in many ways an intellectual continuation of Kaplan's "Coming Anarchy," "Saving Failed States" by Helman and Ratner not only posits the existence of such a phenomenon as a "failed" state, they assert that it was brought about by rapid decolonization since 1945 (Helman & Ratner, 1992–1993). They frame their argument in terms of *risk* and *emergency*, and demand: "something must be done" (Helman & Ratner, 1992–1993, p. 3). Fortunately for them, *intervention* does indeed constitute "something," and it is precisely the kind of "something" for which they were looking.

Nations, they argue, need to be "saved" because self-determination has been a failure (they would let the leader assume it is largely due to internal inadequacies), especially in Africa which becomes the primary focus of their article. They object, almost mock, the "states that achieved independence after 1945," who attach great and "almost exaggerated" importance to the concept of sovereignty (Helman & Ratner, 1992–1993, p. 9). What matters is "survivability" and this only comes from external benefactors, such as a suitably restructured UN which has increasingly become a leading agent of neoliberal transformation (see Cammack, 2006). If it seems like Helman and Ratner are articulating something like a global application of the basic template of residential schooling, as argued above, it is an observation that is commended by their own wording:

> "The conceptual basis for the effort [UN-led nation-saving] should lie in the idea of conservatorship. In domestic systems when the polity confronts persons who are utterly incapable of functioning on their own, the law often provides some regime whereby the community itself manages the affairs of the victim. Forms of guardianship or trusteeship are a common response to broken families, serious mental or physical illness, or economic destitution. The hapless individual is placed under the responsibility of a trustee or guardian, who is charged to look out for the best interests of that person". (Helman & Ratner, 1992–1993, p. 12)

"The very fact that scholars and commentators are seriously advocating this approach," Ruth Gordon comments, "is an indication of how negatively we view certain communities" (1997, p. 907). As Gordon, a professor of international law, further explains, advocacy such as that of Helman and Ratner and other western "humanitarian interventionists" is necessarily based on conceptions of inferiority:

> "The 'civilized' nations of Europe and the United States had the right to control their own destinies free of foreign intrusion. The less civilized Asian and Latin American States, however, were fair targets of intervention. While this view has partially dissipated in this century, 'the power of intervention remains the

power to stigmatize and political meaning is in large measure rooted in historical memory'". (Gordon, 1997, p. 908 fn. 15)

The same binary applies to the military instruments themselves: a US President can declare a "red line" against the alleged use of chemical weapons in Syria, while still using white phosphorous, depleted uranium, and various cluster munitions in the US weapons stockpile. Poisoned gas becomes the weapon of the "uncivilized," and the cruise missile the weapon of the "civilized".

The basic operating premise is that "certain human beings, who were predominately black and brown peoples, were inferior to Europeans and simply incapable of governing themselves" and this is part of the same baggage of assumptions that, to varying degrees, "underlie current paradigms to utilize forms of conservatorship" (Gordon, 1997, p. 909). The abductive narrative here is framed in a manner that "makes this result seem logical and in the interest of both the peoples of the Third World and their kindhearted patrons in the West" (Gordon, 1997, p. 910).

Gordon goes even further, noting that the western tradition on which international law itself was founded, a tradition whose "underlying subcontext...was a belief in racial and cultural inferiority" — indeed, the "very roots of international law are mired in the heritage of colonialism" (Gordon, 1997, p. 911 fn. 30). Again, the basic structural logic of residential schooling comes back to the fore:

> "Once it is determined that particular states have 'failed,' these states would be deemed victims and incapable of managing their own affairs in much the same way we view children as being incapable of managing their own affairs. The international community would then be designated to act on their behalf". (Gordon, 1997, p. 924)

Thus when we in Canada "apologize" for an institution such as residential schooling, for what are we really apologizing? What have we learned about ourselves and our basic values and working assumptions? The answer to both questions unfortunately appears to be: little or nothing.

We thus turn to the contributions by authors in this volume which, I must stress, are not ordered in terms of a rank based on their quality or importance, but are instead grouped according to three broad themes. Part One thus concentrates on the work of "doing good," with a special focus on NGOs and human rights. Part Two deals with the creation of a state of exception in terms of global and domestic political economy. Part Three involves what might be termed the work of ideologically-informed cultural mystification, where the chief opponents and targets of US imperialism are profoundly demonized and thus dehumanized, western troops are bestowed with a monumental status as heroes, and, as we are taught, US military training consists of teaching young Asian girls how to skip rope. After all of this, can "humanitarianism" be redeemed? I address this conclusion at the end of this chapter.

Good Intentions, NGOs, and Violence

In Part 1, chapter 1, "Iatrogenic Imperialism: NGOs and CROs as Agents of Questionable Care," Émile St-Pierre examines the role of NGOs and Contract Research Organizations (CROs) in the formation and propagation of a neoliberal paradigm in health care. As St-Pierre explains, neoliberal policies beginning in the 1980s forced many states to retract from health care provision. NGOs and CROs have emerged as *gap fillers* in the wake of these policies. The activities of NGOs and CROs in conjunction with states and pharmaceutical corporations produce changes in the everyday lives of people, offering new possibilities for some at the same time that they dominate and classify populations in new ways. NGOs, CROs and the actors they are tied to, rely on patterns of illness and inequality to continue existing, and securing revenues. *Iatrogenic imperialism* is used by St-Pierre as an analytic to bring to light the way "good intentions," expertise and humanitarianism play into efficiency-driven, neoliberal configurations of health care that fail to produce benefits for all, that undermine public health systems and that tend to reproduce global inequalities. In exploring the roles of lesser-known but increasingly important actors in health care worldwide, St-Pierre's research critically analyzes some of the newest phenomena in the neoliberal turn health care has been experiencing and speaks to their penetration into the everyday lives of people.

In chapter 2, "US Imperialism and Disaster Capitalism in Haiti," Keir Forgie details some characteristic actions of the new, that is, US imperialism enforced upon Haiti leading up to and following the earthquake of January 2010: military and CIA intervention, the UN-administered MINUSTAH occupation, US-funded NGOs, the militarization of humanitarian aid. These tools of disaster capitalism are all part of the new imperialism, Forgie argues. The US military and CIA have repeatedly intervened against Haitian sovereignty to impose US "democratic" systems that favour neoliberalism. Meanwhile, MINUSTAH enforces US objectives repressing free-speech and effectively acting as a large gang, one opposed to supporters of the overthrown president, Jean-Bertrand Aristide. NGOs, for their part, provide a means through which the US can funnel aid money and pursue self-interests while undermining local authority. In addition, the militarization of humanitarian aid in Haiti exemplifies a masked occupation under the guise of altruistic rhetoric. And as Forgie argues, predatory impositions of neoliberalism and corporate interests that pushed through disaster capitalism serve to subvert Haiti to a US means of production and sponge for capital overflow. Each of these coercive methods ensures US hegemonic globalization, acting as distinguishing features of the new imperialism, Forgie explains.

In chapter 3, "Who Needs Me Most? New Imperialist Ideologies in Youth Centred Volunteer Abroad Programs," Tristan Biehn examines the new imperial ideologies present in narratives manufactured by the websites of youth-centred volunteer abroad organizations. These narratives serve to instil neoliberal, capitalist understandings of the issues of global inequality and poverty in prospective volunteers, resulting in the depoliticization and decontextualization of such issues. Biehn finds that ideas of "change" and "good" are ubiquitous and yet are left undefined, that claims of "helping" and "immersion" are questionable, and that the utility of international student volunteering lies not in the benevolent donation of unskilled western youth labour to underprivileged communities, but in the production of ideal neoliberal subjects. The nebulous concepts of *help* and *change* are commodified and made the responsibility of individuals—the prospective volunteers—who are inundated with the message that actions taken to end global inequality will also benefit them personally. As Biehn explains, such programs contribute to the neoliberal project of redirecting efforts from the pursuit of larger structural changes or solutions to these issues.

Chapter 4 by Hilary King which is titled, "Queers of War: Normalizing Lesbians and Gays in the US War Machine" is a very welcome addition to the subject of gender, sexuality, and corresponding ideas of rights that we first introduced in Volume 3 (see Pas, 2013). In her chapter, Hilary King begins by noting how at a recent Human Rights Campaign (HRC) gala in Los Angeles, US Vice-President Joe Biden, the keynote speaker of the evening, claimed that the rights of LGBT people are an inseparable part of America's promotion of human rights around the world. This speech exemplifies the ways in national sovereignty, and whether or not any nation is deserving of it, has come to be decided by the extent to which a given nation accepts the gay and lesbian subject, King points out. In the past decade, the US has become a vocal advocate for the legal rights of LGBT subjects. Through the careful governance of liberal mentalities, as King explains, the appropriation of these rights by the US government has heavily aided the US in forwarding its imperial war machine. By relying on Jasbir Puar's theoretical framework of "homonationalism," King's chapter looks specifically at the Matthew Shepard and James Byrd, Jr. Hate Crimes Prevention Act, the repealing of Don't Ask Don't Tell (DADT), as well as the HRC, in order to explore the ways in which sexuality has become a formation in the articulation of proper US citizens.

The Political Economy of Exception

One of the defining features of the existence of a global *dictatorship* (hegemon and superpower might be too "soft" in this "human rights era" of invasions and occupations), is where one state gets to set the rules by which others live, while raising itself above those same rules. This leads to the idea of the practiced reality of "American exceptionalism" as an aspect of the global state of exception imposed by the US—two "exceptions" in one, combining both the ideas of emergency and primacy. In this respect, chapter 5, "The International Economic Sovereignty of the United States of America: Integrating the Exception into Our Understanding of Empire," by Karine Perron, addresses the scope of US capacity to influence and set out rules for international economic policies, rules which it then ignores. By examining cases concerning the IMF, the WTO, and even the overthrow of governments, US advocacy of capitalism, free trade, and democracy, each is contrasted with situations in which the US made exceptions for its own benefit. The significance of US power to decide on "the exception" is discussed by Perron in relation to the strategy of enlargement openly promoted by the Clinton administration and pursued by subsequent US governments. As economic growth has been added to the US definition of national security, exceptions have become a permanent feature of American foreign policy. Using Schmitt's definition of sovereignty as the power to decide on the exception, Perron argues that this capacity of the US to decide on exceptions regularly in the international economic realm is significant of its international sovereignty, and its intended supremacy. In these respects, Perron is raising some critical points of interest similar to those of Scheppele (2013): with respect to international law, what the US does by erecting itself as an exception is to create a rule from the exception. The US works to distribute this law, and uses its rule to extract and centralize gain. What Perron also does, like Scheppele (2013), is to pay respect to the fact that apart from a brief period when economic globalization seemed to reign supreme, powerful states (such as the US) have proceeded to seize back much of the power they had allegedly lost or ceded. A demonstration of the synergy between corporate empire and US empire takes us to the next chapter.

In chapter 6, "Life, Liberty and the Pursuit of Wage Labour: The American Legislative Exchange Council and the Neoliberal Coup," Mathieu Guerin produces a fascinating investigation and theoretical discussion of the American Legislative Exchange Council (ALEC), a not-for-profit organization that brings together corporate representatives and state legislators—thus "marrying" both capital and the state. Behind closed doors, Guerin reveals, the representatives and legislators design and vote on model bills. Legislators then bring the model bills home to their respective assemblies and attempt to implement them. The corporate members of ALEC are, in this way, empowered to change citizen's rights without interference from the federal government. By fostering close ties with state legislators, these corporations have the power to impose their vision of society without recourse to military or police violence. Guerin also investigates the connection between the character of gentrification in San Francisco and the bullying might of Silicon Valley's ALEC-affiliated corporate technocracy. This case study demonstrates how capital co-opts the existing state structure as a mode of subjugation and repression. Guerin's research and analysis conclude that ALEC is an organization that symbolizes a *corporate imperium* rooted in the rise of neoliberalism in the early 1970s and emerging within the established imperial state of the US. An in-depth look at the infamous Powell memorandum reveals an imperialistic ideological continuity between its conception in 1971 and ALEC itself.

Pariahs, Princes, and Playthings

John Manicom's "The Terrorist, the Tyrant and the Thug: 'Anti-Anti-Imperialism' in American Media and Policy" (chapter 7), is a powerful examination of the discursive and narrative practices of US politicians and media with regard to non-US opponents of US power. These US actors generate catastrophizing discourse classifying phenomena in politically advantageous ways and seeking to arouse certain reactions to events. The types of evaluations and reactions that occur in this discourse, Manicom observes, are relatively predictable and based on the subject's level of cooperation with US power. The most negative evaluations are assigned to states and sub-state groups which actively oppose US power. Mainstream western media operate from similar ideological perspectives to governments and benefit from a privileged discursive position in society allowing them to produce knowledge seen as generally legitimate, as Manicom demonstrates throughout. Their practices thus help to enable and sustain the narratives of politicians in demonizing and dehumanizing opponents and thus legitimating the often brutal practice of US interventionism.

Chapter 8 by Laura Powell, "Glorification of the Military in Popular Culture and the Media," fits well between Manicom's and the final chapter of the volume. In this chapter Powell argues that while our military members are generally perceived as heroes, this romanticized perception of the military is more damaging than it is helpful. The mainstream media are part of the problem, Powell shows, as news coverage of conflicts is often incomplete or wrong, and based on an idealized version of the military as an unstoppable humanitarian force, while failing to discuss the terrifying realities of war. The Pentagon-Hollywood union also helps propagate this distorted view of the military. Perpetuating this view of the military works to disadvantage the men and women affected by PTSD as a result of their deployments and, Powell argues, attracts potential recruits who may not be aware of the dangers associated with enlisting. In some respects then, Laura Powell is furthering this seminar's long-standing interest in "militainment".

On that note, my chapter 9, "A Flickr of Militarization: Photographic Regulation, Symbolic Consecration, and the Strategic Communication of 'Good Intentions'," is based on a study of the US Department of Defense's Flickr photostream, from 2009 through February of 2014, examining a total of 9,963 photographs (with some key examples reproduced in the chapter), and two dozen US military directives, manuals, and guides on public diplomacy, strategic communication, social media use, and photography. Having said that, the analysis is not a quantitative one; instead, the project builds on Pierre Bourdieu's ideas about regulated images, consecrated works, and the objectification and codification of (militarized) values, as well as the works of a number of visual anthropologists. Rather than an activity that expresses the randomness of individual imaginations, US military photographs register a pattern that reflects the prevailing political norms of a given social order. The patterns to be found among these thousands of images is in fact quite regular, and makes a series of clear points. This public engagement is carried out by the Pentagon with a belief that a major part of "the battle" is a "battle of the narrative," one that takes place in the public's "cognitive space," in what is has been termed "Fourth Generation warfare". These photographs are intended to represent the US military as a humanitarian, charitable organization, working among many communities around the world that are populated by children who are only too happy to be vaccinated and to skip rope with US soldiers. Female US soldiers have smiling close encounters with little girls, or cradle babies. When not displaying pure, motive-less good intentions, the photographs also produce a celebration of the awesome power and sophistication of US military technology: jets flying in formation, shiny drones illuminated at night like alien UFOs, lines of massive ships at sea, etc. Yet, there are virtually no images of actual combat. The photographs collectively portray a world rendered frictionless by the speed and ubiquity of American power and technology. In addition, by being studiously depoliticized, the photographs produce a political effect, for political purposes—they do not tell the horror stories of war, of blood shed and lives lost, of destruction and grief, but rather portray something like a birthday party, with a cycle of endless family reunions. However, as the Pentagon understands that every action is potentially a message, and there is an unresolved tension between "perception effects" and military planning, strategic communication in the form of disseminating photographs through social media faces ultimate pitfalls.

About Those Good Intentions

There are many valid and unimpeachable reasons why students, for example, might be considering humanitarian work and/or working for a NGO. There is no gainsaying that many students have genuine, sincere, and heartfelt reasons for coming to the aid of others: those who come from privileged backgrounds might feel the need to "give back"; those who come from backgrounds of struggle might be determined to lessen the burden of disadvantage on others like them. Having read chapters such as the ones in this volume, or several others, and having been asked to question their beliefs in the value of humanitarian aid or even foreign intervention to prevent atrocities, they might be left wondering whether all forms of altruism are to be forsaken. I would say: not so fast. The real challenge now is to question our assumptions and envision or acknowledge existing alternatives that further solidarity, collaboration, and reciprocity without the paternalism and Eurocentrism of the "white man's burden".

One way to proceed is by questioning why helping others should lead to work abroad. Do you really have any special skills to offer other than the ability to articulate good intentions? Has your assistance been requested by those who would presumably benefit from it? How well do you understand a different society that you can permit yourself to undertake potentially transformative action? What are your motives, and do you think the organization(s) you support, or for which you work, share the same motives? If it is a question of solidarity, is the solidarity spontaneous and one-sided, or the product of actual dialogue and mutual understanding? Why would you not choose to work at home, where presumably you are not a stranger, nor an intruder? Indeed, this last question is one that gains salience particularly with anthropology students. Frustrated with what they perceive as their inability to change the politics of their own nation, some feel that they might make more of an impact in a different nation (Mathers, 2010, p. 169). Yet this assumes that other societies are less complex, easier to change and even receptive to outsiders bringing about change for them. If one feels that Africa is oppressed, then why assume that is to Africa that one must go, rather than work at home to change the policies of one's country, for example, supporting debt forgiveness, challenging unjust trade and aid policies, reining in your corporations, or pushing for the demilitarization of the foreign relations of one's own country? It is important not to assume that others are simply waiting for a stranger to come and lead them, like a Hollywood tale of the usual white messiah who is always the hero of other people's stories. Ifi Amadiume—an African feminist who noted that, increasingly, Black women had begun to expose the racism in the women's movement and accused western feminists of "a new imperialism" (1987, p. 4)— relates to us a story of a young anthropologist in a seminar in which she participated:

> "I asked a young White woman why she was studying social anthropology. She replied that she was hoping to

go to Zimbabwe, and felt that she could help women there by advising them how to organize. The Black women in the audience gasped in astonishment. Here was someone scarcely past girlhood, who had just started university and had never fought a war in her life. She was planning to go to Africa to teach female veterans of a liberation struggle how to organize! This is the kind of arrogant, if not absurd attitude we encounter repeatedly. It makes one think: Better the distant armchair anthropologists than these 'sisters'". (Amadiume, 1987, p. 7)

A second set of questions has to do with whether charity is the best expression for one's altruism. This raises other questions especially when we turn to charity at home. Why is it that in a society such as Canada's where virtually every activity, positive or negative, is taxed, we are called upon more and more to give to charity? Rather than mobilize to "raise awareness" about the homeless (as if we were unaware of them), why do we not instead mobilize the same numbers of those giving to charity to combat austerity? Why should taxes not go to feeding our hungry fellow citizens, instead of into funds to provide "incentives" for corporate investors or into military expenditures so we can bomb Libya? Indeed, by taking up the social welfare slack, are we not facilitating the state in increasing the power of the wealthy, in further militarizing our international relations, and in increasing inequality at home? Sure enough, without presenting heaps of documentary evidence and considering all of the implications, these questions may appear simple, or too ingenuous. Nonetheless, is it acceptable that we do not at least ask such questions to *begin* with?

A third bundle of questions has to do with supporting intervention in another country to supposedly prevent or stop mass violence. Assuming that one is in possession of accurate information, that the information does not come filtered through or created by vested interests, and that one possesses the ability to fairly interpret such information in the historical and cultural context of a given political conflict—something that daunts most "experts"—then which instrument is best suited to end such violence? Whose army, navy and air force are you calling on to carry out your good intentions? Do militaries ever act in the absence of other political and economic agendas or are they answerable only to your personal concerns? What other agendas are facilitated by military intervention, such that the "cure" can end up being worse than the "illness"? How is war consistent with the defense of human rights? How do you avoid the risk of prolonging, widening and further militarizing a local political conflict by intervening militarily? Are you prepared for the aftermath of intervention, and what degree of responsibility and accountability are you prepared to shoulder? Should you feel comfortable in calling for the sacrifice of the lives of your own soldiers, and inevitably of civilians in another country, while you remain physically detached from the conflict? Are you prepared to intervene in all situations of conflict where human rights are endangered, or is it just some, and if so why just some? Which is the "lesser evil" that you are prepared to live with and to justify: is it the survival of a local regime that you consider to be a "dictatorship," or the survival and reinforcement of a global imperial dictatorship that seeks any justification to renew and assert its military dominance? These are just *some* of the *first* questions we need to ask. We should, if we are being honest with ourselves, also consider other norms and practices, such as Cuba's socialist internationalism. In the latter case, no permanent military bases resulted from Cuba coming to the aid of Angola; Cuban assistance was requested and mutually understood as an act of solidarity; there was no lucrative, extractive gain as a result of Cuba mobilizing to send troops and doctors to Angola; and, Angola's sovereignty was not undermined, rather it was defended by Cuba. Therefore, a consideration of the stakes, aims, methods, and the whole politics of intervention need to be clearly thought out and articulated. What there should not be is any more of the reflex "cries": "something must be done," "we cannot stand idly by," and so forth—complex situations require maturity and political acumen, not trivial passion.

A final set of questions concerns the prospect of a graduating student working for a NGO. As I tell seminar participants, no one will benefit from their starving and being homeless; no argument will be "won," or should be won, at the cost of their own suffering. Life in a capitalist society is always full of compromises, such that an extra-systemic stance of total purity is unattainable. As a professor, I should know all about complicity: working in an institution essential to the training of new capitalist cadres, with multiple ties to all sorts of corporate interests, under neoliberal management, and even tied to the military and military industries. The point then is not to automatically forego the chance of earning an income in what is possibly one of the few major growth industries left in the west — that of the NGO complex — but to perhaps treat such employment strategically, as a stepping stone perhaps, where one acts as a critical insider, not allowing oneself to be digested by the system, and always being ready to expose hypocrisies and injustices as they arise. One should also be sober about envisioning change purely by individual means. "What am *I* to do" and "what can *I* change" are always flawed questions because they first assume the centrality of individual action, when transformation can only ever be achieved collectively.

Inevitably (because it always happens) students and others will doubt the value of studies in this area, feeling that such work is not practical or applicable, and that it lacks a "real world" extension — we need to "do". It is true that in sociology and anthropology we lack courses on fundraising, writing brochures, community canvassing, or installing electrical wiring and performing dental work — and that is not a problem. We do not need to try to do everything, and students with such interests and motivations need not see sociology and anthropology as terminal points of qualification. Courses in carpentry and financial management are always available to those who are interested. Yet, this is still not a satisfactory way of addressing the disquiet. The disquiet is itself rooted in a limited understanding and appreciation of what we really *do*, by first of all divorcing thought from action, and secondly not realizing that it is often *thinking* itself that is a woefully absent or minimized action in our society. Certain norms of action in our society are taken for granted, and held as unquestionable, in part because few are those who challenge, criticize, unthink and rethink what is done (military intervention, capitalist development, individualistic consumerism, etc.), and why it is done. It's the generalized absence of such real questioning that precludes the possibility of real debate and consideration of alternatives. Changing what is considered to be *unthinkable* and *unspeakable* is itself a form of practical action, arguably of the most essential kind.

The intention here was not to provide some easy blueprint, or a map of safe or recommended options. The aim was also not to have students abandon their own good intentions. The method is instead one that asks students: what are your good intentions, what makes them good, and how do you put your intentions into practice? *Whose roads are paved by your good intentions, and where do those roads lead?*

Notes

1   From Duke University Libraries' "NGO Research Guide" archived at:
    http://web.archive.org/web/20100611063147/http://librar
    y.duke.edu/research/subject/guides/ngo_guide/igo_ngo_c
    oop/ngo_wb.html.
2   This brought back a slightly ironic realization. While Montgomery McFate, the anthropologist who worked as the senior social scientist of the US Army's Human Terrain System, argued that anthropologists would anthropologize the military by joining HTS, dismissing claims that they would make anthropologists seem like US military agents (even though in uniform, and some carrying weapons), her own husband was saying something different at the same time.

Sean McFate told *Voice of America* that many NGOs and many people in USAID were "leery" of working with AFRICOM or any US military organization "because it might impugn their neutrality or their impartiality which they depend on for their own protection when they're working in countries" (Taylor, 2009/11/1).

3   In this regard I am referring to the African Growth and Opportunity Act (AGOA), first instituted by US president George W. Bush: http://trade.gov/agoa/.

References

Amadiume, I. (1987). *Male Daughters, Female Husbands: Gender and Sex in an African Society*. London, UK: Zed Books.

Anheier, H. K., & Themudo, N. (2005). The Internationalization of the Nonprofit Sector. In R. D. Herman (Ed.), *The Jossey-Bass Handbook of Nonprofit Leadership and Management, 2nd ed.* (pp. 102–127). San Francisco, CA: Jossey-Bass, Inc.

Bloodgood, E., & Schmitz, H. P. (2012). Researching INGOs: Innovations in Data Collection and Methods of Analysis. Paper presented at the International Studies Association Annual Convention, March 31, San Diego, CA.
http://faculty.maxwell.syr.edu/hpschmitz/papers/researchingingos_february6.pdf

Boli, J. (2006). International Nongovernmental Organizations. In W. W. Powell & R. Steinberg (Eds.), *The Nonprofit Sector* (pp. 333–351). New Haven, CT: Yale University Press.

Cammack, P. (2006). UN Imperialism: Unleashing Entrepreneurship in the Developing World. In C. Mooers (Ed.), *The New Imperialists: Ideologies of Empire* (pp. 229–260). Oxford, UK: Oneworld Publications.

Campbell, H. C. (2014/5/2). Understanding the US Policy of Diplomacy, Development, and Defense: The Office of Transition Initiatives and the Subversion of Societies. *CounterPunch*.
http://www.counterpunch.org/2014/05/02/the-office-of-transition-initiatives-and-the-subversion-of-societies/

Chandler, D. (2002). *From Kosovo to Kabul: Human Rights and International Intervention*. London, UK: Pluto Press.

Fassin, D., & Pandolfi, M. (2010). Introduction: Military and Humanitarian Government in the Age of Intervention. In D.

Fassin & M. Pandolfi (Eds.), *Contemporary States of Emergency: The Politics of Military and Humanitarian Interventions* (pp. 9–25). New York, NY: Zone Books.

Ferguson, J. (2007). Power Topographies. In D. Nugent & J. Vincent (Eds.), *A Companion to the Anthropology of Politics* (pp. 383–399). Malden, MA: Blackwell.

Gordon, R. (1997). Saving Failed States: Sometimes a Neocolonialist Notion. *American University International Law Review*, 12(6), 904–974.

Hanieh, A. (2006). Praising Empire: Neoliberalism under Pax Americana. In C. Mooers (Ed.), *The New Imperialists: Ideologies of Empire* (pp. 167–198). Oxford, UK: Oneworld Publications.

Harvey, D. (2005). *A Brief History of Neoliberalism*. Oxford, UK: Oxford University Press.

Helman, G. B., & Ratner, S. R. (1992–1993). Saving Failed States. *Foreign Policy*, 89, 3–20.

International Development Association (IDA). (2007). Aid Architecture: An Overview of the Main Trends in Official Development Assistance Flows. Washington, DC: The World Bank.
http://www.worldbank.org/ida/papers/IDA15_Replenishment/Aidarchitecture.pdf

Kaplan, R. D. (1994/2). The Coming Anarchy: How Scarcity, Crime, Overpopulation, Tribalism, and Disease Are Rapidly Destroying the Social Fabric of Our Planet. *The Atlantic*.
http://www.theatlantic.com/magazine/print/1994/02/the-coming-anarchy/304670/

Kinney, N. T. (2006). The Political Dimensions of Donor Nation Support for Humanitarian INGOs. Paper presented at the International Society for Third Sector Research (ISTR) Conference, July 11, Bangkok, Thailand.
http://c.ymcdn.com/sites/www.istr.org/resource/resmgr/working_papers_bangkok/kinney.nancy.pdf

Makoba, J. W. (2002). Nongovernmental Organizations (NGOs) and Third World Development: An Alternative Approach to Development. *Journal of Third World Studies*, 19(1), 53–63.

Mathers, K. (2010). *Travel, Humanitarianism, and Becoming American in Africa*. New York, NY: Palgrave Macmillan.

Mooers, C. (2006). Introduction: The New Watchdogs. In C. Mooers (Ed.), *The New Imperialists: Ideologies of Empire* (pp. 1–8). Oxford, UK: Oneworld Publications.

Morton, B. (n.d.). An Overview of International NGOs in Development Cooperation. United Nations Development Program.
http://www.undp.org/content/dam/china/docs/Publications/UNDP-CH11%20An%20Overview%20of%20International%20NGOs%20in%20Development%20Cooperation.pdf

Obama, B. (2013/7/1). Remarks by President Obama at Business Leaders Forum. Washington, DC: The White House, Office of the Press Secretary.
http://www.whitehouse.gov/the-press-office/2013/07/01/remarks-president-obama-business-leaders-forum

Overseas Development Institute. (1996). The Impact of NGO Development Projects. Briefing Paper. London, UK: Overseas Development Institute.
http://www.odi.org.uk/sites/odi.org.uk/files/odi-assets/publications-opinion-files/2636.pdf

Pas, N. (2013). The Masculine Empire: A Gendered Analysis of Modern American Imperialism. In K. McLoughlin & M. C. Forte (Eds.), *Emergency as Security: Liberal Empire at Home and Abroad* (pp. 43–71). Montreal, QC: Alert Press.

Philpot, R. (2014). *Rwanda and the New Scramble for Africa: From Tragedy to Useful Imperial Fiction.* Montreal, QC: Baraka Books.

Powell, C. L. (2001). Remarks to the National Foreign Policy Conference for Leaders of Nongovernmental Organizations, October 26. Washington, DC: US Department of State.
http://avalon.law.yale.edu/sept11/powell_brief31.asp

Salamon, L. M. (1994). The Rise of the Nonprofit Sector. *Foreign Affairs*, July-August.
http://www.foreignaffairs.com/articles/50105/lester-m-salamon/the-rise-of-the-nonprofit-sector

Scheppele, K. L. (2013). The Empire's New Laws: Terrorism and the New Security Empire After 9/11. In G. Steinmetz (Ed.), *Sociology & Empire: The Imperial Entanglements of a Discipline* (pp. 245–278). Durham, NC: Duke University Press.

Schuller, M. (2009). Gluing Globalization: NGOs as Intermediaries in Haiti. *PoLAR: Political and Legal Anthropology Review*, 32(1), 84–104.

Taylor, D. (2009/11/1). Aid Workers Anxious about US Military Involvement in African Development - PART 5 of 5. *VOA (Voice of America)*.
http://www.voanews.com/content/a-13-aid-workers-anxious-about-us-military-involvement-in-african-development-part-5-of-5/406576.html

Timmer, A. D. (2010). Constructing the "Needy Subject": NGO Discourses of Roma Need. *PoLAR: Political and Legal Anthropology Review*, 33(2), 264–281.

Whitlock, C. (2013/4/13). Niger Rapidly Emerges as a Key U.S. Partner in Anti-Terrorism Fight In Africa. *The Washington Post*.
    http://www.washingtonpost.com/world/national-security/niger-rapidly-emerging-as-a-key-us-partner/2013/04/14/3d3b260c-a38c-11e2-ac00-8ef7caef5e00_print.html

PART ONE:
Good Intentions, NGOs, and Violence

CHAPTER 1

Iatrogenic Imperialism: NGOs and CROs as Agents of Questionable Care

✫ ✫ ✫ ✫ ✫

Émile St-Pierre

Military interventions by powerful nations have increasingly occurred under the justification of humanitarian values and principles. In deploying a moral imperative to act for the benefit of the maximum number of innocent lives, the destructive aspects and politics of intervening are often overlooked. This chapter concerns a similar pattern being reproduced in healthcare worldwide. In the wake of the retreat of the state in matters of welfare provoked by the pressures of International Financial Institutions (IFIs), various actors have filtered into the daily lives of people across the world and have offered themselves up as options for providing care. I will speak here only of certain health-oriented non-governmental organizations (NGOs) and contract research organizations (CROs) as they relate to neoliberal imperialism.

A modality of empire, in this case, emerges from good intentions and the provision of care to bodies that are said to desperately need it: a humanitarian movement that constructs itself as unexploitative and outside political considerations, but dominates people therapeutically and reproduces global inequalities (Calhoun, 2010, p. 41; Fassin, 2010, p. 273; McFalls, 2010, p. 318). NGOs and CROs have become participants in networks of decentralized and managerial care often operating through exception which ultimately does not realize health benefits equally or for all.

I will first outline how neoliberal policies starting around the 1980s shaped healthcare in states like Brazil and Mozambique and then examine the material and ideological conditions that allowed NGOs and CROs to become involved in global health. I then turn my focus to NGOs like Save the Children and CARE whose drive for efficiency in saving a maximum number of lives, especially in situations described as emergencies, makes for easier partnership with pharmaceutical companies like Merck and government organizations like USAID. Lastly, the role of CROs, as both healthcare providers and profitable subcontractors of pharmaceutical companies, is discussed in relation to the purported social good clinical trials provide.

Neoliberal Imperialism in Healthcare

Policies of privatization of healthcare and international patent regulations can perhaps be best understood as part of a US-led neoliberal imperialism that promotes a system that benefits all parties yet produces and takes advantage of asymmetries in trade and capital flows. When the IMF and World Bank open up the markets of countries, "the wealth and well-being of particular territories are augmented at the expense of others" with capitalist interests based in the US as prime beneficiaries (Harvey, 2005, pp. 31–32, 39). Though this continues to an extent today, I discuss reforms that began in the 1980s.

Healthcare was an important area affected by these reforms. Privatization was pursued as a solution to what were perceived as inefficient government services. While the extent of these measures varied, privatization or *decentralization* took hold in many countries in both the Global North and Global South. Through decentralization, the World Bank continues to believe efficiency can be achieved locally, improving the delivery of services (Reich, 2002, pp. 1670, 1672).

In neoliberal reform, the public sector was not erased, but rather took care of the unprofitable aspects of public health. The World Bank is of the opinion, shared by many in the US government, that market principles should be placed first as they are expected to produce health benefits and prosperity in turn (Waitzkin et al., 2005, pp. 898–899). In other words, the state is only there to ensure "that the conditions are right for capital accumulation" which will improve health (Hanieh, 2006, p. 187). But asking *cui bono* here is important: who benefits in terms of health and wealth? Claims of *pharmaceutical* empire seem relevant when the US can put pressure on South Africa to prevent it from calling a state of emergency over HIV/AIDS and circumventing the WTO rules on importing generic drugs (Cooper, 2008, pp. 52–53). This resonates with Harvey's (2005) description of imperialist practices as states try to retain control of capital flows according to the strengths of the regional economy (in this case, pharmaceuticals) (p. 107).

Alongside healthcare reform, patent regulations were increasingly lobbied for by the pharmaceutical industry and indeed sought to make strong intellectual property laws a prerequisite for countries' continued access to US markets. The use of the word *piracy* to describe unsatisfactory patent protections branded the practices of Brazil and India as tantamount to theft and dangerous. Interestingly, in this instance *lack* of regulation was criminal to a neoliberal government (Harrison, 2001, p. 496).

What were the effects of all this for Brazil and India? In Brazil, just as an AIDS epidemic was making its way to the fore, the state implemented reforms leading to serious understaffing and underfunding in healthcare as it instituted a constitution in 1988 making healthcare a universal right (Biehl, 2004, p. 108). The Brazilian state also changed its philosophy of public health from one focused on prevention and clinical care to one of pharmaceuticalization at the same time as it joined the Agreement on Trade Related

Aspects of Intellectual Property Rights (an international agreement to protect patents). It also imported vast amounts of patented medication on which all taxes were abolished. This created a lucrative market for pharmaceutical companies and made access to specialized care increasingly difficult for those without the capital to purchase healthcare (Biehl, 2004, pp. 112–113). Most international and national funds were allocated to AIDS prevention through NGOs (with the number of these organizations growing from 120 in 1993 to 480 in 1999) and local programs operating like NGOs. Before a law made medicines universally available (to reduce costs on care for opportunistic diseases accompanying AIDS), citizens were represented to their own state through NGOs, who decided who got what care (Biehl, 2004, pp. 108–110).

In Africa, similar stories have unfolded as USAID and the World Bank have pushed for structural adjustment and dismantled state services. These same organizations have also pushed for NGOs to fill in the voids created by compressing the state (Pfeiffer, 2003, p. 726). For example, in Uganda, the World Bank pressured policymakers to implement user fees for healthcare and a Danish aid agency pushed for a policy change concerning essential drugs, using the promise of future benefits and the threat of cutting off aid (Reich, 2002, p. 1669).

Foreign aid itself and Public-Private Partnerships (PPPs), to eradicate disease with drugs and vaccines, became entry points for pharmaceutical companies and NGOs in the 1990s and 2000s. In both cases, the state's inefficiency or incapacity to provide medical services justified these new initiatives, especially as states could no longer turn to the USSR for support with the end of the Cold War. In Mozambique, for instance, aid from USAID and the World Bank (two of the most aggressive proponents of structural adjustment) has been increasingly funnelled through NGOs as these are thought to reach poor communities more efficiently and *compassionately* than public services (Pfeiffer, 2003, pp. 725–726). As a powerful example of what I would call *iatrogenic imperialism*, the influx of compassionate NGOs fragmented the public healthcare system in Mozambique (previously touted as a model for the *developing world* by the WHO) and intensified the already growing social inequality (Pfeiffer, 2003, pp. 726–727). Not only did healthcare professionals find new possibilities for better livelihoods with NGO salaries, but the state found itself busy managing deals with and competition between NGOs rather than dealing with care (Pfeiffer, 2003, p. 732).

Public-Private Partnerships, comprised of governments, academia, international organizations and pharmaceutical companies, have also emerged out of the gaps in the state. These are geared towards improving access to or developing drugs and vaccines for diseases (such as malaria and tuberculosis) often seen as unprofitable objects of research by the pharmaceutical industry. People from the countries concerned are usually a small fraction of those on the board of these partnerships and some PPPs become independent NGOs that use portfolio management approaches, underscoring a certain managerial tendency emerging in this enterprise (Campos, Norman & Jadad, 2011, pp. 986–987, 992–993).

Non-Governmental Organizations

With the retreat of the state in many countries of the Global South, NGOs have stepped in to fulfill some of its roles. As organizations that are not elected by the people they are helping, their direct accountabilities lie elsewhere. In many respects NGOs function like modern states and corporations: they often adopt managerial practices oriented towards efficiency to maximize their objective of saving as many lives as possible. It should be clear in stating this that I am not referring to all NGOs and all their practices, but certain influential NGOs and prominent tendencies in humanitarian practice. The practices of NGOs have many effects: they fill gaps and give legitimacy to the state while also undermining state governance (as previ-

ously argued), they can inflate housing costs, and they offer opportunities for advancement for middle-class, public
sector workers in the Global South which reproduces
global inequalities (Schuller, 2009, pp. 85, 87, 92, 97).

However, these are only some of the externalities of the
capillary forms of therapeutic domination that take place
when NGOs exert the power over life and death in situations of emergency. HIV/AIDS treatment programs offer a
good example of what I mean. Lack of access to treatment
for HIV/AIDS became a global humanitarian emergency
in 2000. Vinh-Kim Nguyen (2009) argues that it was biomedical advances in therapy and diagnosis that allowed
decades of neglect to be reframed as a crisis (pp. 196, 200).
The newly-constituted HIV emergency invited intervention from NGOs in the name of saving lives. Ironically,
their actors and even their tasks are increasingly seen as
indistinguishable from those of intervening military forces.
Indeed, both are concerned with the management of populations to ensure that lives are saved (Nguyen, 2009, p.
201). In the case of HIV, massive treatment programs have
involved enrolling patients, deploying unprecedented
funding, drugs and technologies to better manage the well-
being of populations of individuals with the most intimate
detail.

PEPFAR (President's Emergency Plan for AIDS Relief)
launched under George W. Bush, became the prime example for the administration of its humanitarian foreign policy (Nguyen, 2009, pp. 202–203). Its implementation was
mostly left to local faith-based organizations advocating
abstinence and fidelity as prevention measures, part of a
set of intimate technologies deployed in order to save lives
that change the way people care for and talk about their
bodies and their families. Though PEPFAR differs in its
singularity from assemblages of NGOs, it operates in a
similar mode of therapeutic domination (Nguyen, 2009,
pp. 204–205; McFalls, 2010, p. 318).

To prove the effectiveness of treatment, certain measures of efficiency like the number of lives or *years* of life
saved then become the basis for experimentation and the

generation of evidence in staying accountable to funders (Nguyen, 2009, pp. 209, 211). NGOs must often attract funding from external sources like USAID, which has led to accusations of them being subcontractors for foreign powers as their projects may reflect the priorities of their funders more than grassroots demand (Landolt, 2007, p. 707).

The measures used to explain effectiveness and intervention go beyond the usual humanitarian concern for *bare life*, that is the number of lives saved (McFalls, 2010, p. 324). Other measures such as *quality-of-life* have become important for NGOs working in India in the field of HIV/AIDS, moving beyond its past as a measure of development to become a justification for intervention. Measures such as these minimize the need for political coercion as people become *empowered* to see their actions as a sort of entrepreneurial maximization of their own health. *Empowerment* has a history in biomedicine going back to the 1970s. It emerged out of concerns for efficiency of public health promotion and the limits of biomedicine, leading to a focus on making people responsible for their own health and *empowered* to change *unhealthy* habits (Lock & Nguyen, 2010, p. 295). In this case of HIV/AIDS in India, quality-of-life *empowerment* is a strategy to regulate peoples' behaviour embedded in a neoliberal program of health governance (Finn & Sarangi, 2008, pp. 1569–1570).

It is thus unsurprising that health should be advocated as important to US foreign policy. A report co-sponsored by the Council on Foreign Relations established that the US promoting global public health would be a means of preventing infectious diseases from reaching the US in a time of increased mobility. It would also improve political instability crucial to maintaining economic flows. Surveillance and treatment systems become justified in claiming strategic and *moral* benefits (Kassalow, 2001). The 2010 US National Security Strategy further emphasizes that pandemic diseases are threats to the US and its citizens, and that the US should seek to create a stable international order for its own interests, but also as an end to be sought in and of itself (White House, 2010).

Interestingly, some of the most influential NGOs have significant ties to US state agencies and major corporations. The ones I allude to here are fairly widely known: Christian Action Research and Education International (CARE International) and Save the Children. CARE's areas of concern include water sanitation, economic development and emergency response. Their total assets and liabilities for 2012 amount to €500 million. Their partners include many UN agencies, such as the World Bank, as well as development agencies, including CIDA and USAID, from many governments of the Global North. Their corporate sponsors are unlisted (CARE, 2012; CARE, 2014). However, the current Chairperson of CARE, Ralph Martens, is a former vice president at Merrill Lynch (SourceWatch, 2014a) and the Chairperson before him, Lydia Marshall, had previously worked as a vice president for Citigroup (SourceWatch, 2014b).

Save the Children is another relief-oriented organization. It discloses its numerous corporate partners on its website. These include GlaxoSmithKline, the Merck Foundation, Disney, Mattel, Goldman Sachs and Johnson & Johnson (Save the Children [STC], 2014). However they also receive hundreds of millions of dollars from governments according to a 2005 financial form. Save the Children subsequently retracted the form from their website, obscuring the staggering US $149 million contribution by USAID (SourceWatch, 2014c).

GlaxoSmithKline, a multinational pharmaceutical corporation, recently partnered with CARE International and Save the Children to increase its presence in the Global South. GSK's CEO framed this move in terms of investing in a region where profits were relatively low and where they could "make a difference" (World Pharma News, 2011). Save the Children's Chief Executive called GSK's move brave and said it would help their top priority of "saving the lives of some of the poorest children of the poorest communities" (World Pharma News, 2011).

Further blurring the line between profitable investment and humanitarianism is the Partnership for Quality Medical Donations (PQMD). The executive director of this organization, in a speech entitled, "The Evolving Role of NGOs in the Pharmaceutical Industry's Product Donation Programs," claims that the Global South's markets offer not just an opportunity for future profit, but also the opportunity for "this magnificent industry to show its concern for the world community as a whole, even to the poorest among us" and ensuring some "victory for humanity" (Russo, 2004, p. 1). The mobilization of humanitarian sentiment is quite clear here.

After the WHO changed their guidelines for drug donations in 1999 in favour of the PQMD's recommendations, a 2001 WHO study conducted in *emergency* countries like Mozambique and India found that those in violation were governments and local distributors, not major pharmaceutical corporations and *experienced* NGOs (Russo, 2004, pp. 2-5). Instead of examining the pressures the pharmaceutical industry-NGO alliance itself has placed on governments and local distributors and the way it has turned the pharmacy into the primary site of healthcare after the retraction of the state in countries like India, this statement makes an appeal to efficiency and an objective humanitarian good (Kamat & Nichter, 1998, pp. 779-780). Their position could be summarized in this way: our experts are better at delivering these inherently good drugs according to the best guidelines and those local amateurs are guilty of irrational and *iatrogenic* drug donation practices (since they may harm those who consume them). I use *iatrogenic* here to illustrate its usage as a term of power in medical discourse that pathologizes local practice while obscuring the influence of the *experts* in fostering these *irrational* and *harmful* practices.

Contract Research Organizations

The extent to which neoliberal imperialism in healthcare is felt is not limited to NGOs. Indeed, pharmaceutical companies arguably have a more direct presence through the Contract Research Organizations they hire to conduct pharmaceutical research at low cost and recruit subjects. At the same time, CROs offer the possibility of treatment to local people for the illness they are researching. Since an increasing number of clinical trials are being conducted in the Global South, some claim these offer a new kind of social good that the state cannot provide (Petryna, 2005). Though global clinical trials are a new phenomenon, they have come under scrutiny through the book and film *The Constant Gardener* (Goldacre, 2012, p. 119). The original material is based on the case of a clinical trial in 1996 illegally conducted at the behest of pharmaceutical giant Pfizer in Nigeria, which caused the deaths of eleven children (Stephens, 2006/5/7). One cable shows Pfizer pressured local officials to drop the matter and accept settlement money (US Embassy, Abuja [USEA], 2009). I will return to this example, but before that it may be useful to explore the issues raised by this example through the main facilitators of pharmaceutical clinical trials today: CROs.

If I specify *today* it is because CROs are in part a product of some of the recent history of neoliberal policy I have alluded to previously. In part due to US regulatory limitations implemented in the 1970s on using prisoners as test subjects, the pharmaceutical industry began to look abroad. Interestingly, the FDA's response to the scandal around prisoner testing was to claim ignorance and reiterate its vow to protect intellectual property rights. By the 1990s, with the help of the FDA, drug development had become a booming, globalized and outsourced endeavour. The search for treatment-naive human bodies upon which to conduct cost-effective experiments abroad meant dealing with foreign bureaucracies, a service which newly-formed Contract Research Organizations are apt to provide, having ties to oversight boards in the countries they operate in. It should be noted that CROs have increasingly made their way into situations of emergency, where needs are higher, to gather patients for trials more effectively (Petryna, 2005, p. 185–192).

Though their clients are giants like Merck and Pfizer, some of these organizations also have a significant global presence, conducting trials that can involve tens of thousands of people in dozens of countries, a practice that also precludes FDA audit efforts (Petryna, 2005, pp. 185–192; Petryna, 2007, p. 295). Large, US-based CROs like Charles River Laboratories (SourceWatch, 2014d) and Covance Laboratories (SourceWatch, 2014e) are also beginning to engage in lobbying directly. Capital not only links CROs to pharmaceutical multinationals and governments, but also links these last two together: without even getting into campaign contributions, Pfizer and Merck, for example, both received millions of dollars in contracts from the US Department of Defense in past years (US Office of Management and Budget [OMB], 2014a; OMB, 2014b).

In conducting globalized trials, CROs not only profit, but they bolster the advance of the pharmaceutical industry in health and reproduce global inequalities in various ways. Much like NGOs, CRO trials also draw away locally trained clinicians to better-paying jobs. In addition, testing a new line of drugs can help create new markets for pharmaceuticals in countries like Brazil by changing patients' expectations and exposing them to expensive, patented drugs (Goldacre, 2012). *Seeding trials* are in fact conducted as barely masked attempts to market new drugs (Psaty & Rennie, 2006, p. 2787). And by playing up the markets for patented drugs, trials play into the dominant position in US foreign policy of ensuring medicinal access through patent protection, to the benefit of the research pharmaceutical industry (Gathii, 2003). These marketing tactics have real consequences for local governments, as policy makers in the Global South trying to make healthcare delivery safe and equitable become mired by pressures and potentially unreliable data from the pharmaceutical industry (Petryna, 2010, p. 60).

Moreover, pharmacists then become consultants in a process of consuming health through drugs and encouraging self-experimentation (Kamat & Nichter, 1998, pp. 779–780). People thus engage in subject-making and self-disciplining in relationship with the research and health industry (and occasionally local governments), becoming part of therapeutic markets in an attempt to secure health benefits in a time where the state alone is not providing it. This makes populations visible and allows them to be *managed* and cared for more *efficiently* (Biehl & Petryna, 2011).

Returning to the Pfizer case, it is a useful example to understand some of the wider context embedding the practices of CROs. Pfizer claimed its researchers went purely out of the goodness of their hearts as a meningitis epidemic ravaged the country. Indeed, Pfizer's statement claimed that the drug had undoubtedly "saved lives" (Stephens, 2006/5/7). However, as the panel of Nigerian doctors reviewing the case pointed out, the Pfizer-sponsored researchers left after the trial, even as the epidemic raged on (Stephens, 2006/5/7). Even though the idea that clinical trials are a depoliticized social good may not be convincing, there is a disincentive to point out the harm resulting from a particular CRO trial because they can simply do business somewhere else (Petryna, 2010, p. 62).

Indeed, ideas of emergency and goodwill legitimated Pfizer's intervention, leading to a deadly experiment that would have been impossible under normal clinical conditions in the US (Petryna, 2005, p. 191). But the Nigerian panel's response must also be viewed critically. Borrowing the language of medical ethics, they called it a clear case of the "exploitation of the ignorant" and proposed increased regulation and oversight (Stephens, 2006/5/7). The panel reinforces the liberal ideas in biomedical ethics of people as free subjects that must become informed, emphasizing moral protections rather than addressing concerns like hunger or sickness that might have more to do with why people sought out the trial (Redfield, 2013, p. 37). This is especially salient as people internalize a neoliberal governmentality that makes them entrepreneurs of their own health, and as states of exception are produced not by suspending the law but by CROs posing obstacles to current legal frameworks (Prasad, 2009, pp. 3, 13). These processes should be seen within the context of "neoliberal securitization," in which the erosion of the state also triggers the state to focus aggressively on social stability to attract global capital (McLoughlin & Forte, 2014, pp. 4–6). CROs and the capital their pharmaceutical sponsors are expected to bring can thus be seen as stabilizing forces, especially in periods of *emergency*.

With clinical trials there is a strange blending of the therapeutic, the commercial and indeed the humanitarian. We see this concretely in how Pfizer responded to the accusations coming from Nigeria: the lawsuit froze momentum to do clinical trials in Nigeria and a Pfizer manager "opined that *when another outbreak occurs, no company will come to Nigeria's aid*" (US Embassy, Abuja [USEA], 2009). This statement reflects the convergence of the need to provide health services in the wake of a dispossessed state, the ostensible goodwill of the pharmaceutical industry's trials and the threat to commerce that resistance poses. Though the industry and US regulators do not necessarily codify providing a social good as a justification for promoting clinical trials in poor areas, it has become a norm (Petryna, 2005, p. 187). In other words, the "politicization of bare life" in neoliberal governmentality seems to be an intrinsic part of the ethicality of drug trials (Prasad, 2009, p. 19).

Unlike security risk management, the management of clinical trials seems to proliferate risk for the subjects of the trials, as protecting patents and the rights of CROs rather than test subjects becomes the neoliberal state's agenda (Prasad, 2009, pp. 15–16). Indeed, CROs whether they are based in the US or India, for instance, rely on global inequalities of disease and access to biomedical treatment to be able to gather enough people who haven't been taking drugs beforehand and ensure untarnished data. The therapeutic and the commercial come together in the way that diseases become marketable assets that exist perhaps only as exchange value as it is a commodity with not a result of useful or productive labour (Prasad, 2009, pp. 6-7, 17). Paradoxically, the pharmaceutical industry seeks to extend the reach of its drugs in the global market while relying on large populations of diseased people seeking treatment globally to develop new drugs.

In the film *The Constant Gardener*, the film's protagonist gets warned not to go looking in "foreign gardens" (Meirelles, 2005). As the title suggests, these *gardens* are not naturally occurring: they are produced. Much like what I have tried to bring out through the idea of iatrogenic imperialism, this idea of a constant gardener implies that though *gardens* may fail, the fundamental assumptions that everyone will become more *prosperous, healthy* and *free* are universally true and good. However, we might reconsider the territorialization that the metaphor of the garden implies: increasingly, any one state or region will have significant inequalities within its borders, pointing to a need to look beyond any one state or actor as *the* constant gardener. Indeed, it is problematic to see clinical trials as being created and controlled solely by Western organizations as well as seeing medical narratives within the frame of colonizer-Other or doctor-patient dichotomies (Saethre & Stadler, 2013, p. 115). As I mentioned before, *iatrogenic* is a term of power, one associated with medical discourse. While I have used it to reflect on the influence of humanitarianism and neoliberalism in healthcare, I would caution against buying into the logic that makes some people into *patients* and others into *experts* or *doctors*. Indeed, the word *iatrogenic* seems to have a dual potential through this dichotomy, whereby it can be used to criticize the harmful practices of non-experts and patients, but can also be used to show the limits of expertise.

Conclusion

In sum, NGOs and CROs have become powerful actors in global healthcare, mobilizing the idea of emergency and humanitarian goals to justify their activities, which have undermined public healthcare systems and reproduced global inequalities. Under neoliberal empire, healthcare has become the individual's responsibility, largely absolving the retracted, managerial state from providing it directly. I have focused here on a facet, or perhaps a modality, of empire that I have called *iatrogenic* for its penetrating and far-reaching consequences, which have emerged from the level of state infrastructure down to the level of the everyday. But it is perhaps this level of the everyday which has been insufficiently explored here. It is in everyday practice that we are likely to find empire in its most minute and hegemonic expressions, but it is also perhaps where empire is most likely to be adapted and resisted.

References

Biehl, J. (2004). The Activist State: Global Pharmaceuticals, AIDS, and Citizenship in Brazil. *Social Text, 22*(3), 105–132.

Biehl, J., & Petryna, A. (2011). Bodies of Rights and Therapeutic Markets. *Social Research, 78*(2), 359–386.

Calhoun, C. (2010). The Idea of Emergency: Humanitarian Action and Global (Dis)Order. In D. Fassin, & M. Pandolfi (Eds.), *Contemporary States of Emergency: The Politics of Military and Humanitarian Interventions* (pp. 29–58). Brooklyn, NY: Zone Books.

Campos, K. D. P.; Norman, C. D., & Jadad, A. R. (2011). Product Development Public-Private Partnerships for Public Health: a Systematic Review Using Qualitative Data. *Social Science & Medicine, 73*(7), 986–994.

CARE. (2012). *Annual Report 2012.* Geneva: Care International. http://www.care.org/newsroom/annual-reports

———. (2014). *Partners and Donors.* http://www.care-international.org/about-us/partners.aspx#.U0cVxqLn_0l

Cooper, M. (2008). *Life as Surplus: Biotechnology and Capitalism in the Neoliberal Era.* Seattle, WA: University of Washington Press.

Fassin, D. (2010). Heart of Humaneness: The Moral Economy of

Humanitarian Intervention. In D. Fassin, & M. Pandolfi (Eds.), *Contemporary States of Emergency: The Politics of Military and Humanitarian Interventions* (pp. 269–294). Brooklyn, NY: Zone Books.

Finn, M., & Sarangi, S. (2008). Quality of Life as a Mode of Governance: NGO Talk of HIV 'Positive' Health in India. *Social Science & Medicine, 66*(7), 1568–1578.

Gathii, J. T. (2003). The Structural Power of Strong Pharmaceutical Patent Protection in U.S. Foreign Policy. *The Journal of Gender, Race & Justice, 7*(2), 267–314.

Goldacre, B. (2012). *Bad Pharma: How Drug Companies Mislead Doctors and Harm Patients.* New York, NY: Fourth Estate.

Hanieh, A. (2013). Praising Empire: Neoliberalism under Pax Americana. In C. Mooers, (Ed.), *The New Imperialists: Ideologies of Empire* (pp. 199–228). Oxford, UK: Oneworld Publications.

Harrison, C. S. (2001). Protection of Pharmaceuticals as Foreign Policy: The Canada-U.S. Trade Agreement and Bill C-22 Versus the North American Free Trade Agreement and Bill C-91. *The North Carolina Journal of International Law and Commercial Regulation, 26,* 457–528.

Harvey, D. (2005). *The New Imperialism.* Oxford, UK: Oxford University Press.

Kamat, V. R., & Nichter, M. (1998). Pharmacies, Self-Medication and Pharmaceutical Marketing in Bombay, India. *Social Science & Medicine, 47*(6), 779–794.

Kassalow, J. S. (2001). Why Health is Important to U.S. Foreign Policy. *Council on Foreign Relations & Milbank Memorial Fund.* http://www.milbank.org/uploads/documents/Foreignpolicy.html

Landolt, L. K. (2007). USAID, Population Control, and NGO-led Democratization in Egypt: The Fate of the ICPD Programme of Action. *Democratization, 14*(4), 706–722.

Lock, M., & Nguyen, V.K. (2010). *An Anthropology of Biomedicine.* Oxford, UK: Wiley-Blackwell.

McFalls, L. (2010). Benevolent Dictatorship: The Formal Logic of Humanitarian Government. In D. Fassin, & M. Pandolfi (Eds.), *Contemporary States of Emergency: The Politics of Military and Humanitarian Interventions* (pp. 317–334). Brooklyn, NY: Zone Books.

McLoughlin, K., & Forte, M. C. (2014). Introduction. In K. McLoughlin, & M. C. Forte (Eds.), *Emergency as Security:*

Liberal Empire at Home and Abroad (pp. 1–19). Montreal, QC: Alert Press.

Meirelles, F. (Director). (2005). *The Constant Gardener* [Motion Picture]. United States: Focus Features.

Nguyen, V. K. (2009). Government-by-exception: Enrolment and Experimentality in Mass HIV Treatment Programs in Africa. *Social Theory & Health,* 7(3), 196–217.

Petryna, A. (2005). Ethical Variability: Drug Development and Globalizing Clinical Trials. *American Ethnologist,* 32(2), 183–197.

————— . (2007). Experimentality: On the Global Mobility and Regulation of Human Subjects Research. *PoLar: Political and Legal Anthropology Review,* 30(2), 288–304.

————— . (2010). Paradigms of Expected Failure. *Dialectical Anthropology,* 34(1), 57–65.

Pfeiffer, J. (2003). International NGOs and Primary Health Care in Mozambique: the Need for a New Model of Collaboration. *Social Science & Medicine,* 56(4), 725–738.

Prasad, A. (2009). Capitalizing Disease: Biopolitics of Drug Trials in India. *Theory, Culture & Society,* 26(5), 1–29.

Psaty, B.M., & Rennie, D. (2006). Clinical Trial Investigators and Their Prescribing Patterns: Another Dimension to the Relationship between Physician Investigators and the Pharmaceutical Industry. *Journal of the American Medical Association,* 295(23), 2787–2790.

Redfield, P. (2013) Commentary: Eyes Wide Shut in Transnational Science and Aid. *American Ethnologist,* 40(1), 35–37.

Reich, M. R. (2002). Reshaping the State from Above, from Within, from Below: Implications for Public Health. *Social Science & Medicine,* 54(11), 1669–1675.

Russo, J.B. (2004). The Evolving Role of NGOs in the Pharmaceutical Industry's Product Donation Programs. *The Partnership for Quality Medical Donations.* http://www.marcopolodesign.com/pqmd/resources_other_s2.html

Saethre, E., & Stadler, J. (2013). Malicious Whites, Greedy Women, and Virtuous Volunteers Negotiating Social Relations through Clinical Trial Narratives in South Africa. *Medical Anthropology Quarterly,* 27(1), 103–120.

Save the Children (STC). (2014). *Corporate Partners.* http://www.savethechildren.org/site/c.8rKLIXMGIpI4E/b.6148397/k.C77

B/Corporate_Partners.htm

Schuller, M. (2009). Gluing Globalization: NGOs as Intermediaries in Haiti. *PoLAR: Political and Legal Anthropology Review*, 32(1), 84–104.

SourceWatch. (2014a). *Ralph Martens*.
http://www.sourcewatch.org/index.php/Ralph_Martens

————. (2014b). *Lydia M. Marshall*.
http://www.sourcewatch.org/index.php/Lydia_M._Marshall

————. (2014c). *Save the Children USA*.
http://www.sourcewatch.org/index.php/Save_the_Children_USA

————. (2014d). *Charles River*.
http://www.sourcewatch.org/index.php/Charles_River

————. (2014e). *Covance Laboratories*.
http://www.sourcewatch.org/index.php/Covance_Laboratories

Stephens, J. (2006/5/7). Panel Faults Pfizer in '96 Clinical Trial in Nigeria. *The Washington Post*, p. A01.
http://www.washingtonpost.com/wp-dyn/content/article/2006/05/06/AR2006050601338.html

US Office of Management and Budget (OMB). (2014a). *Prime Award Spending Data for the US Department of Defense for Pfizer-Wyeth*. Washington, DC: US Office of Budget and Management.
http://www.usaspending.gov/explore?tab=By+Prime+Awardee&frompage=contracts&contractorid=001326495&contractorname=PFIZER+INC.&fiscal_year=all&maj_contracting_agency=9700&maj_contracting_agency_name=Department+of+Defense

————. (2014b). *Prime Award Spending Data for the US Department of Defense for Merck & Co. Inc.* Washington, DC: US Office of Budget and Management.
http://www.usaspending.gov/explore?tab=By+Prime+Awardee&typeofview=detailsummary&contractorid=054554290&contractorname=MERCK+%26amp%3B+CO.++INC.&fiscal_year=all&maj_contracting_agency=9700&maj_contracting_agency_name=Department+of+Defense

US Embassy, Abuja (USEA). (2009/4/20).Nigeria: Pfizer Reaches Preliminary Agreement For A $75 Million Settlement [Diplomatic Cable]. *Abuja, Nigeria: US Embassy.* [09ABUJA671].
http://cablegatesearch.wikileaks.org/cable.php?id=09ABUJA671&q=nigeria%20pfizer

Waitzkin, H.; Jasso-Aguilar, R.; Landwehr, A., & Mountain, C. (2005). Global Trade, Public Health and Health Services: Stakeholders' Constructions of the Key Issues. *Social Science & Medicine*, 61(5), 893–906.

White House. (2010). *National Security Strategy*. Washington, DC: White House.

http://www.whitehouse.gov/sites/default/files/rss_viewer/national_sec urity_strategy.pdf

World Pharma News. (2011). GSK Forms Partnership with Three Leading NGOs.

http://www.worldpharmanews.com/gsk/1689-gsk-forms-partnership-with-three-leading-ngos%20%28CARE%20and%20Save%20the%20Children%29

CHAPTER 2

US Imperialism and Disaster Capitalism in Haiti

✯ ✯ ✯ ✯ ✯

Keir Forgie

"Have they not consigned these miserable blacks to man-eating dogs until the latter, sated by human flesh, left the mangled victims to be finished off with bayonet and poniard". — Henri Christophe, 1767–1820.

At 4:53 PM, on Monday, January 12, 2010, a 7.0 magnitude earthquake shocked Port-au-Prince, Haiti. It was the most devastating earthquake the country had experienced in over 200 years, with estimated infrastructure damage between $8 and $14 billion (Donlon, 2012, p. vii; Farmer, 2011, p. 54). This is particularly astounding considering that Haiti is recognized as the poorest country in the Western Hemisphere, with 70% of individuals surviving on less than $2 US per day (Farmer, 2011, p. 60). The quake's epicentre was located 15 miles southwest of Port-au-Prince, which is the most heavily populated area in all of Haiti (Donlon, 2012, p. vii). Approximately three million Haitians, one third of the country's population, live in Port-au-Prince and every single individual was affected by the disaster: the Haitian government reported 230,000 deaths, 300,600 injured persons, and between 1.2 to 2 million displaced people (Donlon, 2012, p. vii). The country presented a "blank slate," with all manner of political, economic, and social services in absolute ruin — an ideal circumstance to exercise the arms of the new (US) imperialism: notably, NGOs, the UN Stabilization Mission in Haiti (MINUSTAH), the militarization of humanitarian aid, and disaster capitalism.

US hegemonic globalization is the current world order—it is the new imperialism. The breadth of US influence across the globe in terms of politics, economics, and military are unparalleled across history, affording the nation the means to orchestrate geopolitics in its favor through coercion, masked by rhetorical altruism (Moselle, 2008, pp. 1, 8). However, the US is currently challenged by a state of economic decline and shifting international relations. In an effort to maintain its dominant position, the US must implement a number of novel strategies. As such, the "new imperialism" is distinguished by certain contemporary characteristics: notably, war in the pursuit of dwindling natural resources, the militarization of the social sciences, war corporatism, the romanticization of imperialism, and as a central focus to this paper, the framing of military interventions as "humanitarian," legitimized through rhetoric of freedom, democracy, and the right to intervene. In truth, the militarization of humanitarian aid serves to facilitate the imposition of neoliberal economic policies through the exploitation of weakened states—a strategy known as "disaster capitalism".

Disaster capitalism is a defining feature of US imperialism. It is used to exploit nation states during times of crises and to implement neoliberal corporate policies that favor US capitalism. Apocalyptic events present the ideal opportunity of a "blank slate" on which free-market economics and US-style "democratic" systems can be established to replace what has been temporarily incapacitated. These exploitative transitions are possible because nations in turmoil, desperate for aid, are not in a position to negotiate the terms of that aid; therefore, controversial policies are passed while the victimized nation and its people are emotionally and physically shocked and collectively dependent (Klein, 2007, p. 17). The result is an extortion of state sovereignty swaddled by mutual consent: privatization, government deregulation, and reduced social welfare are beneficial for US capitalism and detrimental for the long-term security and development of shocked nations (Klein, 2007, p. 9).

The US imposes its imperial will upon Haiti via military intervention, US-funded NGOs, and the US-sponsored UN-mission, MINUSTAH. The US has repeatedly used its military and the CIA to intervene in Haitian politics and guarantee neoliberal commercial interests. MINUSTAH has contributed to the country's state of ontological insecurity, preventing democratic organization and fair representation. In addition, US-sponsored NGOs have undermined the authority of the Haitian government locally and on a global political scale, which facilitates the implementation of US interests in Haiti. Combined with Haiti's history of colonial oppression, these injustices help explain the economic and structural vulnerability of the nation leading up to the earthquake of 2010. Haiti may be the poorest country in the Western Hemisphere, in dire need of assistance (and fair political relations) from more developed nations. However, not all assistance is created equal—given that altruistic rhetoric and appeals to humanitarianism are used to mask US intentions of conquest, the focal point of any analysis of US imperialism in Haiti must be the political and economic conditions that result from US impositions, not the propaganda used to foster a favorable international appeal for foreign aid. Claims of good intentions do not negate imperial outcomes that prevent independent development and exacerbate indebtedness.

US imperialism and disaster capitalism in Haiti are enforced by military intervention, US-funded NGOs, and the MINUSTAH occupation of Haiti, all of which have undermined Haitian governmental autonomy, societal structure, and economic development. Furthermore, the militarization of humanitarian aid within Haiti following the cataclysmic earthquake of January 2010 facilitated US-style disaster capitalism. Taken together, militarization of aid and disaster capitalism are the exemplars of the new imperialism. The US capitalized upon the crisis to pursue its own politico-economic interests under the guise of altruistic rhetoric. These actions are imperialist because of the coercive methods used to usurp the power of national decision-making in relation to infrastructure development and economic policy, which ultimately subverts Haiti and reduces it to the status of a US means of production and a sponge for capital overflow.

US Military Intervention

The US military has a long history of intervening in Haiti to impose imperial interests: noteworthy US interventions include the military occupation of 1915-1934, support for the Duvalier dictatorships of 1934-1986, the CIA sponsored coup of 1991, and the CIA orchestrated exile of President Aristide in 2004. In 1915, US Marines invaded Haiti and occupied the country for a period of 19 years in order to secure US interests. The US privatized the National Bank, re-instituted forced-labour, and left behind a military force that would become the precursor for the Haitian Army (Podur, 2012, pp. 13-14). From 1957 to 1986, the US supported the dictatorial regimes of the Duvaliers because of their anti-communist agendas and their favouring US corporate investors (Smith, 2010/1/14). The Duvalier reign was overcome by revolt in 1986, and in 1991 Jean-Bertrand Aristide of the Lavalas political party was elected president with a campaign of progressive reforms to serve Haiti's poor (Podur, 2012, pp. 16-17). Following a CIA military backed coup in 1991, Aristide was removed from power only to be restored to the presidency by the Clinton administration under the condition that Aristide impose the US neoliberal plan (referred to by Haitians as "The Plan of Death") (Chossudovsky, 2004/2/29; Smith, 2010/1/14). In February 2004, the Pentagon and Haiti's elite organized yet another coup that exiled Aristide to South Africa. To quell the pro-Aristide uprising, the US instigated a UN military occupation of Haiti and appointed a puppet government led by René Préval to enforce the US neoliberal plan (Chossudovsky, 2004/2/29; Frantz, 2011;

Smith, 2010/1/14). According to President Aristide, he was kidnapped and forced to resign under pressure by the US, although these accusations have been denied (CNN, 2004/3/1; Frantz, 2011). Even this brief chronology attests to the fact that the real state power belongs to the US military, which seems to intervene against Haitian sovereignty as it sees fit. Currently, UN military forces originally deployed to control "unrest" (dissent) following the coup of 2004 continue to occupy Haiti under the guise of security and stabilization. MINUSTAH has, however, contributed considerably to the state of ontological insecurity in Haiti, functioning as an arm of US imperialism.

MINUSTAH

MINUSTAH functions to enforce US politico-economic interests in Haiti by suppressing democracy and contributing to ontological insecurity that interferes with national sovereignty. MINUSTAH's continued occupation of Haiti is based on the proposition that the international community is threatened by local political violence (Frantz, 2011). However, with the US paying one-quarter of MINUSTAH's budget, the support for occupation is much more sinister.

MINUSTAH enforces US government objectives by preventing social and political movements that run counter to neoliberalism and US corporate investment. According to a US Embassy cable from October 2008, then Ambassador Janet Sanderson explicitly states, "The UN Stabilization Mission in Haiti is an indispensable tool in realizing core USG (US government) policy interests in Haiti," including the prevention of resurgent "populist and anti-market economy political forces" (US Embassy Port-au-Prince [USEP], 2008/10/1). MINUSTAH has suppressed electoral democracy and free speech in Haiti though fraudulent elections and the killing of civilians during peaceful protests, thereby eliminating any opportunity for the poor majority to be heard (Frantz, 2011). According to Camille Chalmers, executive director of the Haitian Platform to Advocate for Alternative Development (PAPDA), "in terms of the construction of a democratic climate and tradition, we have regressed in comparison with the periods preceding MINUSTAH's arrival". This perception is based on the 2006 and 2010 presidential elections supported by the UN in which the most popular political party, Fanmi Lavalas led by Aristide, as well as many other political opponents, were banned from participating (Coughlin, 2011/10/6). Furthermore, in April 2008, UN troops killed a handful of demonstrators who were protesting against the rising costs of food, exemplifying the violent repression of political free speech.

In addition to such acts of armed violence, MINUSTAH has been accused of several accounts of sexual assault and the spread of disease. Together, these acts contribute to the state of ontological insecurity in Haiti, thereby undermining national sovereignty. For instance, in November 2007, 111 Sri Lankan soldiers were discharged for the sexual exploitation of Haitian minors (Coughlin, 2011/10/6). Furthermore, evidence suggests that UN soldiers introduced a virulent strain of Nepalese cholera just ten months following the earthquake. Approximately 7,000 Haitian have died and 700,000 have fallen ill (Engler, 2012/12/20). Outbreaks began after excrement from a MINUSTAH base in Mirebalais was released into the Artibonite River, used by the inhabitants of local slums for bathing and drinking. There is also reason to believe that UN officials were aware of the cholera strain's presence prior to the outbreak due to illness among soldiers, yet did nothing to prevent the contamination of local water sources (Coughlin, 2011/10/6; Engler, 2012/12/20).

For these reasons, Haitians are indignant towards MINUSTAH—it represents US interests in Haiti, functioning as a large anti-Aristide gang (Coughlin, 2011/10/6). In this sense, MINUSTAH enforces political repression of the poor majority, serves the dominant status quo of Haiti's elites, and facilitates imperial interests that prevent Haitian self-determination. These effects are mirrored and compounded by those imposed via the overwhelming presence of US-funded NGOs.

NGOs

NGOs function as arms of US imperialism by undermining the Haitian government: NGOs confuse the locus of sovereign authority for Haitians, possess agendas tied to global political influence, and offer a means for the US to invest aid money towards projects that suit imperial ambitions. It is estimated that prior to the earthquake of 2010, between 3,000 and 10,000 NGOs were present in Haiti, earning the country the title "Republic of NGOs" (United States Institute of Peace [USIP], 2010).

The excessive number of non-state organizing bodies produces a sense of hypergovernance, thereby undermining the authority of the Haitian government. A perception of statelessness among residents ensues and a confusion as to who governs the country results from a dependence on NGOs for essential services. A lack of coordination between NGOs and the state results in a mismatch of social development projects that are unsustainable, further contributing to the impression that no local authority is truly in charge (Kivland, 2012, pp. 248, 261; USIP, 2010).

Furthermore, NGOs provide a channel through which foreign governments and donors can funnel aid money, which draws away from potential state resources. This funding greatly increases NGO infrastructure, which in turn lures educated personnel from the public sector towards the greater financial opportunity, benefits, and improved working conditions offered by NGOs. The result is a "brain-drain" and further incapacitated government (USIP, 2010, pp. 1–2).

NGOs also possess their own agendas and political influence while being heavily influenced by donor interests, therefore decisions are made to support the donors and deliverers more than the recipients (Cunningham, 2012, p. 113). Humanitarian aid is inherently political, which fos-

ters a form of political coercion that elicits policies at the
discretion of the donor (Bueno de Mesquita, 2007, p. 254).
To illustrate, many NGOs were involved in the political
maneuvers—partnered with the governments of the US,
Canada, and France—that resulted in the exile of democratically elected president Aristide in 2004 (Engler,
2009/3/8). Considering that Aristide's constituency is
comprised of the poor majority, it is questionable exactly
whom NGOs are trying to help.

Although recipients do benefit from the aid conferred,
the greatest gains are made by donors, and NGOs offer a
means of pursuing business and political opportunities
abroad with substantial returns on investment. Despite the
$12 billion US funneled into Haiti through foreign aid and
NGOs following the quake, the country remains in dire
straights because the nature of the humanitarian aid regime conspires to prioritize donor-interests, particularly
those of the US. These interests include militarizing the
Caribbean Basin in pursuit of manifest destiny while per-
manently subverting Haiti to a means of production for US
capital.

The Militarization of Humanitarian Aid

The US has used the militarization of humanitarian aid in
Haiti to mask a forced occupation and imperial ambitions
under the guise of stabilization. The US government initiated a military invasion of Haiti before President Préval
indicated any security concern, thereby undermining Haitian sovereignty. The US greatly exaggerated the threat of
internal violence and political uprising to justify an excessive military deployment, which criminalized the victims.
Furthermore, the US used its military force and political
influence to immediately usurp control of the rescue operation, resulting in the subversion of food and medical security in favor of military priorities. In this sense, the US
demonstrated two things: the military's inability to trans-
fer combat skills to humanitarian action and the willing-

ness of the US to capitalize upon any opportunity in the Caribbean in pursuit of self-interests.

As mentioned, the US government initiated a military deployment in Haiti before any request was made by the Préval government, demonstrating US self-entitlement to usurp national decision making. According to a cable from Secretary of State, Hillary Clinton, the US deployed 4,000 military personnel to arrive in Haiti by January 15, followed by an additional 6,000 two days later. In a January 16 cable, President Préval established the following key priorities in the aftermath of the quake: communications, coordination, transport, food, water, medicine, and burials—no formal request for military personnel had been made (Herz, 2011/6/15). On January 17, a "joint communique" issued by Préval and Hillary Clinton stated the first request from Haiti for increased security assistance by the US military (Herz, 2011/6/15). Although the sense of unilateral US intervention was diminished, it did not entirely calm criticism from the international community of the US militarization of aid to Haiti. This forced the US to begin a campaign of rhetorical appeasement that reinforced the role of the US military as an assistant, not a leader, to the Haitian rescue mission (Clinton, 2010/1/22). Thus began the third US military occupation of Haiti within the previous twenty years.

The US deployed an excessive amount of military personnel to support the MINUSTAH security effort and justified this action through an exaggeration of the threat of looting and violence; however, the reality is that such incidences were sporadic and the preconceived notions of savagery served only to criminalize the victims who were in need of real humanitarian assistance, not law enforcement. In a January 14 cable to US Embassies and Pentagon commands worldwide, Hillary Clinton warned of significant looting related to food shortages; however, according to Ambassador Merten in Haiti, such incidences occurred only sporadically (Herz, 2011/6/15). The expectation of large-scale violence that could interfere with the delivery of essential supplies was the justification behind the US decision to deploy military forces before medical aid, water, or food. Considering that incidences of violence were relatively rare, the militarization of humanitarian aid in Haiti appears to have been an effort to assert political control rather than provide genuine assistance. As explained by Camille Chalmers, "the first response [has been] a military response. It is a militarization of humanitarian aid. Today there are 32,000 foreign soldiers in the country, and I don't think we need 32,000 soldiers to distribute humanitarian aid" (Mennonite Central Committee [MCC], 2010/2/8). According to the Pentagon, at the height of its intervention, there were approximately 22,000 US military personnel in Haiti, with 7,000 present on the ground and the remaining forces mobilized in 58 aircraft and 15 nearby vessels. In addition, the Coast Guard was assisting in the interception of any potential refugees (Herz, 2011/6/15). On January 19, Sebastian Walker, a reporter stationed in Haiti, explained, "most Haitians here have seen little humanitarian aid so far. What they have seen is guns, and lots of them....This is what much of the UN presence actually looks like on the streets of Port-au-Prince: men in uniform, racing around in vehicles, carrying weapons" (Democracy Now!, 2010/1/19). With an additional 10,000 MINUSTAH soldiers present on the island, claims of an overwhelming military presence and sense of US domination are understandable.

The US used its military force and political influence to usurp control of the rescue operation and subvert food and medical security in favor of military priorities. The effects of this interference were most evident and criticized in relation to the US military control of the Port-au-Prince airport, which it seized within the first 72 hours after the quake. The US pushed forward an agenda that prioritized military flights over planes that were carrying medical personnel, essential supplies, and relief experts. The primary concern of the military was to establish a secure atmosphere, which interfered with the delivery of aid. The result seems contradictory, as civil unrest, one might assume, could be more likely to develop as supplies run low and aid is slow to arrive (Way, 2010/2/2). The preferential treatment of US military flights carrying weapons and equipment elicited serious criticism from mid-level French, Italian, and Brazilian officials. The medical aid organization Médecins Sans Frontières (MSF) was particularly frustrated by the US' control. Five MSF planes carrying vital supplies and personnel were refused landing for extended periods and were forced to land in Santo Domingo, Dominican Republic (Democracy Now!, 2010/1/19; Herz, 2011/6/15; Way, 2010/2/2). Similar difficulties were encountered with flights supplied by the UN World Food Program (WFP), which carried food, water, and medicine as well (Bennis, 2010/1/20). Such instances have led to the accusation that the US in fact interfered with the progress of the rescue mission. As Patrick Elie, a reporter in Port-au-Prince, explains, "the priorities of the flight should be determined by the Haitians. So, otherwise, it's a takeover" (Democracy Now!, 2010/1/19). Clearly, the US was more concerned with its agenda of military control over humanitarian relief — arguably an expected outcome with the militarization of humanitarian aid — which paved the way for disaster capitalism to follow.

Disaster Capitalism

Disaster capitalism describes the predatory actions of governments and corporations that identify market opportunities in times of crisis and take advantage of incapacitated nations to carry out extensive neoliberal reform that would otherwise be highly resisted and difficult to implement. Once the US military had established emergency control of Haiti in 2010, the US government overtook the state and enforced a series of policies that favored neoliberalism and US corporations. In this regard, the US possessed a preconceived ideology of structural reform that it sought to impose on Haiti immediately following the earthquake. Following from that, the US took control of the aid money that was destined for Haiti and invested it in corporations and organizations that supported US interests. US food aid was dumped into the country, further exacerbating the dire state of the peasant farming industry, which had been previously handicapped by the Clinton administration.

Four years after the earthquake that devastated Haiti, over 170,000 people continue to sleep under makeshift tents while foreign aid is funneled into private enterprise and the creation of industrial areas: luxury tourism, mining, and an expanded sweatshop industry have been pushed on the country as the easy economic solutions to a complex problem (Fresnillo, 2014/3/5). The US has taken advantage of this natural disaster, and from its acquisition of emergency power, has pushed to implement the same old neoliberal "Plan of Death"—masked by rhetorical good intentions, disguising imperial ambitions.

Immediately following the earthquake, imperial ideology and predatory capitalism were evident in the commentaries of several right-wing institutions, academics, and politically powerful individuals. For example, the Heritage Foundation (HF) explicitly stated an intention to capitalize upon the natural disaster. Immediately following the quake, the right-wing think tank released the following comment: "In addition to providing immediate humanitarian assistance, the US response to the tragic earthquake in Haiti offers opportunities to reshape Haiti's long-dysfunctional government and economy as well as to improve the public image of the United States in the region" (Eaton, 2010/1/17). The original paper, titled "Amidst the Suffering, Crisis in Haiti Offers Opportunities to the US," was removed the following day, as the opportunistic intentions received sharp criticism, particularly from Naomi Klein, who coined the term "disaster capitalism" and published the essay on her own website the day after the earthquake (Fresnillo, 2014/3/5). Simultaneously, Bill Clinton, US special envoy to Haiti, was busy advocating for the implementation of a neoliberal plan in Haiti published by Oxford University professor and economist Paul Collier. The details of the plan, drawn up in January 2009 and outlined in a paper titled "Haiti: From Natural

Catastrophe to Economic Security," stipulates that powerful international bodies must intervene militarily and occupy failed states to ensure economic reconstruction and development (Smith, 2010/2/8). Specifically, Collier and Clinton advocate for the investment in luxury tourism and the expansion of the garment industry, despite the fact that these projects contribute little to the social fabric of Haitian society and serve exclusively the needs of major businesses. Collier advises for the exploitation of the low labour wages by corporations in Haiti as a viable means to compete with China's textile industry. Furthermore, Collier proposes extensive privatization of the country's port and electrical systems (Smith, 2010/2/8). As a result, the plan functions to exacerbate the inequalities already experienced by the Haitian poor and does little to develop the crumbling Haitian infrastructure, which has historically developed around similar endeavors.

The excitement of US officials concerning the financial opportunity in Haiti is best represented by a cable released in February 2010 from the US Ambassador in Haiti, which contains the exclamation, "THE GOLD RUSH IS ON!" referring to potential business opportunities available for the reconstruction of Port-au-Prince (USEP, 2010/2/1; Fresnillo, 2014/3/5). The US government was quick to recognize the financial significance of the natural disaster and used its political influence to impose control over the aid money destined for Haiti. Two institutions were established by the international community to oversee the management of relief and recovery funds: the Interim Haiti Recovery Commission (IHRC), co-chaired by Bill Clinton and the Haitian Prime Minister, and the Haiti Reconstruction Fund (HRF). Almost none of the money donated to Haiti actually went directly into the country or to local businesses. Instead, funds were primarily funneled back into US infrastructure and private US corporations (Quigley & Ramanauskas, 2012/1/3).

The greatest financial beneficiaries of aid money destined for Haiti were in fact the US government and US private corporations. Although the US donated an impressive

$379 million immediately after the quake, the Associated Press reported in January 2010 that 33 cents of each dollar was reimbursed back to the US military, and 42 cents of every dollar was invested into private and public US NGOs—very little aid was directly invested in the Haitian government (Quigley & Ramanauskas, 2012/1/3). In August 2010, the US Congressional Research Office revealed that the $1.6 billion donated by the US for relief efforts followed a similar pattern of self-indulgence. For example, some noteworthy recipients include the Department of Defense, which was reimbursed $655 million; the US Agency for International Development (USAID)—which funneled extensive contracts into US disaster relief, debris removal, and reconstruction corporations—received $350 million; and, individual US states received grants of $220 million to cover services for Haitian evacuees (Quigley & Ramanauskas, 2012/1/3). Reconstruction contracts followed a similar trend: of the 1,500 contracts worth over $267 million, only 20% were allocated to Haitian firms. The rest have been awarded to US firms that rely on US suppliers, yet exploit the low-wages of Haitian workers (Dupuy, 2011/1/7; Flaherty, 2011/1/13). Specifically, $76 million in contracts were doled out to the Washington, DC area, encompassing nearly 30% of the total allocated funds (Quigley & Ramanauskas, 2012/1/3). Haiti received a meager 1% of emergency aid and 16% of reconstruction aid directly (Fresnillo, 2014/3/5). Relatively speaking, the Haitian government and local businesses were almost entirely bypassed in the reconstruction of their own country, whereas the US received substantial capital investment.

In the immediate aftermath of the earthquake, US food aid was needed to nourish the country in its shocked state; however, in the long-term, food aid has had a disastrous effect on the local agricultural industry. Local peasant farmers are unable to compete with the low prices of surplus US rice, corn, and sugar that were dumped into Haiti in 2010. Local demand for Haitian foods dropped along with prices as American food was being given away (Webster, 2012/1/10). In this manner, foreign food aid creates a parallel structure that inhibits economic development and undermines local markets. Indeed, food aid can have the deleterious effect of establishing a dependency on agricultural imports and ultimately serves the interests of donors (Cunningham, 2012, pp. 110, 112).

This is not the first time that local agricultural markets in Haiti have been undermined by US food policy. During the Clinton Administration, neoliberal policies and IMF-World Bank sponsored trade reforms lifted trade barriers and opened Haiti to the US agricultural market. This led to the dumping of surplus US food capital into Haiti. Due to the 2008 US Farm Bill, which subsidizes American farmers and agricultural products, the US is able to undersell Haitian peasant farmers. Food aid and food dumping into newly opened markets, enables the US to maintain high prices locally while disposing of surplus capital abroad. Here, the long-term effects of food aid on the recipient country do not discourage the donor as the arrangement actually benefits the US economy and provides the opportunity to pursue strategic welfare and economic policies (Cunningham, 2012, p. 104; Friedmann, 1993, p. 35). Even former President Bill Clinton, who instigated the tariff cut-offs on imported rice in Haiti, recognizes that the policies have "failed everywhere [they've] been tried" (Dupuy, 2011/1/7). The end result is a food market perpetually dependent on the foreign supply of foods that can be grown locally.

Conclusion

The behaviour of the US towards Haiti can be described most accurately as imperial. This is evident from well-documented US military and CIA interventions, US masked political influence via MINUSTAH, disguised state manipulation through NGOs, forced occupation following the earthquake, and predatory neoliberal impositions and exploitative capitalism during Haiti's incapacitated state. It is true that the US presence in Haiti

following the earthquake was not entirely detrimental—it
did in fact help to some extent; however, based on the evidence, the primary concern of the US military and government seems to have been an exercise of control and
promotion of corporate self-interests, not genuine concern
for Haiti's suffering people. Much of the "help" that the US
provided, in fact hurt Haiti instead. It is therefore essential
to establish that "good intentions," whether truly sincere
or honestly sinister, do not negate responsibility for the final result. As such, the US is entirely deserving of criticism
for its exploitative relationship with Haiti. During the last
several decades, the US has clearly imposed its imperial
rule over Haiti through repeated military and CIA interventions that aim to establish US-style democratic systems
that favour neoliberalism, thus opening markets for the
disposal of surplus US capital. The mission of MINUSTAH
appears to be an occupation with the sole purpose of supporting a US-established puppet government system,
which in turn, amplifies the security threat in Haiti and
undermines national sovereignty. Furthermore, the US
strategically uses NGOs to pursue political interests in
Haiti and is able to avoid responsibility due to the unac-
countability of NGOs: NGOs are typically exempt from
critical analysis due to their adoption of a humanitarian
morality, protected by the consensus of a right to intervene. The imperial ambitions of the US are epitomized by
the militarization of humanitarian aid in Haiti, which offers the most blatant example of usurped national sovereignty through forced occupation. Finally, an
overwhelming military presence enabled the imposition of
political control and facilitated the ensuing disaster capitalism of privatization, deregulation, decentralization, and
corporate profiteering. The US took advantage of the
"blank slate" presented in Haiti and pushed forward its
old plan of structural reform to increase trade and further
open up the Haitian market, subverting Haiti to the position of a US means of production and sponge for capital
overflow.

With friends like these, who needs enemies? The US military and its soldiers are not humanitarians, and the US government is no economic or political saviour—rather, they are the embodiment of the "new" imperialism.

References

Bennis, P. (2010/1/20). Haiti Needs Aid, Not Militarization. *YES! Magazine*.
http://www.yesmagazine.org/peace-justice/haiti-needs-aid-not-militarization

Bueno de Mesquita, B. (2007). Foreign Aid and Policy Concessions. *Journal of Conflict Resolution*, 51(2), 251–284.

Chossudovsky, M. (2004/2/29). US Sponsored Coup d'Etat: The Destabilization of Haiti. *Centre for Research on Globalization*.
http://globalresearch.ca/articles/CHO402D.html

Clinton, H. (2010/1/22). Demarche Request: Haiti: U.S. Humanitarian [Diplomatic Cable]. Washington, DC: Secretary of State [10STATE6918].
http://wikileaks.org/cable/2010/01/10STATE6918.html

CNN. (2004/3/1). Aristide says U.S. Deposed him in 'Coup d'État'. *CNN*.
http://www.cnn.com/2004/WORLD/americas/03/01/aristide.claim/

Coughlin, D. (2011/10/6). WikiLeaks Haiti: US Cables Paint Portrait of Brutal, Ineffectual and Polluting UN Force. *The Nation*.
http://www.thenation.com/article/163846/wikileaks-haiti-us-cables-paint-portrait-brutal-ineffectual-and-polluting-un-force

Cunningham, O. (2012). The Humanitarian Aid Regime in the Republic of NGOs: The Fallacy of 'Building Back Better'. *The Josef Korbel Journal of Advanced International Studies*, 4, 102–126.

Democracy Now! (2010/1/19). US accused of Militarizing Relief Effort in Haiti. *Democracy Now!*
http://www.democracynow.org/2010/1/19/us_accused_of_militarizing_relief_effort

Donlon, R. A. (2012). Preface. In R. A. Donlon (Ed.), *Haiti Earthquake and Response* (pp. vii–viii). New York, NY: Nova Science Publishers, Inc.

Dupuy, A. (2011/1/7). One Year after the Earthquake, Foreign Help is Actually Hurting Haiti. *The Washington Post*.

http://www.washingtonpost.com/wp-dyn/content/article/2011/01/07/AR2011010703043_pf.html

Eaton, G. (2010/1/17). Haiti Becomes a Target for Economic "Shock Therapy". *New Statesman*.

http://www.newstatesman.com/print/node/167115?title=&text=

Engler, Y. (2009/3/8). Haiti—The UN and NGOs are the New Tools of Neo-Imperialism. *Melange*.

http://www.counterpunch.org/2009/03/01/haiti-s-harsh-realities/

————. (2012/12/20). MINUSTAH's Disregard for the People of Haiti. *Dissident Voice*.

http://dissidentvoice.org/2012/12/minustahs-disregard-for-the-people-of-haiti/

Farmer, P. (2011). *Haiti after the Earthquake*. New York, NY: PublicAffairs.

Flaherty, J. (2011/1/13). One Year after the Earthquake, Corporations Profit While People Suffer. *Truthout*.

http://www.truth-out.org/archive/item/93894:one-year-after-haiti-earthquake-corporations-profit-while-people-suffer

Frantz, C. (2011). Leta Restavek: The Suppression of Democracy in Haiti (COHA). *Institute for Justice and Democracy in Haiti*.

http://www.ijdh.org/2011/10/topics/politics-democracy/leta-restavek-the-suppression-of-democracy-in-haiti-coha/#.Uyyt5f3a6FI

Fresnillo, L. (2014/3/5). Haiti, Four Years after the Earthquake: The Mirage of Reconstruction. *El Diario*.

http://haitiotrosterremotos.info/lang/es/haiti-four-years-after-the-earthquake-the-mirage-of-reconstruction/

Friedmann, H. (1993). Political Economy of Food: A Global Crisis. *New Left Review*, 197, 29–57.

Herz, A. (2011/6/15). WikiLeaks Haiti: The Earthquake Cables. *The Nation*.

http://www.thenation.com/article/161459/wikileaks-haiti-earthquake-cables#

Kivland, C. L. (2012). Unmaking the State in "Occupied" Haiti. *PoLAR: Political and Legal Anthropology Review*, 35(2), 248–270.

Klein, N. (2007). *The Shock Doctrine: The Rise of Disaster Capitalism*. New York, NY: Metropolitan Books.

Mennonite Central Committee (MCC). (2010/2/8). Militarization of Aid. Mennonite Central Committee.

http://mccottawa.ca/system/files/Militarization%20of%20Aid%20Talking%20Points_0.pdf

Moselle, T. S. (2008). *The Concept of World Order*. Cambridge, MA: Harvard Kennedy School.

http://www.hks.harvard.edu/cchrp/research/ConceptOfWorldOrder_Mo
selle.pdf

Podur, J. (2012). *Haiti's New Dictatorship: The Coup, the Earthquake and the UN Occupation.* London, UK: Pluto Press.

Quigley, B., & Ramanauskas, A. (2012/1/13). Haiti After the Quake: Where the Relief Money Did and Did Not Go. *Counterpunch.*

http://www.counterpunch.org/2012/1/03/haiti-after-the-quake/print

Smith, A. (2010/1/14). Catastrophe in Haiti. Socialist Worker.

http://socialistworker.org/print/2010/1/14/catastrophe-in-haiti

———— . (2010/2/8). The "Shock Doctrine" for Haiti. *Socialist Worker.*

http://socialistworker.org/print/2010/02/08/shock-doctrine-for-haiti

United States Institute of Peace (USIP). (2010). *Haiti: A Republic of NGOs?* Washington, DC: United States Institute of Peace.

http://www.usip.org/events/haiti-republic-ngos

US Embassy, Port-au-Prince (USEP). (2008/10/1). Why we need continuing MINUSTAH presence in Haiti [Diplomatic cable]. Port-au-Prince, Haiti.[08PORTAUPRINCE1381_a].

https://wikileaks.org/plusd/cables/08PORTAUPRINCE1381_a.html

———— . (2010/2/1). Embassy Port au Prince Earthquake SITREP [Diplomatic cable]. Port-au-Prince, Haiti. [10PORTAUPRINCE110].

http://wikileaks.org/cable/2010/02/10PORTAUPRINCE110.html

Way, J. (2010/2/2). Haiti: The Impacts of Militarized Aid. *Upside Down World.*

http://upsidedownworld.org/main/international-archives-60/2346-the-impacts-of-militarized-aid

Webster, D. (2012/1/10). Fault Line: Aid, Politics, and Blame in Post-Quake Haiti: Two Years After the Earthquake, Where Did the Money Go? *Global Post.*

http://www.globalpost.com/dispatch/news/regions/americas/haiti/1201
10/haiti-earthquake-aid-rice?page=0,3

Who Needs Me Most? New Imperialist Ideologies in Youth-Centred Volunteer Abroad Programs

★ ★ ★ ★ ★

Tristan Biehn

David Harvey describes the new imperialism as the imposition of American neoliberal values and policies on other nations (Harvey, 2003). The new imperialist project is supported in part by narratives which aim to produce good neoliberal capitalist subjects both at home and abroad. One of the spaces in which this becomes evident is in the messages, both explicit and implicit, within student or youth-centred volunteer abroad programs. Examinations of the narratives produced by these programs in their recruitment efforts and mission statements reveal deeply ingrained and unquestioned neoliberal values and assumptions. Youth are encouraged to consider self-improvement and individual efforts as solutions to issues of global inequalities, rather than addressing political and economic systems and underlying relationships of exploitation and domination. The language used in these recruitment messages to youth enforces neoliberal, capitalist understandings of the problem of and potential solutions to global inequalities. Problems are thus decontextualized and depoliticized. The messages reinforce a desired image of the Western youth as a powerful actor, an impetus for change, and an inspiration to the underprivileged, stagnant, victimized target populations elsewhere. Change is constructed as a concept which stands in for vague and unspecified promises. Through an examination of the messages conveyed by the websites of two key examples of youth-centred international volunteer organizations, I hope to show the neoliberal assumptions evident within these narratives and to illustrate the ways these narratives serve the new imperialism.

Cross Cultural Solutions: The Leading Authority on International Volunteering

Cross Cultural Solutions (CCS) calls itself, "the leading authority on international volunteering," boasting of nearly 20 years of experience (since 1995) and claiming to have, "virtually invented short-term international volunteering" and "set the standards of excellence in the field of international volunteering". It is a US-based, non-profit organization, started by Steve Rosenthal in 1994 after his own positive experiences abroad, which he hoped to make available on a larger scale (Cross Cultural Solutions [CCS], 2014b). Projects are created by members of local communities, a system by which CCS attempts to address local needs and goals without "imposing outside ideas" (CCS, 2014b). CCS is serious about its transparency and responsibility to local people. It does try to encourage an attitude of respectful hard work and learning on the part of the volunteer. I chose CCS as one of my case studies because of its position as a respected organization which does avoid some of the obvious critiques of these types of projects, and as an organization which serves to demonstrate the flaws of even a thoughtful and well meaning approach to international volunteering.

Depoliticizing Global Inequalities and the Effortlessness of Change

On their homepage, detailing their organization's philosophy, CCS uses the word "change" 15 times in a 237 word message. Change is wished for by an unspecified mass of "people around the world" who "want change" in "inequities," "corrupt systems that prevent self-determination," and "unjust repression". According to their philosophy, "the change we all wish to see won't be realized through big, sweeping acts—not by governments, or armies, or the UN. Instead, lasting change will be achieved through small, personal acts of kindness and selflessness" (CCS, 2014c). They propose that it is this small change in people that CCS can bring about, and this change in volunteers will bring change to communities in a "ripple effect". The message ends with their motto: "Change their world. Change yours. THIS CHANGES EVERYTHING" (CCS, 2014c, capitalization in the original). Here, volunteers are cast as modest heroes, saving the world and bettering themselves at the same time. This philosophy is repeated throughout their site and those of other organizations, and seems to be the ideal picked up by journalists who wish to describe the *voluntourist* trend (the term "voluntourism" is commonly used to refer to the amalgamation of aspects of volunteering and tourism). Thus, I believe it is worthy of a great deal of unpacking.

The idea of change is used as a vague promise which is repeated frequently but is never tied down to any specifics. What is emphasized is its achievability. This makes it possible for potential volunteers to imagine change their own way and to simply insert their personal vision in the organization's broad philosophy. At the same time, this change is transformed into something each and every reader can actually carry out. Potential volunteers are also assured that only through changing themselves through the organization's program can they cause this change to happen for others (however they have imagined it). It is specifically asserted that change will not come about via certain large-scale organizations, but only through personal achievement. This is particularly interesting, as it effectively shifts the burden of responsibility from governments and the UN to volunteers and the organizations that coordinate their efforts. It is important to note that it is not only this burden that is shifted, but that there is an accompanying shift in power and control over an area, from that area's (elected) government or local leadership to (unelected) NGOs (Baptista, 2012, p. 641). The dismissal of "big, sweeping acts" serves to guide readers away from political action and instead leads them to self-improvement and small-scale efforts. This is representative of a common and oft utilized neoliberal move, one which successfully quashes mass movements of resistance before they even form. Through this narrative, the energies of dissatisfied people are redirected to international volunteering.

How CCS Promises Real Social Change and Immersion

CCS' website has a specific section which targets high school students (ages 15–17). The high school volunteer recruitment page immediately mentions the favourable effect completion of their program would have on one's CV. The students are promised that just one trip will allow them to become more confident and adventurous, and to become better leaders with superior college resumes. Through the narratives present in these websites, prospective volunteers are reminded constantly of the direct, personal benefits that they will receive in exchange for their volunteer efforts. In this way, solutions to inequality and suffering are articulated as worth pursuing as part of a capitalist exchange: volunteer labour in return for marketable skills and better CVs. CCS outlines multiple locations which are available for volunteer opportunities, mostly describing places as safe, beautiful, warm, and welcoming. Teaching children English, doing crafts with them, organizing soccer matches, planting gardens and painting murals are listed as ways, "you'll be able to effect real social change while being completely immersed in a new culture and welcoming community" (CCS, 2014a). English is presented as the key to gain access to global economy and to progress (Jakubiak, 2012, p. 442). Learning English is put forward as a way for the underprivileged members of local communities which host such programs to improve themselves and rise above and out of their local, rural communities, a narrative which reproduces images of an inferior periphery which successful, driven individuals abandon in search of opportunity in the centre (Jakubiak, 2012, pp. 445-446). The projects are nearly identical as described above no matter which location is viewed, casting into doubt the degree to which specific local issues are addressed. The messages go on to describe the "Home-Base" ("equipped with working fire extinguishers, first aid kits, and smoke detectors [and] providing all high school volunteers with personal lockers for valuables") that the youth will live in during their stay, as well as the translators that will be on hand at all times (CCS, 2014a). This highlights the odd nature of the term "immersion" as found on these websites. According to these narratives, cultural immersion can occur while living segregated from the host communities, without the ability to speak the local language, with staff guiding a volunteer's every movement. This conveys a questionable understanding of immersion as something which happens painlessly, easily, and simply by being in a place. Apparently, just "being there" is enough to legitimize and validate this experience.

The organization created a short video introducing prospective volunteers to their operations in Kilimanjaro, Tanzania, that includes statements made by staff members and volunteers about the program, all to entice the potential volunteer. One volunteer (18, American), talks about the instantaneous positive impact a volunteer has, "within minutes of walking in the door you can see the impact that you make on the kids, they love volunteers" (TV1Productions, 2013, 1:30). Another volunteer (22, American) admits that at first she thought she would teach the kids perfect English, but then realized, "the English that I teach them is not as important as the love and attention that I can give" (TV1Productions, 2013, 1:55). The country director states that, "it is more of a matter of creating awareness...the moment they meet those people they are already making a difference...just by smiling to them, talking to them, these people feel recognized, feel appreciated" (TV1Productions, 2013, 3:07). Here we hear again that "making a difference" is instant, effortless, and requires nothing more than the presence of a Western volunteer. Later, the 18 year old we heard from earlier tells us about how safe the "home-base" is, while the video shows us a van pulling through the gates of an enclosed compound which are then closed by the uniformed house guards (TV1Productions, 2013, 5:15). This image serves to underline previously raised questions concerning the legitimacy of claims of immersion. The video is a painfully illuminating example of the problematic narratives being produced and distributed by these organizations.

International Student Volunteers, Inc.

International Student Volunteers, Inc. (ISV) is a US-based, non-profit organization which boasts of being the world's highest-rated student volunteer program (according to the average rating given by over 30,000 student participants). ISV has over ten years of experience, has 32 members of the US Senate and Congress who serve on their Board of Reference (endorsing their global efforts), and has been named, "one of the Top Ten Volunteer Organizations by the US Center for Citizens Diplomacy in conjunction with the US State Department" (International Student Volunteers, Inc. [ISV], 2014d). ISV was founded in 2002 by Randy Sykes, growing from his wish to develop "a volunteer program to help address the tremendous needs around the world while providing an opportunity for young people to travel with a purpose; to give of themselves and contribute to something meaningful, educational and fun" (ISV,

2014a). I selected ISV as my second case study due to its internationally recognized, award-winning status.

How ISV Practises Responsible Tourism

ISV's website emphasizes its ties with local communities and "grassroots" organizations. It also claims to offer "the highest quality projects that are safe, meaningful, sustainable and achievable" which are formulated to appeal to students with an emphasis on "combining life-changing volunteer work with adrenaline filled adventure travel" (ISV, 2014d). In their description of "Responsible Tourism," ISV states that they, "aim to bring about positive economic, social, cultural and environmental impacts" (ISV, 2014b). What is meant, specifically, by such statements? While it is easy to dismiss such terms as mere buzzwords, it would be a mistake to do so. An examination of the ISV's use of these terms, and the messages surrounding them, serves to illustrate the problematic ideologies present in their projects, the ways they seek to create the expectations of an ideal student volunteer experience, as well as issues of expense and the manufactured need for international volunteers.

Safety Concerns, Cost, and the Inexperienced Volunteer

ISV addresses the issue of students' safety by listing various precautions taken by the organization on behalf of prospective volunteers. Their website describes the potential volunteer's position: "You'll be participating on [sic] tasks you may not be trained in, possibly in a foreign speaking country [sic], you may not have much international travel experience and therefore many questions about vaccinations and other safety concerns" (ISV, 2014c). This anticipates a volunteer's position as inexperienced and unprepared. One may wonder why inexperienced individuals would be shipped around the world to take part in various activities for which they are not properly trained. If an individual must be trained to take part, why are locals not trained to work in their own communities? Why are Western youths flown across the globe, at great expense, to temporarily fill these positions? ISV goes to great lengths to address imagined safety concerns, listing support structures, supervision, and routine risk assessment and site inspections of supported local projects (ISV, 2014c). These support structures are another expense made necessary by the movement of western youth to these communities.

A standard four week "volunteer and adventure tour program" with ISV will cost nearly $4,000. This amount varies (slightly) depending on program and country, and does not include airfare, half of one's meals during the "adventure tour" portion, or the required travel insurance package. In the section entitled "What am I Paying For," ISV provides a breakdown of where a volunteer's money goes, in helpful bullet-point form. Administration, volunteer recruitment, volunteer support, volunteer management, volunteer supervision, meals and accommodation, transport, in-country support staff, connections between organizations, and finally the project itself are listed (ISV, 2014e). Most of these expenses, obviously, are only required because of the insistence on international volunteer labour. Since this is a significant amount of money, particularly for students, ISV suggests ideas for fund raising. A volunteer blog offers examples of how individuals, following ISV prescriptions, attempt to raise thousands of dollars for their trips abroad. A young Australian woman details her plans for "raising funds through a blog, and...planning on having a trash and treasure sale, movie night, pyjama party and exercising my creative writing skills to obtain exposure about my cause in my local news paper" (Katieannie09, 2014). There are many such descriptions of similar efforts, including an assortment of commercial enterprises such as selling chocolates and doughnuts. Friends and family are enlisted to contribute to these efforts, as well as strangers who can be reached through media outlets and the internet. All of this time, energy, and money (valuable commodities by any capitalist reckoning) go toward financing a student's vacation. Volunteering is presented as the "good" being done by the student in order to justify such expense. Donors are thanked for their "generosity" and updates on one's progress are provided via ISV's blog. How do these donors, and the volunteers themselves, come to see such efforts as necessary or beneficial?

This necessity is presented in the persuasive narratives of international volunteer organizations. ISV assumes the need of communities for foreign volunteers, stating (in reference to local NGOs), "these organizations rarely have the funding required to recruit and support international volunteers themselves. To help recruit international volunteers, many local NGOs partner with volunteer service organizations" (ISV, 2014e). They do not attempt to explain why international volunteering is a good way to address global inequalities. In fact, much effort is made to convince prospective participants that international volunteering is worth doing (as evidenced by the constant bombardment of the reader with messages of "making a difference" and "positive impact"). In a section explaining the difficulties of volunteering independently, ISV unintentionally highlights the problematic nature of this assumption, asserting that, "the difficult part is finding an organization you want to work for that meets your needs as a volunteer, will support you should something go wrong, and is willing to accept you as a volunteer" (ISV, 2014e). They note that local organizations may be seeking volunteers with specific skill sets, thus making many potential volunteers unwanted. However, if a volunteer joins an organization such as ISV, suddenly there is a plethora of need and want for their service. How then do such organizations respond to charges that they themselves create this need? Additionally, even if we uncritically accept the proposal that "underprivileged" communities must be helped to "develop," surely there are more efficient methods that can be imagined to achieve this.

Producing Ideal Neoliberal Subjects

The organizations presented here, as well as the volunteers who take part in their programs, may well be sincere in their hopes for change and their wishes to help. The sentiment, although vague, is laudable. I do not seek to vilify those who make an effort to ease the suffering of others. However, as the above narratives have demonstrated, volunteer abroad organizations propagate and reinforce new imperialist ideologies. Youth centred volunteer abroad programs are part of a process of indoctrination wherein young people and members of target communities are recruited as ideal neoliberal capitalist subjects. The hope that mutual understanding and respect, along with individual efforts, can "make an impact" on inequality and suffering around the globe is a neoliberal narrative which obfuscates the complex causes of inequalities. Policies (such as those instituted by the IMF) which undermine the abilities of states to support their own health care and education systems are not a result of misunderstanding. Voluntourism aims to recast consumers as the solution to issues of global inequality, instead of the problem (Baptista, 2012, p. 639). The volunteers produced by these narratives are encouraged to believe that it is reasonable that changing the world should be an effortless and fun process. The prospective volunteers are trained to help others with the promise of reward in the forms of self improvement, more appealing resumes, and self satisfaction. This is problematic, in part, because real, viable solutions toward solving global inequalities will probably not benefit over privileged westerners. Prospective youth volunteers, having been fed narratives which assure them that their mere presence, smiles, and energy are all that is needed to change the world, do not seem likely to take steps to seriously address poverty and oppression. Meanwhile, they have been assured that spending money and individual efforts are the best way to positively influence their world. In the world under the new imperialism, even the wish to help initiate change and alleviate suffering is commodified and harnessed to suit US neoliberal capitalist goals.

References

Baptista, J. A. (2012). The Virtuous Tourist: Consumption, Development, and Nongovernmental Governance in a Mozambican Village. *American Anthropologist*, 114(4), 639–651.

Cross Cultural Solutions (CCS). (2014a). High School Volunteer Abroad.
http://www.crossculturalsolutions.org/discover-what-you-can-do/high-school-volunteer-abroad

————. (2014b). Our History.
http://www.crossculturalsolutions.org/about/our-history

————. (2014c). Our Philosophy.
http://www.crossculturalsolutions.org/

Harvey, D. (2003). *The New Imperialism*. Oxford, UK: Oxford University Press.

International Student Volunteers, Inc. (ISV). (2014a). Our Story.
http://www.isvolunteers.org/our-story

————. (2014b). Responsible Travel.
http://www.isvolunteers.org/responsible-travel

————. (2014c). What to look for in a Volunteer Provider.
http://www.isvolunteers.org/what-to-look-for-in-a-volunteer-provider

————. (2014d). Why Students All Over the World Prefer ISV's Volunteer Program.
http://www.isvolunteers.org/why-isv

————. (2014e). Why Pay to Volunteer?
http://www.isvolunteers.org/why-pay-to-volunteer

Jakubiak, C. (2012). "English for the Global": Discourses in/of English-Language Voluntourism. *International Journal of Qualitative Studies in Education*, 25(4), 435-451.

Katieannie09. (2014). Overwhelmed with Generosity.
http://isvolunteers.goabroad.net/Katieannie09/journals/7261/overwhelmed-with-generosity

TV1Productions. (2013, March 22). Cross-Cultural Solutions Kilimanjaro, Tanzania [Video File].
http://www.youtube.com/watch?v=N2whqVlgIIg

CHAPTER 4

Queers of War: Normalizing Lesbians and Gays in the US War Machine

★ ★ ★ ★ ★

Hilary King

When considering the legacy of the US as a nation, of all the characteristics available, "gay-friendly" should not be one that readily comes to mind first. Being a nation born of white supremacy, settler colonialism, and patriarchy, it is perhaps not remarkable that the nation has been a site of heteronormativity since its inception. Yet in recent years, the US (as well as other western countries) has begun to represent itself as a leader in rights for lesbian, gay, bisexual and transgendered people (LGBT), setting examples for the rest of the world in the view of some US human rights activists. Much of this excitement has to do with the work the Obama administration has done putting forward laws that allegedly further said rights. From expanding the legal scope of "hate crimes" to include those attacked as a result of their sexual orientation, to repealing "Don't Ask Don't Tell" (DADT), Obama has been deemed a favourite amongst mainstream gay and lesbian activists (HRC, 2011). Through producing exceptional narratives of the US as an advocate of gay and lesbian rights, the Obama administration has thus not only effectively erased America's history of violence against LGBT individuals, but has also oversimplified this violence as one that can only be stopped through what many activists deem to be neoliberal inclusion (Spade, 2011, p. 208).

In her book *Terrorist Assemblages* (2007), Jasbir Puar develops the conceptual frame of "homonationalism" to understand how the mainstream lesbian and gay movement has not only stifled the more radical anti-neoliberal LGBT movements, but has also become an effective tool for the advancement of US imperialism. I will explore this theory by looking closely at the *Matthew Shepard and James Byrd, Jr. Hate Crimes Prevention Act*, the 2011 repeal of DADT, and the recent growth in prominence of the Human Rights Campaign (HRC) as one of the most important LGBT nonprofit organizations in the US. What does the seemingly progressive organization HRC have to do with military violence overseas? What is the link between the Hate Crimes Act and the increase of military spending? In addition to addressing these questions, I will provide an overall analysis of how the incorporation of gay rights into the US national discourse has governed US citizens into believing that they have not only the right, but the responsibility to propagate their values and beliefs overseas.

Homonationalism

Homonationalism describes the contemporary racial and economic relations in western sexual rights discourses, and explains the global narratives around sexual human rights, immigration, freedom and democracy. Natalie Kouri-Towe explains how it functions similarly to Orientalism:

> "Homonationalism functions in complementary ways to Edward Said's concept of Orientalism, which describes how the West produces knowledge and dominates 'the Orient' through academic, cultural and discursive processes. Like Orientalism, [it] speaks to the ways Western powers circulate ideas about other cultures (like Arab and Islamic cultures) in order to produce the West as culturally, morally, and politically advanced and superior. However, unlike Orientalism, homo-

nationalism speaks particularly to the way gender and sexual rights discourses become central to contemporary forms of Western hegemony". (Kouri-Towe, 2012)

Thus through sexual rights discourses, the US has been able to construct itself as a progressive and morally superior nation in relation to countries with different, more discriminatory laws and legislation towards their LGBT citizens. Since the US grants its lesbian and gay citizens some measure of legal rights (however uneven), government leaders such as Barack Obama and Hillary Clinton feel that they are entitled to denounce the anti-gay laws in countries such as Russia, Uganda, or Senegal. It is important to interrogate how this arrogance comes to be justified, because arguably the individuals still among the most vulnerable to violence within the US are those who fall under the LGBT umbrella (Spade, 2011, p. 89). Therefore, how could the country's leaders possibly declare themselves to be leaders of this movement? The narrative of homonationalism also operates as a script that normalizes the homosexual as a white, cisgendered subject (Puar, 2007, p. 48). That is, this narrative's focus on the affluent white gay man as the central body in the movement, effectively displaces the queer "ethnic," and the violence inflicted upon them.

If gay rights movements incorporate individuals into a system such as neoliberalism, it must be understood that this system, in practice, operates on the accumulation of capital through dispossession (Harvey, 2003, p. 137). In other words, neoliberalism is a system that ultimately operates on the marginalization and exploitation of others, for the benefit of an elite class. This provides some insight into how the inclusion of LGBT people into neoliberal structures only benefits a select few. Those less likely to benefit from gay marriage, for example, would be lower class individuals, *trans* individuals, or racialized individuals with limited opportunities (Spade, 2011, p. 81). Therefore, LGBT rights narratives in the US produce representations of the gay citizen as white, middle class, and often, male, because they are the easiest to incorporate. Ultimately, this disqualifies "racial others" from the homonational imaginary (Puar, 2007, p. 48).

Human Rights Campaign and the Construction of Just Gay Subjects

Founded in 1980 as a relatively small political action committee, the HRC fund was initially developed to raise money for gay-supportive congressional members in the US (Encarnación, 2014). It has since become the largest civil rights organization in America that advocates for the rights of its LGBT citizens, with its reach extending well beyond the country's borders. In 2011, HRC endorsed Obama for re-election (HRC, 2011). This was not only a testament to their faith in his administration's ability to create positive change for LGBT citizens at home, but also demonstrated their strong belief in the US' responsibility to protect LGBT rights around the world. Amongst the administration's alleged victories for LGBT rights outlined in the HRC's official endorsement, the Obama administration was applauded for having added the US to a UN General Assembly resolution calling for an end to criminal penalties based on sexual orientation or gender identity (HRC, 2011). Further, HRC recognized the administration's support for the first ever UN Human Rights Council resolution condemning violence and discrimination against LGBT people (HRC, 2011). Since Obama's re-election, with support from HRC, the US continues to grant itself legitimacy in its role to fight LGBT inequalities across the globe.

On March 22, 2014, Vice-president Joe Biden was the keynote speaker at a HRC gala in Los Angeles. In this speech he asserted LGBT rights should be a vital part of US foreign policy (HRC, 2014, March 22), in which he also denounced cultural differences around this issue:

> "The single most basic of all human rights is the right to decide who you love....It is the single most important

human right that exists...and hate, hate can never, never be defended because it's a so called cultural norm. I've had it up to here with cultural norms".

There are two concepts from this quote that require some interrogation. Firstly, Biden's myopic use of the term "cultural norms" fails to account for cultures that have been stunted, robbed or shaped in some way by legacies of colonial power and imperialism. For example, he makes a point to shame Uganda for their laws that punish people for "aggravated homosexuality," but conveniently omits the fact that these laws have been passed in large part due to groups of evangelical Christians from the US, who have been working with politicians and religious leaders in Uganda to promote the passing of these laws (Kaoma, 2012). Moreover, despite all this, Biden at no point scrutinizes the US for its cultural norms. He refers to the legal discrimination that still occurs against LGBT Americans as "barbaric" acts, but does not trace them back to America's longstanding culture of heteronormativity. Secondly, by defining LGBT rights as the "right to decide who you love," Biden removes LGBT identities from its intersections with race, gender, class, and ethnicity, and reduces it solely to a matter of sexual preference.

In *Terrorist Assemblages*, Puar draws from Miranda Joseph's theory of analogic inclusion to critique the ways in which gay and lesbian rights discourses have framed sexuality as something not only separate from race, but as "a form of minoritization parallel to ethnicity and race" (Puar, 2007, p. 118). In reasoning that civil rights have already been bestowed upon people of colour, Puar suggests that mainstream gays and lesbians have ultimately relieved themselves of the duty to incorporate any form of critical race or anti-racist critique into their agenda (Puar, 2007, p. 118; see also Puar, 2008). HRC specifically is not a group exempt from reproducing narratives of the "just gay" citizen. However it is worth considering that a mainstream LGBT movement with a strong emphasis on intersectionality would be of little interest to the US government, considering its recent and well-documented reliance on the LGBT movement for fuelling its racist war machine.

Producing Exceptional
Narratives of Citizenship

In 2009, after tireless lobbying by the HRC, Barack Obama signed into law the *Matthew Shepard and James Byrd, Jr. Hate Crimes Prevention Act*. A response to the horrific killing of Matthew Shepard, this act expanded on the 1960 US federal hate crime law to include crimes prompted by a victim's sexual orientation, gender identity, or disability (US Senate, 2009). It aimed to protect LGBT rights by providing millions of dollars to enhance police and prosecutorial resources (Spade, 2011, p. 89). This law, however, was also the rider to the controversial *National Defense Authorization Act* for the fiscal year of 2010, an act that had authorized $680 billion for the Pentagon in the fiscal year 2010, making it the largest military budget ever (Martin, 2009/10/30). Therefore when people were rallying around what they considered to be the advancement of gay civil rights in the US, they were also rallying around increased US military spending, as well as military expansion overseas (US Senate, 2009).

In reference to the *Hate Crimes Prevention Act*, Dean Spade questions how the veterans of stonewall and Compton's cafeteria uprisings against police violence would feel about an act that provides millions of dollars to police and prosecutorial resources (Spade, 2011, p. 89), to the extent that this Act effectively erases the state's role as a perpetrator of this violence. At the reception commemorating the enactment of the *Hate Crimes Prevention Act*, Barack Obama made the following statement:

> "We have for centuries strived to live up to our founding ideal, of a nation where all are free and equal and able to pursue their own version of happiness. Through conflict and tumult, through the morass of

hatred and prejudice, through periods of division and discord we have endured and grown stronger and fairer and freer. And at every turn, we've made progress not only by changing laws, but by changing hearts, by our willingness to walk in another's shoes, by our capacity to love and accept even in the face of rage and bigotry". (White House, 2009/10/28)

This history that Obama produces is one in which the US has stood in exception to such acts of "rage and bigotry," and further, continues to prevail in times when "hatred and prejudice" rear their ugly heads. Thus the discourse put forward is not only one that individualizes acts of oppressive violence, but one that also constructs them as something that exists only as an exception within the US. Further, the US is not only exceptional in the rights it bestows upon its citizens, but is in a state of exception whereby extreme measures of the state are justifiable in that it seeks to protect their exceptional citizens.

At a time when the American public was becoming more and more disillusioned with their country's role in allegedly "spreading democracy" in countries such as Afghanistan and Iraq (Agiesta & Cohen, 2009/8/20), the passing of the *Hate Crimes Prevention Act* gave Americans an opportunity to rally around their dedication as a nation to protecting the human rights of every individual. The fact that it also masked details of the US' contentious military budget for 2010 was simply an added bonus. The timing of the passing of this law, as well as its role as a rider to the *National Defence Authorization Act* should not be considered a mere coincidence.

On December 22, 2010, the Obama administration repealed DADT (HRC, 2011/10/20). DADT was a policy instituted by the Clinton administration in 1994, which essentially banned lesbians and gays from openly serving in the military. In repealing the policy, Obama was hailed by LGBT activists for his clear stance on advancing LGBT rights in the US. Unsurprisingly, HRC was at the forefront of campaigning for the repeal of this policy, working zealously for public support. With the support of government liaisons, they constructed it as the civil rights issue of this generation, a fairly troubling notion considering the state-inflicted violence that is still meted out to marginalized peoples within the US who supposedly have already been allotted their civil rights. Ultimately this repeal relied entirely on the framing of the matter as one of civil rights. Here the use of liberal ideological gambits is crucial for masking the fact that the policy repeal is first and foremost one that allows more people to become both perpetrators and victims of imperial violence. During the special ceremony for the repeal, Obama shared the following anecdote:

> "As one special operations warfighter said during the Pentagon's review—this was one of my favourites: We have a gay guy in the unit. He's big, he's mean, he kills lots of bad guys. No one cared that he was gay. And I think that sums up perfectly the situation". (White House, 2010/12/22)

Here Obama reproduces the narrative Puar spoke of that suggests the other must be killed in order for American life to be valorized. Similar to the *Hate Crimes Act*, the repealing of DADT could be read as an opportunity to rally around the US and its military at a time when its role in Afghanistan was under heavy scrutiny, to say the least. Effectively, it acted as a giant PR campaign to remind the world that the US does stand for freedom, equality, and justice, thus legitimizing their role in spreading democracy abroad, even if in the figure of "warfighters" of the kind that perpetrated night raids in Afghanistan that killed scores of civilians.

Lesbian and Gay Subjects on the Right Side of History

In March 2014, a letter was sent to Barack Obama by a coalition of civil and human rights groups requesting a meeting with senior administration officials to discuss the human rights violations of LGBT people in countries such as Nigeria, Uganda and Russia (Gregg, 2014/3/14). As reported by the HRC, the recommendations included:

> "Reprogramming aid away from discriminating governments to civil society organizations that are committed to proven evidence-and rights-based intervention; using the full weight of US diplomatic weight to press countries to repeal anti-LGBT laws; and providing on-the-ground training protection and support to people put at risk because of anti-LGBT laws or harassment. These recommendations are carefully crafted to ensure that the people who most need foreign assistance are not punished for the actions of leaders who are standing on the wrong side of history". (Gregg, 2014/3/14)

The rhetorical device of "the wrong side of history," used here by an HRC blogger, constructs a dichotomy between the civilized and the backward, or more historically speaking, the European and the non-European. Specifically, this dichotomy is posited by narratives produced through international law (Philipose, 2008, p. 105). Most of the laws objected to by the HRC are in direct violation of international human rights law (Amnesty International [AI], 2013/12/20). It is important to note here the extent to which the US, and other imperial nations, has historically relied on international law to justify the interventions, annexations, occupations, and sanctions of non-western territories. Thus it is a tool used for the purpose of incorporating the "uncivilized" into modernity (Philipose, 2008, p. 108).

Philipose indicates that one of the factors involved in being considered civilized in the eyes of international law is determined by one's sexuality and self-regulating capacity to be sexually appropriate (Philipose, 2008, p. 111). Therefore it is unsurprising how international law has been preoccupied with the prosecution of rape as a weapon of war (Philipose, 2008, p. 112). She states further:

"The opportunity to construct a war zone as a place of sexual deviance reflects a colonial impulse that mobilizes international law to justify armed intervention, foreign occupation, incarceration, criminal trials and the use of torture against those who came to be understood as sexual deviants". (Philipose, 2008, p. 112)

This sexual deviance Philipose refers to, once solely associated with queerness, has progressed to also encompass those who are portrayed as monstrous by association of "hypertrophied heterosexuality" (Puar, 2007, p. 38). Those who oppose gay rights are thus constructed as barbaric misogynists.

In his keynote speech at the HRC gala, Joe Biden quoted Andrei Sakharov saying, "a country that does not respect the rights of its citizens will not respect the rights of its neighbours" (HRC, 2014, March 22). This quote was made in direct reference to Russia and its military intervention in Ukraine. Biden creates a direct link between Russia's failure to adhere to international law and protect LGBT rights with its failure to be a diplomatic country. That is not to suggest there cannot be links between the two, but rather to suggest that this dichotomy of diplomatic and non-diplomatic countries is overly simplistic and relies heavily on another country being constructed as sexually deviant, so that the one may define oneself in relation to it as superior.

Conclusion

Angela Davis notes that in order to dismantle US imperialism, it is important not to view peace as merely the cessation of war. The anti-imperialist battle is not one that looks toward only an end goal, but rather is one that engages constantly in a critique of the methodologies it deploys (Davis, 2008, p. 22). Thus to view struggles against imperialism as one separate from struggles against patriarchy, heteronormativity, colonialism, and white supremacy, would be a mistake.

A few years prior to the US invasion of Afghanistan, American liberal feminists had begun mobilizing to "save" the Afghan women living under the Taliban. While much of this mobilization was laced with good intentions and anti-war sentiments, it produced a narrative of the Afghan woman as someone who needed to be saved from her culture, and thus produced Afghan cultures as monolithic, backward cultures that needed to be corrected. The issue was largely that women were organizing on the basis of a global sisterhood: "the abstract spiritual solidarity often based on scarce knowledge of the actual conditions of and absence of real relationships with the 'other'" (Arat-Koc, 2002, p. 128). Arguably a similar thing is occurring within the field of LGBT activism.

By reducing queer identities to one's sexual preference or gender identity, one effectively erases the ways in which systems of colonialism, imperialism, and white supremacy shape how one experiences queer identities. It is not enough to direct the gaze onto countries with repressive laws towards their LGBT citizens. Rather, we must reverse the gaze, and be critical of the ways in which we, as westerners, are complicit in continuing legacies of colonialism and imperialism, and that these cannot be removed from the promotion of LGBT rights.

References

Agiesta, J., & Cohen, J. (2009/8/20). Poll Shows Most Americans Oppose War in Afghanistan. *The Washington Post.*
http://www.washingtonpost.com/wp-
dyn/content/article/2009/08/19/AR2009081903066.html

Amnesty International (AI). (2013/12/20). Uganda: Anti-Homosexuality Bill must be Scrapped. *Amnesty International.*
http://www.amnesty.ca/news/news-updates/uganda-anti-
homosexuality-bill-must-be-scrapped

Arat-Koc, S. (2002). Hot Potato: Imperial Wars of Benevolent Interventions? Reflections on "Global Feminism" Post

September 11th. In B. Crow and L. Gotell (Eds.), *Open Boundaries: A Canadian Women's Studies Reader*, (pp. 126–133). Toronto, Pearson's Education Canada.

Davis, A. (2008). A Vocabulary for Feminist Praxis: On War and Radical Critique. In C. Mohanty, M. Pratt & R. Riley (Eds.), *Feminism and War: Confronting US Imperialism*, (pp. 19–26). New York, NY: Zed Books.

Encarnación, O.G. (2014). Human Rights and Gay Rights. *Current History*, 113(759), 36–39.

Gregg, R. (2014/3/14). Coalition Calls for White House Meeting on Human Rights Violations in Nigeria, Uganda. *HRC Blog*.
http://www.hrc.org/blog/entry/coalition-calls-for-white-house-meeting-on-human-rights-violations-in-niger

Harvey, D. (2003). *The New Imperialism*. Oxford, UK: Oxford University Press.

Human Rights Campaign (HRC). (2011). *HRC Endorses President Barack Obama for Reelection*.
http://www.hrc.org/blog/entry/hrc-endorses-president-barack-obama-for-reelection

———. (2011/12/20). Don't Ask Don't Tell Repeal Act of 2010.
http://www.hrc.org/laws-and-legislation/federal-laws/dont-ask-dont-tell-repeal-act-of-2010

———. (2014, March 22). *Vice President Biden's Remarks from the 2014 HRC Gala*. [video file].
https://www.youtube.com/watch?v=iFXz2DMrU-c

Kaoma, K. J. (2012). Colonizing African Values: How the U.S. Christian Right is Transforming Sexual Politics in Africa. Somerville, MA: Political Research Associates.
http://www.sxpolitics.org/wp-content/uploads/2012/08/colonizingafricanvaluespra.pdf

Kouri-Towe, N. (2012). Trending Homonationalism. *No More Potlucks*.
http://nomorepotlucks.org/site/trending-homonationalism/

Martin, P. (2009/10/30). Obama Signs Bills for Record Pentagon Homeland Security Spending. *World Socialist Web Site*.
http://www.wsws.org/en/articles/2009/10/dfns-o30.html

Philipose, E. (2008). Decolonizing the Racial Grammar of International Law. In C.T. Mohanty, M.B. Pratt and R.L. Riley (Eds.), *Feminism and War: Confronting US Imperialism*, (pp. 103–116). New York, NY: Zed Books.

Puar, J. (2007). *Terrorist Assemblages: Homonationalism in Queer Times*. Durham, NC: Duke University Press.

———— . (2008). Feminists and Queers in the Service of Empire. In C. Mohanty, M. Pratt & R. Riley (Eds.), *Feminism and War: Confronting US Imperialism*, (pp. 47–55). New York, NY: Zed Books.

Spade, D. (2011). *Normal Life: Administrative Violence, Critical Trans Politics, and the Limits of Law*. Brooklyn, NY: South End Press.

US Senate. (2009). *National Defence Authorization Act for the Fiscal Year 2010*. Washington, DC: U.S. Senate.

http:// www.intelligence.senate.gov/pdfs/military_act_2009.pdf

White House. (2009/10/28). Remarks by the President at Reception Commemorating the Enactment of the Matthew Shepard and James Byrd, Jr. Hate Crimes Prevention Act. Washington, DC: Office of the Press Secretary, The White House.

http://www.whitehouse.gov/the-press-office/remarks-president-reception-commemorating-enactment-matthew-shepard-and-james-byrd-

———— . (2010/12/22). Remarks by the President at Signing of the Don't Ask, Don't Tell Repeal Act of 2010. Washington, DC: Office of the Press Secretary, The White House.

http://www.whitehouse.gov/the-press-office/2010/12/22/remarks-president-and-vice-president-signing-dont-ask-dont-tell-repeal-a

PART TWO:
The Political Economy of Exception

CHAPTER 5

The International Economic Sovereignty of the United States of America: Integrating the Exception into Our Understanding of Empire

☆ ☆ ☆ ☆ ☆

Karine Perron

Championing itself as the leader of capitalism, more obviously so since the Cold War, the US has led the world into an era of neoliberalism in which the free market is deemed to be the ultimate way to prosperity (Ellwood, 2010). In fact, after memories were cleared of the factors that led the US into the Great Depression of the 1930s, the end of World War II was followed by the rebirth of the belief in the free market, a belief which was best expressed through the creation of the Bretton Woods trio: the International Monetary Fund (IMF), the World Bank, and the General Agreement on Tariffs and Trade (GATT), the latter succeeded by the World Trade Organization (WTO). Since then, the US has controlled a good deal of the financial world and it can be argued that the country has both written the rules and enforced them.

However, a simple look at the course of US economic history allows one to realize that the US feels free to break the rules of capitalism it advocates whenever the occasion demands it for the benefit of the country and especially its corporations. Michael Ignatieff has addressed the exceptionality of US capacity to both be an advocate of human rights, while disrespecting them on multiple occasions: "What needs explaining is the paradox of being simultaneously a leader and an outlier" (Ignatieff, 2005, p. 2). It is with this paradox in mind that this chapter examines what we might call a state of exceptionalism: the various ways in which the US influences the international economy in its favour and imposes on the rest of the world rules it does not apply to itself. The role of multilateral international economic and politic institutions in which the US holds sway, with a focus on the IMF, will first be examined. Then, the claims of the US to economic liberalism will be contrasted with the managed trade policy that has actually been applied and the way the WTO has been both advocated and disregarded according to the situation. The overthrow of the government of Guatemala in 1954, as just one notorious case, will provide an example of the extent to which the US has gone to control the economic and political direction of dissident countries and to protect American corporate interests (Kinzer, 2006). Finally, the US strategy of enlargement will be used to open up a discussion about the significance of this international economic control, as well as the implications of the US deciding on the exception.

US Influence in Multilateral Economic Institutions: The International Monetary Fund

International economic institutions have proven to be some of the most effective organisms through which the US has advanced its economic agenda. After World War II, there was a desire among developed countries to create a set of rules that would prevent crises such as that of the 1930s (Ellwood, 2010). The "challenge of peace," as the post-war period was heralded, was to produce economic growth and to locate markets for the productive capacity of the US in a period when vast regions of Europe and

Asia were badly damaged by war (Nixon, 1971; Ellwood, 2010). These realities shaped the goals of the Bretton Woods meeting in 1944, and the proposals that followed set the tone of early post-war US liberalism, including the implementation of a fixed exchange rate with the US dollar as the international currency, and free trade as the ideology (Harvey, 2003; Ellwood, 2010). The IMF and the World Bank were born out of the Bretton Woods meeting and were meant to promote free trade. They were also powerful instruments for the US to use to its advantage (Harvey, 2003). This fact did not, however, come as a surprise to everyone present at this meeting:

> "Keynes, Britain's delegate to the meeting, advocated a balanced world trade system with strict controls on the movement of capital across borders. He held that the free movement of all goods and capital, advocated most powerfully by the US delegation, would inevitably lead to inequalities and instabilities". (Ellwood, 2010, p. 36)

The IMF was designed by the representatives attending the Bretton Woods meeting, and the US had the strongest voice. The functioning of the organization itself gives a clear idea of the weight of America in the decision-making process: voting power is directly correlated with the member country's monetary contribution to the Fund (International Monetary Fund [IMF], 2014). To illustrate this, when the IMF was first founded, the American quota, on which the number of allocated votes is based, was $2.75 billion, over twice that of the closest member country's quota, the Union of Soviet Socialist Republics, which was $1.2 billion (IMF, 2011, Schedule A). Today, there are 188 member countries of the IMF, and the US still possesses by far the largest voting share, with 16.75% of votes. The second country in terms of voting power is Japan, with 6.23% (IMF, 2014). If there were to be any doubts about the degree of control America has over the IMF, the information available on the official website of the organization should help to dispel them.

The IMF states as its objective (among others) the creation of economic stability and growth. In order to allow
this, the organization deems it necessary to break down
trade barriers and unfair competition tactics, such as the
devaluation of national currencies (IMF, 2011, Article 1). It
is interesting to note that these objectives were disregarded
by the US on various occasions since the foundation of the
Fund. The *Job Development Act* of 1971, also called the
Nixon Shock, was an obvious case, since it implied the
President's unilateral decision to abolish the Gold Standard (the direct convertibility of gold into US dollars) precisely in order to devalue the dollar and dramatically
reduce the US' foreign debt. This measure led to the end of
the fixed exchange rate and a return of floating rates and
risky speculations (Harvey, 2003, p. 62; Ellwood, 2010).
The President was well aware of the repercussions of this
decision on international trade, as demonstrated by this
quote from his address to the nation: "Now, this action
will not win us any friends among the international money
traders. But our primary concern is with the American
workers, and with fair competition around the world....As
a result of these actions, the product of American labor
will be more competitive, and the unfair edge that some of
our foreign competition has will be removed" (Nixon,
1971). The meaning of "fair competition" fluctuated; it was
apparently contingent on the economic situation of the US.
Another issue with which the IMF concerns itself are the
economic policies of the countries to which it lends money
(IMF, 2014). Structural adjustment measures imposed by
the IMF include the devaluation of the national currency;
significant cuts in government spending, such as social
services and subsidies for products that meet basic needs;
privatization of state-owned enterprises and reduction of
the public sector; and, of course, the abolition of trade barriers (Ellwood, 2010). While in 1999 the Structural Adjustment Facility was replaced with the Poverty Reduction
and Growth Facility, and the measures have officially been
rendered more social-friendly (IMF, 2009), multiple studies
have shown the disastrous social effects of such measures,

and the IMF itself has been forced to recognize their inef-
fectiveness in some cases (IMF, 2013; Stevis, 2013/6/5).
However, debtor nations were not given the privilege of
choice:

> "Countries were forced to adopt the austerity measures
> if they wanted to get the IMF 'seal of approval'. Without
> it they would be ostracized to the fringes of the global
> economy". (Ellwood, 2010, p. 56)

Again, when examining structural adjustment measures advocated by the IMF, one quickly notices that the US
has not been a model for these measures when it itself has
been in economic difficulty, especially after the 2008 financial crisis. The country with the largest debt in the world
apparently saw no contradictions in continually promoting
economic liberalism and spending $350 billion dollars in a
bailout of private banks, and proposing the largest budget
deficit since World War II (Meyerson & Roberto, 2009). As
David Harvey summarizes:

> "Any other country in the world that exhibited such
> macroeconomic conditions would by now have been
> subjected to ruthless austerity and structural adjustment
> procedures by the IMF. But the IMF is the United
> States". (Harvey, 2003, p. 72)

Clearly the US, in not considering itself bound by the same
obligations as others, decides that it is the exception.

Unilateral Decisions:
Using and Disregarding WTO

While the IMF plays a central role in multilateral international economic decisions and influence, most trade
agreements are made on the bilateral level (Laïdi, 2008).
Considering the necessity for US companies to sell their
products outside the home country, because of the domestic market saturation, US trade policy consists of what can
be called an offensive or market access strategy (Laïdi,

2008). In fact, most of the trade interests of the country are about exporting American products and services to other countries, with as little in the way trade barriers as possible. However, as we will see, the US also has defensive interests, and its advocacy for market liberalization has limitations when it comes to imports of products that compete with American-made merchandise (Ashbee & Waddan, 2010).

When conflicts arise between member nations concerning trade, the World Trade Organization comes into play, and it has been particularly useful for the US in the last 20 years. The WTO offers a number of advantages for the US, both in terms of effectiveness towards reaching its trade goals of opening markets abroad and in terms of perceived international legitimacy in doing so. In fact, unlike the IMF, voting power in the WTO is not as glaringly skewed and the rulings are based on law rather than on internal policies (World Trade Organization [WTO], 2014). According to Sanchez (2002), resorting to the WTO for dispute resolution, as opposed to so-called "managed trade policies," which include the dispositions of Section 301 of the Trade Act of 1974 (International Trade Administration [ITA], 2013), is ideal for the US in terms of projecting legitimacy regarding US trade policy decisions, as the WTO's ruling system is objectively equitable. Sanchez expresses this opinion as a critique of the Clinton administration's policies, which relied heavily on unilateral market-opening strategies that consisted of threatening noncompliant countries with trade sanctions, such as retaliatory taxes on certain products (Sanchez, 2002; ITA, 2013). Japan was one of the countries most heavily targeted by US pressure to open up its market to American products during the Clinton years, and it was the country that proved most responsive to retaliation threats (Zeng, 2002). Remarkably, Japan was also successfully constructed in the American population's mind as the country most likely to challenge US economic dominance with its unfair competition tactics. This belief, fallacious to say the least, made the application of Section 301 acceptable to the public regardless of the pretended commitment to free trade (Sanchez, 2002; Zeng, 2002). For the 42nd President of the US, free trade was to be applied only when it served US interests, and this belief arguably has stayed consistently in place with the following administrations. We will get back to this in the following section. Yet, notwithstanding US entitlement to making exceptions for itself, this openly unilateral trade-first policy has not been particularly effective in terms of international acceptance (Sanchez, 2002), which is why the resort to the WTO has become increasingly important thereafter (WTO, 2014).

However equitable the rules of the WTO might appear to be on paper—because its system is based on the capacity of the countries in a quarrel to make their legal cases in front of the Dispute Resolution Body (WTO, 2014)—the economic capacity of the countries in question definitely influences the process and the results. Ellwood takes notice of this situation: "All nations have the right to use DRB to pursue their economic self-interest. But the fact is that the world's major trading nations are also its most powerful economic actors. So the tendency is for the strong to use the new rules to dominate the weaker countries" (2010, p. 43). Moreover, nearly all the propositions of the 16 multilateral agreements that all 159 members of the WTO have agreed to largely favour the offensive interests of richer countries such as the US (Laïdi, 2008), which is congruent with the first point of the description of the activities of the WTO stating that the reduction or elimination of obstacles to trade is a primary goal (WTO, 2014).

Abundant examples of occasions the US brought countries reluctant to open up their markets to American exports in front of the WTO's Dispute Resolution Body and won its case can be found in Ellwood (2010) and Harvey (2003), as well as in the archives of the WTO (WTO, 2014). Ranking higher in the interests of this chapter, of course, are the cases in which the US disrespected the rules set by the WTO. One such instance can be found quite recently in the *American Recovery and Reinvestment Act* (ARRA) of 2009 presented by the Obama administration to counter the disastrous effects of the 2008 financial crisis (Ashbee & Waddan, 2010). Indeed, the stimulus package included a "buy American" stipulation that demanded the use of local steel and iron rather than cheaper foreign material (National Conference of State Legislatures [NCSL], 2009). These provisions, of course, disrespected the conditions of the North American Free Trade Agreement (NAFTA) that the US had signed with Mexico and Canada (Ashbee & Waddan, 2010).

This disregard for the free trade agreement should not necessarily have come as a surprise, since another case of the US privileging American steel for the construction of its infrastructure occurred a few years earlier: "US abandonment of the spirit if not the letter of the WTO rules against protectionism by the imposition of tariffs on steel imports in 2002 was a particularly ominous sign" (Harvey, 2003, p. 71). The WTO's Dispute Settlement Body ruled in November 2003 that the decision was illegal (WTO, 2003), whereas the Bush administration disagreed and ignored both the WTO's decision and the European Union's threats of retaliation (Tran, 2003/11/11). A month later, and a little under two years after the imposition of the tariffs, the President lifted them (Bush, 2003; WTO, 2003). Never did he formally accept the WTO's decision (Bush, 2003), which is quite telling as the Bush administration was a fervent proponent of free trade ideology (Ashbee & Waddan, 2010).

Regime Change

The previous sections intended to present the ways in which the US seeks to achieve its economic goals through both multilateral means, with the use of the IMF, and through bilateral agreements settled by the WTO. What is striking from the examples provided is the inconsistency of the US' policy regarding free trade, which is at once strongly advocated or ignored according to the situation. In spite of official statements from Presidents, of IMF decisions, or of the brutal opening of foreign markets by means that go from economic sanctions to overthrowing governments that refused to grant market access to American corporations (Kinzer, 2006), there is no such thing as a US commitment to free trade *as such*. What there is, however, is a commitment to American corporate interests and to the belief in the right of America to decide on exceptions (Chomsky, 1993).

Stephen Kinzer provides numerous cases in which the US not only exercised influence in countries to advance corporate interests, but planned and executed the overthrow of governments (Kinzer, 2006). The example of Guatemala in 1954 is especially useful in showing to what lengths the US will go to enhance its corporate interests, especially given how blatant the facts of US intervention were, even sixty years ago when the American economy unlikely would have been qualified as weak. The government of Guatemala was democratically elected and nationalist, and its president was not willing to abide to any and all US demands. The United Fruit Company, an American corporation, dominated the Guatemalan economy: it was responsible for the great majority of banana exports and consequently much of the employment (Kinzer, 2006). What became an issue between the government and the United Fruit Company, however, were the millions of acres of land that the company owned but did not use, while parts of the population of Guatemala were landless and going hungry. The government demanded that United Fruit sell it the land at the price evaluated by the company in its last tax returns (Kinzer, 2006). United Fruit refused, arguing that the land was worth a lot more than had been declared, but the President moved ahead with the law reform, which led the corporation to seek the assistance of the US government with which it had close ties. In the midst of the Cold War, little effort was required to convince the US government that the decision of the Guatemalan President was a result of anti-American sentiment and pressure from the Soviet Union (Kinzer, 2006). Regardless of how American leaders have taken pride in their work towards defending democracy in Guatemala (Lake, 1993), the truth is that an overthrow of the democratically elected government was then prepared and executed, and a dictatorship that would prioritize American interests over national ones was established (Brockett, 2002; Kinzer, 2006). The US promised Guatemala to become a "showcase for democracy," but reality was that the goal of liberalization of the economy, or "anticommunism," had priority over democratization (Brockett, 2002). The priority given to economic interests over the development of democracy was mentioned by Harvey when he wrote about the contradiction of the US strategy from 1945 to 1970 to expand its influence around the world: "whenever there was a conflict between democracy, on the one hand, and order and stability built on propertied interests on the other, the US always opted for the latter" (Harvey, 2003, p. 59).

The Strategy of Enlargement

One might be tempted to believe that the end of the Cold War could have brought changes to the foreign and economic policies of the US, given the passing of the "communist threat". Anthony Lake, a foreign policy and national security advisor for the Clinton administration, addressed the question of American post-Cold War vision (Chomsky, 1993; Lake, 1993). In his discourse Lake clearly outlined a vision of the global role the US should play. He first reminded us that Bill Clinton, who was president at the time, promised to work towards heightened US engagement internationally with his priorities being economic growth, national security, and the promotion of democracy (Lake, 1993). It is interesting to note how these three objectives effectively become one, as he clearly indicated what was at stake: "Whether Americans' real incomes double every 26 years, as they did in the 1960s, or every 36 years, as they did during the late '70s and '80s" (Lake, 1993). According to Giorgio Agamben, anything that is seen as endangering national security justifies the declaration of a state of exception, and to paraphrase Balladore-Pallieri (as cited in Agamben, 2003) and Schmitt (2005), the notion of exception rests upon the concept of necessity, which is entirely subjective and contingent on what the decision-maker wishes to achieve. Therefore, declaring economic growth to be the main concern of the US' strategy of enlargement has important implications for national security policies.

The leadership of the US has always deployed the definition of exception in the international sphere. When examining US economic policy, it is clear that free trade agreements and international economic policies favourable to American corporations are considered to be of high priority. Moreover, Lake's discourse clearly states that the most important threat the US faces since the end of the Cold War is lethargic economic growth, and consequently identifies the strengthening and broadening of the community of market democracies, as well as the fight against anti-capitalist states, as the way to achieve economic growth (Lake, 1993). It is irrefutable that economic growth has become a question of national security for the US: both the actions and the discourses of US leaders point to this direction. Following this idea is the fact that the protection of national security, which includes economic growth, is reason enough to install a state of exception that has slowly come to be permanent. Whereas states of exception have been declared numerous times in the past, such as during the civil war, when Lincoln suspended Habeas Corpus, and during World War I, when President Wilson assumed even broader powers, there was a shift during the Great Depression when the state of exception was for the first time defended on economic grounds. In fact in his inaugural discourse Roosevelt addressed the economic crisis metaphorically as a war: "I shall ask the Congress for the one remaining instrument to meet the crisis—broad executive power to wage war against the emergency, as great as the power that would be given to me if we were in fact invaded by a foreign foe" (Roosevelt, 1933). The heritage of installing measures of exception to situations of economic duress was continued by Nixon in the 1970s (Ellwood, 2010), and by the International Emergency Economic Powers Act (IEEPA), enacted in 1977 under Carter (Office of the Law Revision Counsel of the United States House of Representatives [OLRC], 1977). The IEEPA has legally allowed the President of the United States, in cases of emergency, to use a series of economic measures that usually would be prohibited:

> "Any authority granted to the President by section 1702 of this title may be exercised to deal with any unusual and extraordinary threat, which has its source in whole or substantial part outside the United States, to the national security, foreign policy, or economy of the United States, if the President declares a national emergency with respect to such threat". (OLRC, 1977, Title 50, Section 1701)

The IEEPA has been used against at least 30 countries and groups, on several occasions in most of these particular cases, and many of the measures are still effective today (OLRC, 1977). National security issues and emergencies appear to be extremely recurrent and long lasting for the US.

Discussion

The evidence presented in the previous sections point towards the conclusion that the US strategy of enlargement and of economic growth heavily relies on declarations of exceptions, whether official or not. US action within the IMF and the influence it has over the policies of the organization, as well as its power to impose structural adjustment programs on other countries while itself disregarding the measures advocated by the IMF, give an idea of how the US can both set the rules and break them. The same can be said about American leadership's relation with the WTO: simultaneously advocating for the principles of the WTO, and using force to open up select markets to American exports, and yet disrespecting the WTO's decisions when they are not to its advantage. The enactment and multiple uses of Section 301 of the Trade Act of 1974 and of IEEPA of 1977 only reinforces how large the scope of what constitutes national security and measures of exception can be for the US. When other options have failed or have been deemed not to resolve the problem swiftly enough, declassified documents prove that overthrows have been executed in order to protect and expand American corporate interests.

The primary purpose of this chapter was to show US exceptionalism when it comes to neoliberalism, that is, by sidestepping neoliberal prescriptions whenever convenient while upholding them globally. Neoliberalism is advocated and enforced solely if it is to the advantage of US corporations. The rules can and will be broken whenever they do not serve US corporate interests. Official statements barely, if at all, disguise this reality, as demonstrated by Lake's discourse, in which he both advocates international rules and subtracts the US from them: "But for any official with responsibilities for our security policies, only one overriding factor can determine whether the US should act multilaterally or unilaterally, and that is American interests" (Lake, 1993). In *Political Theology*, Schmitt (2005) discussed sovereignty in these terms: "Sovereign is he who decides on the exception" (p. 5). It is a question of who appropriates for oneself the power to decide what constitutes order and safety without being significantly challenged (Schmitt, 2005). For the US, order and safety necessitate market economies and democracy, as well as American leadership, which Lake believes is desired and appreciated throughout the world (Lake, 1993). This leadership consequently entails that the US sets out the rules, but is also empowered to deviate from them when it judges it necessary. The information provided in this chapter leads us to the conclusion that the US is sovereign, since it shows little hesitation to decide on undertaking exceptional measures on economic grounds, and has furthermore made exceptions a recurrent practice.

While the discussion of this chapter was limited to the economic aspect of exceptions and US hegemony, it could be extended to the political and military realms. Lake's discourse can be used as an interesting starting point, since it specifically addresses the idea that the US is the dominant power in the contemporary world, and mentions its unrivalled military might, while in the same breath argues that the proliferation of weapons of mass destruction is one of the major threats the world faces (Lake, 1993). He clearly states the aspiration to expand the scope of US influence and the intention to engage militarily in other countries' intra-national ethnic conflicts (Lake, 1993). "American exceptionalism" is more than an overly proud and arrogant self-reflection (Hongju Koh, 2003). US hegemonic ambitions are barely hidden and the idea of an American empire is now endorsed and advocated by a number of influential writers (Boot, 2001/10/15; Kaplan, 2001; Ignatieff, 2005). The power of the US to frequently decide on exceptions in the international economic realm is a significant feature of its international sovereignty; this type of sovereignty should be understood as integral part of the meaning of contemporary empire.

References

Agamben, G. (2003). *State of Exception*. Chicago, IL: The University of Chicago Press.

Ashbee, E., & Waddan, A. (2010). The Obama Administration and United States Trade Policy. *The Political Quarterly*, 81(2), 253–262.

Boot, M. (2001/10/15). The Case for American Empire. *The Weekly Standard*, 7(5).
http://www.weeklystandard.com/Content/Public/Articles/000/000/000/318qpvmc.asp

Brockett, C. D. (2002). An Illusion of Omnipotence: U.S. Policy toward Guatemala, 1954–1960. *Latin American Politics and Society*, 44(1), 91–126.

Bush, G. W. (2003). President's Statement on Steel. Washington, DC: The White House, President George W. Bush.
http://georgewbush-whitehouse.archives.gov/news/releases/2003/12/20031204-5.html

Chomsky, N. (1993). The Clinton Vision. *Z Magazine*, December.
http://www.chomsky.info/articles/199312--.htm

Ellwood, W. (2010). *No-Nonsense Guide to Globalization (3rd ed.).* Cornwall, ON: New Internationalist Publications.

Harvey, D. (2003). *The New Imperialism.* Oxford, UK: Oxford University Press.

Hongju Koh, H. (2003). On American Exceptionalism. *Stanford Law Review.* 55(5) 1479–1527.

Ignatieff, M. (2005). *American Exceptionalism and Human Rights.* Princeton, NJ: Princeton University Press.

International Monetary Fund (IMF). (2009). The Poverty Reduction and Growth Facility (PRGF). Washington, DC: International Monetary Fund.
https://www.imf.org/external/np/exr/facts/prgf.htm

————. (2011). Articles of Agreement of the International Monetary Fund. Washington, DC : International Monetary Fund.
http://www.imf.org/External/Pubs/FT/AA/index.htm#art4

————. (2013). IMF Executive Board Reviews Greece Misreporting, Remedial Steps. Press Release No. 13/166. Washington, DC: International Monetary Fund.
http://www.imf.org/external/np/sec/pr/2013/pr13166.htm

————. (2014). IMF Members' Quotas and Voting Power, and IMF Board of Governors. Washington, DC: International Monetary Fund.
http://www.imf.org/external/np/sec/memdir/members.aspx

International Trade Administration (ITA), (2013). *Section 301.* Washington, DC: International Trade Administration, U.S. Department of Commerce.
http://www.trade.gov/mas/ian/tradedisputes-enforcement/tg_ian_002100.asp

Kaplan, R. (2001) *Warrior Politics: Why Leadership Demands a Pagan Ethos.* New York, NY: Vintage Books.

Kinzer, S. (2006) *Overthrow: America's Century of Regime Change from Hawaii to Iraq.* New York, NY: Times Books/Henry Holt.

Laïdi, Z. (2008). How Trade Became Geopolitics. *World Policy*

Journal, 25(2), 55–61.

Lake, A. (1993). From Containment to Enlargement. Washington, DC: John Hopkins University, School of Advanced International Studies.

https://www.fas.org/news/usa/1993/usa-930921.htm

Meyerson, G. and M. J. Roberto. (2009). Obamas's New New Deal and the Irreversible Crisis. *Socialism and Democracy*, 23(2), 55–69.

National Conference of State Legislatures (NCSL). (2009). Buy American Provisions in the American Recovery Provisions in the American Recovery and Reinvestment Act (ARRA). Washington, DC: National Conference of State Legislatures.

http://www.ncsl.org/print/statefed/BuyAmericanGuidanceSummary.pdf

Nixon, R. (1971) Address to the Nation Outlining a New Economic Policy: "The Challenge of Peace". Santa Barbara, CA: The American Presidency Project.

http://www.presidency.ucsb.edu/ws/?pid=3115

Office of the Law Revision Counsel of the United States House of Representatives (OLRC). (1977). *Unusual and Extraordinary Threat; Declaration of National Emergency; Exercise of Presidential Authorities*. Washington, DC: United States Code Annotated.

http://uscode.house.gov/view.xhtml?req=(title:50%20section:1701%20editi on:prelim)%20OR%20(granuleid:USCprelimtitle50section1701)&f=treesort& edition=prelim&num=0&jumpTo=true

Roosevelt, F. D. (1933). *Inaugural Address*. College Park, MD: The U.S. National Archives and Records Administration.

http://www.archives.gov/education/lessons/fdr-inaugural/#documents

Sanchez, O. (2002). The Perils of a Trade-First US Foreign Policy. *Australian Journal of International Affairs*, 56(1), 143–160.

Schmitt, C. (2005). *Political Theology, Four Chapters on the Concept of Sovereignty*, Chicago, IL: University of Chicago Press.

Stevis, M. (2013/6/5). The IMF Concedes It Made Mistakes On Greece. *The Wall Street Journal*.

http://online.wsj.com/news/articles/SB100014241278873242991045785272 02781667088

Tran, M. (2003/11/11). US Steel Tariffs. *The Guardian*.

http://www.theguardian.com/world/2003/nov/11/qanda.usa

Life, Liberty and the Pursuit of Wage Labour: The American Legislative Exchange Council and the Neoliberal Coup

★ ★ ★ ★ ★

Mathieu Guerin

A challenge in studying the new imperialism lies in overcoming the expectation of features belonging to archetypal empires, for example: colonies, military might, state infrastructure, technological and economic superiority, or national identity and the demographics of a corresponding citizenry (Magdoff, 2003). Here, Harry Magdoff proposes that we examine monopoly capitalism, because it characterizes the contemporary global system (Magdoff, 2003, pp. 91–92). In parallel with this proposal, David Harvey argues that the rise of neoliberal hegemony in the early 1970s endowed the American empire with the "financial orthodoxy" of free market enterprise, a timely way to assert itself around the globe (Harvey, 2003, p. 62). The proliferation of neoliberal values and the advent of Americanization (imperialistic cultural capitalism) are historical contingencies of today's global state of affairs (Harvey, 2003, pp. 62–74), and the oligarchs that head the monopolies that create and manage this dominance are thus themselves a key part of contemporary empire. This assumption proves valid in light of evidence that the corporate imperium, like the nation-state, imposes its interests on both domestic and foreign policies.

In the domestic arena, some of the corporate engines that are vital to the exercise of US soft power are information-technology corporations like Google, Twitter, Yahoo, and Facebook. These corporations encourage their extravagantly paid employees to purchase expensive homes in San Francisco, a short chartered bus ride to their campuses in Silicon Valley. The new technocratic San Franciscans have caused the cost of rent to skyrocket, forcing mass evictions and displacing people from their homes with the non-violent and legal power of money-capital.

Following Magdoff and Harvey, this chapter begins with an inquiry into the inspiration, operation, and impact of the American Legislative Exchange Council (ALEC). ALEC is an organization which facilitates the implementation of US state laws at the hands of global corporations (Center for Media Democracy [CMD], 2014/4/5). The front page of the CMD's website dedicated to investigating ALEC states in bold text:

> "Through the corporate-funded American Legislative Exchange Council, global corporations and state politicians vote behind closed doors to try to rewrite state laws that govern your rights. These so-called 'model bills' reach into almost every area of American life and often directly benefit huge corporations". (CMD, 2014/4/5)

ALEC identifies itself as nonpartisan, although its affiliation with oil giants and the NRA, as well as its arduous labouring against environmental sciences and activism, reveal a clearly conservative agenda (CMD, 2014/4/5). I ask how imperialism functions in our time, one where corporations not only circumscribe and permeate the nation-state infrastructure through organizations like ALEC, but also co-opt it to change policy and thus to impose their vision of society without necessarily resorting to military or police violence.

Imperialism without Colonies

An important aspect of corporate imperialism is its ability to permeate national boundaries. In principle, capital does not owe its allegiance to any flag, nor is its power directed against any one nation. However, as Adam Hanieh argues, although "the capitalist world order...is based upon exploitation and extraction of profit," the nation-state serves an important role in the neoliberal ideal (Hanieh, 2006, p. 187). He explains that:

> "[The capitalist world order's] inability to meet real human needs means that the existing social order always generates opposition and therefore must be maintained by force....The state is critical in ensuring that the conditions are right for capital accumulation". (Hanieh, 2006, p. 187)

ALEC epitomizes this role for the nation-state, by literally putting corporate representatives and government legislators together in the same room. The Powell memorandum of 1971 serves as an empirical record of neoliberal frustration in the face of broad opposition on behalf of the existing social order and marks a pivotal moment in the emergence of the corporate imperium.

The Powell Memorandum

On August 23, 1971, corporate lawyer Lewis F. Powell Jr. sent a confidential memorandum entitled "Attack on American Free Enterprise System" to the Chairman of the US Chamber of Commerce Education Committee (Powell, 1971). The memo deplored a perceived attack on "the American economic system" by what was ostensibly the entirety of the American intelligentsia, media and the majority of the political scene (Powell, 1971, pp. 1-3). The memo inveighed against the discourse that criticizes "American business," and it vilified such public figures as Ralph Nader, Charles Reich, and William Kunstler, while lauding the socio-economic diagnoses of Milton Friedman and Stewart Alsop (Powell, 1971, pp. 4–6). Powell wrote in this regard:

> "The most disquieting voices joining the chorus of criticism, come from perfectly respectable elements of society: from the college campus, the pulpit, the media, the intellectual and literary journals, the arts and sciences, and from politicians....these often are the most articulate, the most vocal, the most prolific in their writing and speaking". (Powell, 1971, pp. 2–3)

Powell called for an aggressive attitude on behalf of American business, prescribed counter-measures to be pursued, and denounced businesspeople apathetic to public criticism, albeit conceding that no business person is trained to retaliate against "propaganda, political demagoguery, or economic illiteracy" (Powell, 1971, p. 7). The author's gun-related metaphors revealed much about his outlook as he continued by writing: "The foregoing references illustrate the broad, *shotgun attack* on the [free enterprise] system itself. There are countless examples of *rifle shots* which undermine confidence and confuse the public" (Powell, 1971, p. 7, emphasis added). With a tone of urgency, Powell claimed:

> "The overriding first need is for businessmen to recognize that the ultimate issue may be survival— survival of what we call the free enterprise system, and all that this means for the strength and prosperity of America and the freedom of our people". (Powell, 1971, p. 10, underlining in the original)

Clearly, when he wrote "our people," Powell was referring to what he believed was the American public. Yet the intelligentsia, media and politicians against whom he was mobilizing in this memo were the intellectual lifeblood of the American public. They represented competing beliefs and values in the American intellectual and political spheres. The polemic that was the object of Powell's frustration originated from these discursive spheres, which largely represented the social order of the early 1970s in the US, and which Powell intended to shirk, supersede, and "defeat" rather than engage. This attitude, in combination with his characterization of the American people as duped by propaganda and demagoguery and as economically illiterate, exposed a belief that is common in colonial and imperialistic ideologies. Specifically, the ideal of divine providence, or a contemporary equivalent of a "manifest destiny," wherein it would be the corporate world's responsibility to help the American people improve themselves and it would be the American people's duty to obey. The following statement from the memo characterizes today's corporate modus operandi:

> "The day is long past when the chief executive officer of a major corporation discharges his responsibility by maintaining a satisfactory growth of profits, with due regard to the corporation's public and social responsibilities. If our system is to survive, top management must be equally concerned with protecting and preserving the system itself. This involves far more than an increased emphasis on 'public relations' or 'governmental affairs' – two areas in which corporations long have invested substantial sums". (Powell, 1971, p. 10)

Reneging on any sense of corporate responsibility is a fundamental feature within the neoliberal narrative, where human needs are to be met by the market, and where the importance of human needs are secondary to capital accumulation – and this is also a fundamental contradiction, since capitalists impoverish the workers whose incomes are needed to purchase commodities (Hanieh, 2006, p. 190). The passage above was thus a call to reverse the power relations between the corporate and social order. Where corporations putatively foster economic growth which is deemed to be beneficial to the social order (for example, by providing tax revenue for the state, increasing employment rates, and increasing the standard of living), Powell's aim was to politicize American business and for corporations to take action against the public (represented by the intelligentsia, the media, and politicians). Powell provided several strategies to the Chamber of Commerce to the end of implementing this reversal. The strategies in question target specific aspects of public life, and are organized under the headings *What Can Be Done about the Campus, What Can Be Done about the Public, The Neglected Political Arena, Neglected Opportunity in the Courts,* and *Neglected Stockholder Power* (Powell, 1971, pp. 15–28). Notably, Powell encourages the Chamber of Commerce to intervene in the staffing of colleges and universities, to monitor and evaluate the "quality" of textbooks and of national television programs, to monitor "news analyses," and to pay for advertisements aimed at "the overall purpose of [informing] and [enlightening] the American people" (Powell, 1971, p. 24). In light of what Powell's marshaling of corporate force meant for the American populace, as well as the subservience it envisioned for the state, it is apt to call what is being staged in the Powell memo as a non-violent coup d'état.

According to Bill Moyers, the Powell memo was the inspiration behind the establishment of lobbying groups and think-tanks such as the Heritage Foundation, the Business Roundtable, the Manhattan Institute, Americans for Prosperity, the Cato Institute, and of course, the American Legislative Exchange Council, inaugurated by Paul Weyrich only two years after the memo had been circulating in the corporate world (Moyers, 2011/11/2).

The American Legislative Exchange Council

ALEC's website reports that the council was founded in 1973, by "a small group of state legislators and conservative policy advocates [who] met in Chicago to implement a vision" (ALEC, 2014a). The top of the webpage showcases three pillar values of the group: "limited government, free markets, and federalism" (ALEC, 2014b). The webpage divulges very little information on the organization and its activities, and no information at all on its corporate members. As I searched for information on ALEC, I was systematically referred to the Center for Media and Democracy itself, or to a source which lead back to it in very few steps. It is worthy of note how secretive ALEC has been in the past 40 years, as well as the story behind its public exposure.

In 2011, ALEC came into the American media spotlight via the shooting of 17 year old Floridian Trayvon Martin (Nichols, 2012/3/21). According to John Nichols, ALEC was impressed by Florida's now infamous "Stand your Ground" law when it was enacted in 2005: "ALEC members introduced, advocated for and passed not just 'Castle Doctrine' laws (which allow for the violent defense of homes) but 'Stand Your Ground' laws (which extend home-defense principles into the streets)" (Nichols, 2012/3/21). The extensive media coverage throughout the aftermath of the killing eventually turned up the passing of similar laws based on ALEC's model bills in 16 states (Nichols, 2012/3/21). In the spring following Martin's death, an ALEC insider contacted Lisa Graves, executive director and editor-in-chief of the Center for Media and Democracy, with the intent of making all of ALEC's current model bills available to the CMD (Moyers, 2012/9/28). This instigated the launch of an investigation at the Center for Media and Democracy that continues to focus exclusively on ALEC. In a following episode of the Bill Moyers and Company show entitled "United States of ALEC," Lisa Graves comments on what she originally found in the leaked files:

> "Bills to change the law to make it harder for American citizens to vote, those were ALEC bills. Bills to dramatically change the rights of Americans who are killed or injured by corporations, those were ALEC bills. Bills to make it harder for unions to do their work were ALEC bills. Bills to basically block climate change agreements, those were ALEC bills". (Moyers, 2012/9/28)

The CMD stresses that ALEC is much more powerful than a lobby or a front group, and argues that ALEC's activities in fact render "old-fashioned lobbying obsolete" (CMD, 2014/1/23). According to the CMD, ALEC is almost entirely funded (more than 98%) by corporations and corporate foundations (CMD, 2014/1/23). Moreover, the CMD indicates that "the organization boasts 2,000 legislative members and 300 or more corporate members" (CMD, 2014/1/23). These legislative members and representatives of corporations sit together behind closed doors to discuss and vote on model bills designed by one of eight ALEC Task Forces (CMD, 2014/1/23). Legislators return to their respective capitals, with ALEC's model legislature in hand, and proceed to implementing the model bills into state law (CMD, 2014/1/23). In the words of the CMD,

> "ALEC boasts that it has over 1,000 of these bills introduced by legislative members every year, with one in every five of them enacted into law. ALEC describes itself as a 'unique,' 'unparalleled' and 'unmatched' organization. We agree. It is as if a state legislature had been reconstituted, yet corporations had pushed the people out the door". (CMD, 2014/1/23)

The last sentence of this statement quite exactly echoes Powell's call to forfeit corporations' social responsibilities. More data reminiscent of the Powell memo can be found on ALEC.org, specifically concerning ALEC's task forces. The structure of the organization is its division into eight task forces, each with its own focus on particular aspects of life. The task forces bear titles that correspond to the headings by which Powell organized his prescriptive strategies to the Chamber of Commerce in 1971: *Civil Justice; Education; Health and Human Services; Tax and Fiscal Policy; Commerce, Insurance, and Economic Development; Communications and Technology; Energy, Environment, and Agriculture;* with the curious addition of *International Relations* (ALEC, 2014b). ALEC explains that the role of its task forces may be to "commission research, publish issue papers, convene workshops and issue alerts, and serve as clearinghouses of information on free market policies in the states" (ALEC, 2014b). The influence of the Powell memo on the "vision" of ALEC is salient in the design of its operations. It intends to accord the corporate world, or what Powell referred to as "American Business" in 1971, the tools to do its "duty" of educating the public to improve itself, and to coerce the people to obey by changing their rights.

There are hundreds of corporations, corporate trade groups, special interest groups, law and lobbying firms, and government groups whose affiliation with ALEC is minutely documented and published by the CMD (CMD, 2014/1/23). To give a sense of the scale and power behind ALEC, however, I find it helpful to highlight the membership of at least a subset of its corporate affiliates.[1] I have chosen only a few and organized them according to sectors which best represent their pertinence to everyday life (see Table 1).[2]

Table 6.1: Current or Recent Corporate Members of ALEC by Sector	
Media	AT&T, AOL, Comcast Corporation, DirecTV, FedEx, News Corporation, Time Warner Cable, Verizon Communications Inc., Wall Street Journal, Washington Times
Energy and Agriculture	ExxonMobil Corporation, BP America Inc., Chevron Corporation, PG&E, Peabody Energy, Shell Oil Company, EnCana Corporation, Dow Chemicals, Monsanto
Information Technology	Dell Inc., Enron Corporation, Facebook, Google, eBay, IBM, Microsoft Corporation, Yahoo!, Hewlett Packard, Sony, Northrop Grumman
Everyday Consumer Products	Johnson & Johnson, Kraft Foods Inc., Coca-Cola, Wal-Mart, VISA, Pepsi, McDonald's, Nestlé USA, Ticketmaster, Coors Brewing Company, Reynolds American, Home Depot, JC Penney, Scantron
Finance, Banking and Insurance	Bank of America, State Farm Insurance, Geico Insurance, Prudential Financial
Pharmaceutical and Industrial Conglomerates	Koch Industries, GlaxoSmithKline Pharmaceutical, Takeda Pharmaceutical, Roche Diagnostics Corporation, Honeywell, General Motors Corporation, Chrysler Corporation, Ford Motor Company, General Electric

The CMD also publishes actual ALEC model bills total-ing in the hundreds and makes them available to be downloaded and read by anyone. Model bills may concern such topics as voter, worker, or consumer rights, the priva-tization of education, crime and the privatization of incar-ceration institutions, health, environment, energy, agriculture, national government power, or taxes. Between these topics, ALEC's specialized task forces, and the list of corporations I have divided into sectors, it should be clear that ALEC is Lewis Powell Jr.'s vision of a neoliberal coup, of engulfing the American public in a corporate imperium, and of "the rich man's burden" to educate people as to their own improvement via the free enterprise system.

ALEC's Agenda: International Relations, Policies for the Keystone XL Pipeline and Cybersecurity

Given that ALEC operates mainly via the legal infrastruc-ture of state-levels of government, it is not surprising to find them in support of federalism and implicated in tak-ing power from Washington to place it in the hands of state-level governments. This is explained by John Nichols as follows:

> "If you really want to influence the politics of this country, you don't just give money to presidential campaigns, you don't just give money to congressional campaigns. The smart players put their money in the states. It's state government that funds education, social services, and it taxes. And so, the smart donors can change the whole country without ever having to go to Washington, without ever having to go to a congressional hearing, without ever having to lobby on Capitol Hill, without ever having to talk to a President". (Moyers, 2012/9/28)

One of the task forces that ALEC has developed is named "International Relations". This suggests that ALEC intends to circumscribe the national-level power of Congress and of the President while maintaining an agenda with foreign nations, allowing it to operate simultaneously on the planes of domestic and foreign policy. ALEC's website thus explains:

> "The members of the International Relations Task Force (IRTF) believe in the power of free markets and limited government to propel economic growth in the United States *and around the globe* and that these guiding principles *are just as relevant overseas* as they are in the States [*sic*]." (ALEC, 2014c, emphasis added)

The central object in this statement is "economic growth". As David Harvey argues, over-accumulation is a problem that is inherent to the logic of capitalism, and one that has lead to a variety of imperialistic modus operandi in the past (Harvey, 2003, pp. 162–182). The geographical expansion of capitalism, for example, constitutes a solution to this problem by availing the system of new opportunities for investment, production, and consumer bases (Harvey, 2003, p. 139). This geographical expansion can be achieved via coercion by armies or colonizing forces, but also via more consent-oriented methods such as the co-option of existing state mechanisms governing social relations and relations of authority (Harvey, 2003, p. 146). ALEC's initiative to develop a task force to focus on foreign policies indexes their espousal of this solution to the problem of over-accumulation which follows exactly from the logic of capital as it is outlined by Harvey.

The key initiatives of this task force, according to ALEC's webpage, are to "increase exports, safeguard intellectual property rights, promote the nation's security and restore the Constitutionally-designated balance of power between the states and the federal government" (ALEC, 2014c). The policies put forth by the IRTF are typically designed in collaboration with another task force. Examples of model bills produced by the IRTF are entitled, "Resolution for Reform of Counterproductive Export Control Policies"; "Resolution in Support of the Keystone XL Pipeline";

and, "Statement of Principles for Cybersecurity; and Federalism Education Requirements for Public Attorneys" (ALEC, 2014c). I will briefly discuss the "Resolution in Support of the Keystone XL Pipeline" as well as the "Statement of Principles for Cybersecurity," two of the model policies from this list which deal with more timely and popular issues.

The model bill designed in support of the Keystone XL Pipeline is a cooperation between ALEC's *International Relations* and *Energy, Environment and Agriculture* task forces, the latter of which has welcomed the membership of BP America Inc., Chevron Corporation, Dow Chemical Company, ExxonMobil Corporation, General Motors Corporation, Koch Industries, and Shell Oil Company, to name the predominant players. Formatted with a blank space in which to insert the name of the state for which it is destined, the model policy lists no less than ten "whereas" statements before finally arriving at two resolution statements (ALEC, 2014d). In sum, the "whereas" statements cover the assumption that the US relies and will rely on the petroleum industry, the statement that national security is threatened by the US's dependence on "difficult geopolitical relationships," and the speculation that the construction of the Keystone XL Pipeline will yield jobs and economic growth for years to come (ALEC, 2014d). The resolution itself simply states that the legislative body supports the continued and increased development of the pipeline and urges Congress to approve the project, a seemingly innocuous resolution (ALEC, 2014d). However, the CMD published a list and description of 17 related model bills, now passed into law, which were designed by the *Energy, Environment and Agriculture* task force, aiming to repeal pollution protection, to oppose public health safeguards, to criminalize environmental protection, and to encourage the disavowal of climate change. The bills listed and explained in CMD's publication are nowhere to be found on ALEC's website.

In light of the Snowden leaks published in June 2013, it is noteworthy that Facebook and Google had a hand in designing the "Statement of Principles for Cybersecurity" as members of ALEC's *Communications and Technology* task force. The statement was approved by the ALEC Board of Directors on January 9, 2014 (ALEC, 2014e). The very first principle of this policy states that:

> "While recognizing government's important role to protect its citizens, the state and the U.S. governments should exercise leadership in encouraging the use of bottom-up, industry-led, and globally-accepted standards, best practices, and assurance programs to promote security and interoperability. We must also collaborate with trusted allies both to share information and to bolster defenses". (ALEC, 2014e).

This curious statement leaves the reader wondering who, if not the technocracy, the NSA and their allies, is referred to by the words "trusted allies". Moreover, the statement begins with a disclaimer concerning the government's role to protect its citizens, which logically entails that the following part is expected to override that role at some point. In other words, the statement suggests that "the US government's exercise of leadership" to "promote security and interoperability" jeopardizes the safety of its citizens.

The principles that follow in the model bill emphasize the ability to respond to "new technologies, consumer preferences, business models, and emerging threats," and to "enable governments to better use current laws, regulations, efforts, and information sharing practices to respond to cyber bad actors, threats, and incidents domestically and internationally" (ALEC, 2014e). In addition, cybersecurity measures are intended to "help consumers, businesses, governments, and infrastructure owners and operators" manage risk with respect to their "assets, property, reputations, operations, and sometimes businesses" (ALEC, 2014e). The mention of economic entities such as consumers, businesses, assets and property suggest that these principles have in fact to do with more than security; they have to do with securing capital and securing the profitable task of risk management for the technocracy and this, as revealed by the disclaimer, at the expense of citizens' protection.

The final principle clearly places the responsibility to enact this policy in the hands of currently existing corporations (such as those involved in the creation of this very statement):

> "Partnerships between government and industry has [sic] provided leadership, resources, innovation, and stewardship in every aspect of cybersecurity since the origin of the Internet. Cybersecurity efforts are most effective when leveraging and building upon these existing initiatives, investments, and partner-ships". (ALEC, 2014e)

In the end, this policy seems to be a legally recognizable statement that secures the capital of information technology corporations, that legitimates their actions, and that praises their role "since the origin of the internet" which, as is now popular knowledge, was created by the US military. This statement arguably constitutes an attempt to "enclose the commons" (Harvey, 2003, p. 148), and to procure control over the degree and manner of enclosure in question. Shedding light on the intentions underlying the IRTF's "Statement of Principles for Cybersecurity," Harvey explains that, "wholly new mechanisms of accumulation by dispossession have opened up" (Harvey, 2003, p. 148), and I claim that ALEC's conception of cybersecurity in this statement constitutes the corporate imperium's creation of an opportunity to instill such a mechanism.

Corporate Imperialism in Silicon Valley

In her article about the battle for the soul of San Francisco, Rebecca Solnit discusses how, throughout the last decade, San Francisco has succumbed to a phenomenon that is arguably beyond gentrification. The labour force created by the technocratic corporations that operate out of Silicon

Valley is moving into the San Francisco area and causing the cost of living and housing to skyrocket (Solnit, 2014/2/20 and Doucet, 2014/1/8). Solnit proposes that, "2013 may be the year San Francisco turned on Silicon Valley" (Solnit, 2014/2/20). Trust in the technocratic giants—Google, Facebook, Yahoo—wavered in June 2013 as Edward Snowden blew the whistle on the clandestine relations between Silicon Valley and the NSA (Solnit, 2014/2/20). The souring public perspective of information technology corporations is only aggravated by the fact that Silicon Valley is effectively buying San Francisco. Isabeau Doucet summarizes the dire state of property value and eviction in San Francisco:

> "City public health officials estimate that someone earning minimum wage would need to work more than eight full-time jobs to be able to afford a two-bedroom apartment downtown....Home prices have risen by 22 percent in the past three years while evictions under the Ellis Act have gone up 170 percent in the same period. A time-lapse info-graphic produced by the anti-eviction mapping project shows the city being pockmarked by 3,678 no-fault evictions from rent controlled apartments in the past 16 years with 2013 an 11-year high". (Doucet, 2014/1/28)

In 2013 and continuing into 2014, protests erupted in certain neighbourhoods with protesters blocking the private buses that take Facebook, Twitter, Google and Yahoo employees to and from work each day (Solnit, 2014/2/20). Ironically, tenants and tenant organizations can be found on Facebook under the banner of the San Francisco Anti-Displacement Coalition where they organize to combat evictions and rent increases. While technocrats are eager to set trends and to identify as one of the counterculture currents for which San Francisco is recognized, "the corporations doing this are not the counterculture, or the underground or bohemia," Solnit adds, "only the avant-garde of an Orwellian future" (Solnit, 2014/2/20).

The Technocrat's Money, the Caveman's Brawn

What seems to be going on in San Francisco is an unchallenged affront to property rights. People who have lived in the same property, sometimes for their entire lives, are finding their right to that property revoked via the power of capital. As a result, they are forced out of the community they know as their home. They are not being displaced by a violent or terrorizing use of repressive force, but by the quiet co-option of existing legal institutions and economic apparatuses. This usurping only requires the rise of property values, which is effortlessly achieved by the superior wealth of employees of the technocracy, this wealth bestowed via the concentrated money-capital of Silicon Valley's corporate cluster of Google, Facebook, Twitter, and Yahoo. In other words, it is the power of capital, accumulated and redistributed by the corporate imperium, which achieves the function of repression and subjugates tenants and property owners in the San Francisco area.

The evicted tenants are forced out from a property for which they were already buying the right to use, the use of which was therefore already commodified and secured as capital. This phenomenon, described by Solnit as "beyond gentrification," is occurring as an effect of Silicon Valley's over-accumulation of capital. It follows the logic of "accumulation by dispossession" as discussed by Harvey (Harvey, 2003, pp. 145–152). At the moment of eviction resulting from tenants' failure to compete with the technocracy's exorbitant wealth, the technocrat's over-accumulated capital is immediately available to "seize hold" of the newly appraised real estate. In Harvey's work on the new imperialism, "accumulation by dispossession" is a phenomenon that is explained in an international context (Harvey, 2003, pp. 180–182). I argue that this exact phenomenon is happening in San Francisco, practiced domestically by imperialistic corporations who are subjugating certain niches of the American class structure, thereby creating a market for over-accumulated capital.

In terms of property rights, the neoliberal narrative would maintain that the evicted tenants or dispossessed owners simply lost the right to their property because a denser concentration of wealth (in this case that of technocrats) has the right to take it from them. The logical conclusion is that evictions *are not an affront to property rights*, but rather the result of proper interactions between rights and capital, a vision in which property rights (and by analogy rights in general) go to the highest bidder. As this narrative goes, every individual is out to accumulate capital, and the measure of this accumulation corresponds to one's right over the rights of others. The resulting schema is analogous to Foucault's notion of governmentality, whereby "power" consists of one's power over the power of others, although "power" becomes conflated with "capital" within the neoliberal ideology (Ferguson & Gupta, 2005, and see Foucault, 1991). The logic of "one's capital over the capital of others," the free enterprise logic that Powell envisioned as permeating all aspects of society, concentrates privilege and serves the most privileged.

What do rights protect if procedural guarantees legitimate, via legal infrastructure and the institution of the market, a person's loss of their property due to their inferior wealth? What is the difference, aside from the implicit rather than explicit role of violence, between being forced out of one's home by the police enforcing a wealthier person's "right," or by the soldiers of an army imposing the will of an imperialistic state, or, for that matter, being forced out of one's cave by a stronger caveman? The neoliberal ideal, which is the reigning ideology of the corporate imperium, equates capital with power. In San Francisco, the technocrat's money is equivalent to the policeman's gun, the soldier's rifle, or the caveman's brawn.

Here, I am not seeking a more just or egalitarian version of property rights, which is a flawed notion by virtue of being designed *by* and *in favour of* the most dominant and exploitative sectors of society. Rather, I simply wish to illustrate how, under the logic of free-enterprise, capital mobilizes state infrastructure (legal institutions and economic mechanisms) and comes to repress and subjugate, in and of itself, in the interest of capital. Moreover, the situation in San Francisco epitomizes the "immanent drive of capital to...establish a disciplinary system that maximizes the extraction of wealth from those who produce it" (Hanieh, 2006, p. 190), which operates in parallel with ALEC's direct intervention in state legislature. As it is corporate imperialism rather than gentrification, Silicon Valley's non-violent colonization of San Francisco exposes the neoliberal narrative's inherent contradiction with respect to human interests, and demonstrates its rapacious appetite for privatization at its most insidiously repressive.

The Orwellian Future

In order to tether the foregoing discussions of ALEC itself and of the situation in San Francisco to a more common context, it is useful to revisit a passage from the Powell memorandum. Recall how the author preached that corporations no longer ought to seek the accumulation of capital "with due regard to the corporation's public and social responsibilities" (Powell, 1971, p. 10). As I argued when discussing the Powell memo, the move to protecting and preserving the free enterprise system in lieu of benefiting society entails a reversal of power wherein corporations use the state to carry out their will over people. The development of ALEC's law-making ability (alarmingly boasting a 20% success rate) is an indicator of the actual implementation of this reversal. The technocracy's exorbitant purchase of San Francisco real estate, which is accompanied by the co-option of the state's legal institutions and law enforcement measures as evidenced by mass evictions, indexes an effect of the neoliberal logic that underpins the reversal in question. As the narrative goes, if it serves the corporate world to evict people from their homes, then so it should be. And, strangely, if it serves the corporate world to archive and trade information with a government agency such as the NSA, then so it should be. In this narrative, the social order, people, humans, only exist to serve free enterprise. In the following section I discuss what this reversal signifies in theoretical terms for the corporate imperium's subjects.

The Circuit of Capital Revisited

Adam Hanieh claims that Marx's notion of the circuit of capital captures the commodities of labour power and means of production, which constitute the "basic capitalist *social relation*" by which "workers are employed by capital in order to produce a commodity" of greater value than the commodity employed at the outset of the production process (Hanieh, 2006, p. 178). As Hanieh remarks,

> "the neoliberal view asserts that the purpose of production under capitalism is exchange, and that our individual consumption choices drive this production. The reality is exactly the opposite: the aim of capitalist production is the accumulation of profit and it is production that shapes our consumption choices". (Hanieh, 2006, p. 177)

The "basic capitalist social relation" which Hanieh invokes importantly encompasses the individual as labourer, but in the socio-economic climate of oligopoly, financial engineering, and massive outsourcing of labour, it must also represent the predictions about human behaviour that become formalized in risk calculation and transformed to the end of financial speculation. In the engineering of demand that ensues from this socio-economic climate, which effectively includes an attempt to take consumption choices into consideration, prices no longer *only* correspond to a cost of labour and raw materials required to produce commodities, be they for computer operating systems, cell phones, utilities, information, or even a soft drink. In other words, the circuit of capital should also represent the individual as an idealized *consumer*.

Where accumulation of profit trumps competition, purchasing power is no longer a "vote" coveted by competing businesses, but instead takes the form of a "contract" which affords the consumer an access fee to a product distributed by the sole provider, or in another light, a *rent* to an oligarchic lord. American citizens (who constitute a large majority of the consumer basis of the corporate empire) are no longer employed to the sole end of production, but rather to earn the wage that will enable them to purchase goods produced predominantly by outsourced labour. Moreover, the marketing, advertising and retail industries constitute massive sectors of employment in America which are entirely devoted to the facilitation of consumption. The institutionalization of this facilitation is reminiscent of (and perhaps, finds its roots in) the ideologies underpinning Fordism as discussed by Antonio Gramsci in 1934 (Gramsci, 2000). That the internet is slowly but surely growing as a retail service itself only shows how a more systematic and tireless performance trumps human endeavour in the logic of maximizing consumption.

Imperialistic corporate capitalism aims to produce a subject that believes in the accumulation of capital, but who is never in a position to actually accumulate any. Not only by labouring, but crucially by *consuming*, the individual is coerced and subserviently perpetuates the accumulation of profits by oligarchic overlords, much like in the feudal era preceding modern civilization.

The Corporate Imperium, the Standardized Consumer, "Improving" the Human Condition

The idea of a corporate imperium raises questions concerning the status of the consumer, who constitutes both a foundational component of globalized capitalism and the object of the corporations' powers of subjugation. In *Seeing like a State*, James Scott reveals the diffusion of the influence of states over all aspects of life as they tended toward modernity in the course of the last few hundred years (Scott, 1998). In his conclusion, he attempts to draw together certain points that tie together all of his case studies:

"The power and precision of high-modernist schemes depended not only on bracketing contingency but also on standardizing the subjects of development. Some standardization was implicit even in the noblest goals of the planners". (Scott, 1998, p. 345)

Lewis Powell Jr., Milton Friedman, and Paul Weyrich each qualify as "visionary intellectuals and planners" whose neoliberal schemes depend on standardizing the subjects of capitalism (Scott, 1998, p. 342). Whether their actions, "far from being cynical grabs for power and wealth, were animated by a genuine desire to improve the human condition," or otherwise, the neoliberalism that they embodied and that persists today via organizations like ALEC conflates "grabs for power and wealth" with "improving the human condition" (Scott, 1998, p. 342). This conflation is in danger of legally permeating all aspects of life for which organizations like ALEC have a "task force". ALEC represents the emergence of a consumerism girded by laws which are designed by the same corporate imperium that benefits from said consumerism, which is, *de facto*, a transgression of the notion of the rule-of-law by which all members of society are bound on equal terms by a common set of rules (see Greenwald, 2011).

In the Powell memorandum, the reversal of corporate and social responsibilities ultimately has the effect of homogenizing the American public: on the one hand as the oppositional force of neoliberal hegemony, and on the other by subordinating it to the free enterprise system as a vehicle for capital. If a person represents an opportunity for the superior production and extraction of capital, that person is more valuable. If an algorithm can squeeze profits out of stocks better than a human can, it is also valuable and becomes subjugated by the imperium. If beavers could purchase lumber, corporations would seek their patronage. In this way, the standardization of subjects is extreme in the case of the corporate imperium, in which life is relegated to a vertex in a network of capital, and a human is simply a path by which the accumulation of profit can be maximized.

Conclusion

The emergence of a corporation-oriented rule-of-law, embodied in the American Legislative Exchange Council, is tantamount to the emergence of a social order which operates on the basis of free enterprise logic without impunity, which is to say "without recognizing human needs". This is empirically salient, for example, in ALEC's proliferation of legislature akin to that which legitimated the killing of Trayvon Martin, ALEC's devotion to climate change disavowal, and ALEC's espousal of (and foundation upon) neoliberal ideologies which would encourage Silicon Valley's nonchalant take-over of the San Francisco area. ALEC constitutes an organization by which the corporate imperium, emerging out of the established imperial state of the US, comes to practice a domestic imperialism that operates primarily with respect to capital, and secondarily with respect to other modalities of imperialism such as ethnicity, beliefs, and so on. It achieves this by permeating and co-opting the existing imperial state's infrastructure and altering the rights of individuals via legal apparatuses, and through the violence of dispossession ensuing from the free enterprise logic of neoliberal orthodoxy.

Notes

1   Each of these corporations are or were recently members of ALEC. I include certain members that have reportedly cut ties with ALEC because I only wish to demonstrate the breadth and scale of this organization via its typical membership, not to produce an up to date list of current members, their task force affiliations, financial contributions, or level of involvement within ALEC, which would be beyond the scope of this paper (for a detailed account, see CMD, 2014/1/23).

2   Information for this table was compiled from (CMD, 2014/1/23). http://www.sourcewatch.org/index.php/ALEC_Corporati ons

References

American Legislative Exchange Council (ALEC). (2014a). History. *American Legislative Exchange Council.*
http://www.alec.org/about-alec/history/
————. (2014b). Task Forces. *American Legislative Exchange Council.*
http://www.alec.org/task-forces/
————. (2014c). International Relations. *American Legislative Exchange Council.*
http://www.alec.org/task-forces/international-relations/
————. (2014d). Resolution in Support of the Keystone XL Pipeline. *American Legislative Exchange Council.*
http://www.alec.org/model-legislation/resolution-in-support-of-the-keystone-xl-pipeline/
————. (2014e). Statement of Principles for Cybersecurity. *American Legislative Exchange Council.*
http://www.alec.org/model-legislation/statement-principles-cybersecurity/
Center for Media and Democracy (CMD). (2014/1/23). What is ALEC. *The Center for Media and Democracy.*
http://www.alecexposed.org/wiki/What_is_ALEC%3F
————. (2014/4/5). ALEC Exposed. *The Center for Media and Democracy.*
http://www.alecexposed.org/wiki/ALEC_Exposed
Doucet, I. (2014/1/28). The Fight for the Soul of San Francisco. *Al-Jazeera Magazine.*
http://www.isabeaudoucet.org/2014/01/28/al-jazeera-magazine-the-fight-for-the-soul-of-san-francisco/
Gramsci, A. (2000). *The Gramsci Reader: Selected Writings 1916-1935.* Ed. Forgacs, D. New York: New York University Press.
Greenwald, G. (2011). *With Liberty and Justice for Some: How the Law Is Used to Destroy Equality and Protect the Powerful.* New York, NY: Metropolitan Books
Ferguson, J., & Gupta, A. (2005). Spatializing States: Toward an Ethnography of Neoliberal Governmentality. In Jonathan Xavier Inda (Ed.), *Anthropologies of Modernity: Foucault, Governmentality, and Life Politics* (pp. 105–131). Oxford, UK: Blackwell Publishing Ltd.

Foucault, M. (1991). Governmentality. In Graham Burchell, Colin Gordon & Peter Miller (Eds.), *The Foucault Effect: Studies in Governmentality* (pp. 87–104). Chicago, IL: University of Chicago Press.

Hanieh, A. (2006). Praising Empire: Neoliberalism under Pax Americana. In Colin Mooers (Ed.), *The New Imperialists: Ideologies of Empire* (pp. 167–198). Oxford, UK: Oneworld Publications.

Harvey, D. (2003). *The New Imperialism.* Oxford, UK: Oxford University Press.

Magdoff, H. (2003). *Imperialism without Colonies.* New York, NY: Monthly Review Press.

Moyers, B. (Reporter). (2012/9/28). United States of ALEC. In Gail Ablow (Producer), *Moyers & Company.* New York, NY: Public Affairs Television Inc.
http://billmoyers.com/episode/full-show-united-states-of-alec/

————. (2011/11/2). How Wall Street Occupied America: Why the Rich Keep Getting Richer and Our Democracy is Getting Poorer. *The Nation.*
http://www.thenation.com/article/164349/how-wall-street-occupied-america

Nichols, J. (2012/3/21). How ALEC Took Florida's "License to Kill" Law National. *The Nation.*
http://www.thenation.com/blog/166978/how-alec-took-floridas-license-kill-law-national

Powell, L. (1971). Confidential Memorandum: Attack on American Free Enterprise System.
http://law.wlu.edu/deptimages/Powell%20Archives/PowellMemorandumTypescript.pdf

Scott, J. (1998). *Seeing Like a State: How Certain Schemes to Improve the Human Condition Have Failed.* New Haven, CT: Yale University Press.

Solnit, R. (2014/2/20). Diary. *London Review of Books,* 36(4), 34–35.
http://www.lrb.co.uk/v36/n04/rebecca-solnit/diary

PART THREE:
Pariahs, Princes, and Playthings

CHAPTER 7

The Terrorist, the Tyrant and the Thug: "Anti-Anti-Imperialism" in American Media and Policy

✯ ✯ ✯ ✯ ✯

John Manicom

Modern imperialism can be seen as the militarization of neoliberal ideology seeking to maximize the area of the market available for capitalist penetration (Hanieh, 2006, p. 171). In order to maintain support for the near-permanent war entailed by this logic, manufacturers of public opinion in core capitalist states must produce and propagate moral and ideological justifications for the invasions, airstrikes, and interventions constituting the more overt forms of imperial aggression (Wood, 2006, p. 16). Proponents of imperialism have selectively applied liberal conceptions of humanitarianism to legitimize interventions (Fassin, 2010, p. 270) and opponents of imperialism are discredited by being painted as opponents of the moral imperatives of humanitarianism, or worse. Recently the narrative surrounding the war on terrorism has been an integral part of US efforts to discursively construct catastrophes to which interventionist strategies can be administered, as another set of justifications for war.

Mainstream western media routinely participate in the perpetuation of such narratives. Along with US politicians, the media habitually treat governments and non-state actors inimical to the interests of multinational corporations and NATO member-states in excoriating terms while reserving more nuanced language for those favourable to western and business interests. Catastrophizing rhetoric emanating from Washington is repeated, often with little critical discussion. Dynamics of discursive authority privileging the statements of government officials and mainstream media analysts allow these discourses a public legitimacy often not enjoyed by more critical analyses.

Catastrophization as the Rationale for "Humanitarian" Interventions: Breaking a Few Eggs

A crusade against evil itself, if expressed in and on those terms, needs no justification and is virtually immune from criticism. "An enemy that rejoices in the murder of the innocent" (Bush, 2003/9/12) is pitted against "the cause of freedom" (Bush, 2001/11/8) in a narrative that provides a "self-evident rationale" for militarist adventures around the world (Hodges, 2011, p. 59) and rhetorically conflates critics with "those who hate innocent life" (Bush, 2003/1/3). In the last decade this narrative of foreign intervention constructed by the George W. Bush administration has demonstrated "its ability to subsume a variety of foreign policy objectives under the rubric of the war on terror" (Hodges, 2011, p. 41). The occupations of entire countries can thus be justified not only as acts of self-defence in the national interest, but as moral imperatives springing from a humanitarian ethic couched in the rhetoric of human rights.

The war on terror narrative can be seen as a form of catastrophization. In cognitive psychology the term denotes a cognitive bias in which mildly negative events are magnified into catastrophes with severely negative implications (Ophir, 2010, p. 59). More globally it can refer to the process by which the volume of negative events/outcomes in a given situation is seen to rise, whether objectively, discursively or both, marking a point in which "catastrophe is imminent" (Ophir, 2010, pp. 61, 62). Discursive catastrophization identifies causes of imminent disaster and seeks to prepare for them (Ophir, 2010, p. 65), often employing the kind of moral rhetoric exemplified in Bush's addresses. As a political strategy it allows discourse-generating entities to classify negative phenomena, "arouse moral and political reactions," identify enemies, and potentially justify the creation of actual catastrophes as a means of thwarting those enemies (Ophir, 2010, pp. 63, 64, 65, 66). A catastrophizing narrative can thus directly affect "sociopolitical reality [through] its capacity to organize experience and human happenings" (Hodges, 2011, p. 63). These organizing discursive processes can be identified, for example, in the war on terrorism narrative's classification of terrorism as a military threat, in political reactions to 9/11 such as the passage of the PATRIOT Act, in the proclamation that "states like [Iraq] and their terrorist allies constitute an axis of evil" (Bush, 2002), and in the prolonged and bloody occupations of Afghanistan and Iraq.

As a rhetorical strategy catastrophization is applied selectively by American power. For example, the war on terror has been emphasized much more than the threat of climate change, resulting in the fact that total US federal war spending from 2001 to the present runs upwards of US $3 trillion (Crawford, 2013, p. 1), while spending on climate change stood at US $8.8 billion a year in 2010 (Government Accountability Office, 2011, p. 5). Within the realm of geopolitics, traditional allies such as Saudi Arabia, a Wahhabist absolute monarchy which was ranked as fifth to last on the Economist's 2012 Democracy Index (The Economist Intelligence Unit, 2013, p. 8), are discursively treated with kid gloves in comparison to countries with governments inimical to American interests. The American National Security Strategy for 2006 approvingly stated that "Saudi Arabia has taken some preliminary steps to give its citizens more of a voice in their government" (Bush, 2006, p. 2), while saying of the democratically elected government of Venezuela that, "a demagogue awash in oil money is undermining democracy and seeking to destabilize the region" (Bush, 2006, p. 15). Meanwhile the Sahara-Sahel region, an important source of American oil imports (Keenan, 2013, p. 11) was described by General Charles Wald in no uncertain terms as a "Swamp of Terror," which "we need to drain" (Powell, 2004), even though "extremist Islamist movements are not particularly strong and popular in the Maghreb" (Byman, 2013/7/10). Selective catastrophization reflects US foreign policy objectives.

Governments or organizations selected for discursive catastrophization by US authorities are generally those that oppose US international power. As such, the selection criteria may be said to be one of anti-anti-imperialism. Algeria, run by an "authoritarian and repressive regime" (Keenan, 2013, p. 224) with a history of state involvement in terrorism (Byman, 2013/7/10; Keenan, 2013, p. 184) has not been selected as a candidate for regime change by Washington, as it has not historically challenged US hegemony; instead the two governments "consult closely [...] on regional issues" (Bureau of Near Eastern Affairs, 2012). Libya under Gaddafi, on the other hand, historically exhibited a tendency to challenge US power, fund the wrong kind of paramilitaries and pursue pan-Africanist and pan-Sahara policies which alarmed American planners (Keenan, 2013, pp. 60–63). Even writing more than two decades ago, Lieutenant Paul Bremer III referred to Libya's embassies as "terrorist infrastructure" and to the country as a "terrorist state" (Bremer, 1993, p. 258), and today Gaddafi has been removed from power with the help of swiftly deployed American discourse ("Those who perpetrate violence against the Libyan people will be held accountable" [Obama, 2011/3/3]), and bombs. Iraq, under a Ba'athist Arab socialist regime which nationalized oil resources, threatened US ally Israel and pursued regional power, was invaded and occupied, while Turkmenistan, ranked sixth from last above Saudi Arabia on the Democracy Index (The Economist Intelligence Unit, 2013, p. 8), provides refueling and "essential overflight clearances" for US military aircraft (Rice, 2008/5/29), has a most favored nation trade agreement with the US (Bureau of South and Central Asian Affairs, 2013) and received military and other funding (Office of the Coordinator of US Assistance to Europe and Eurasia, 2011). Saudi Arabia remains a pivotal US ally while Iran remains the target of substantial but recently more muted discursive catastrophization. In perhaps the most ironic case, the Taliban government in Afghanistan was overthrown for its harbouring of al-Qaeda, both organizations having come about partly as a result of catastrophizing US rhetoric and subsequent interventionist policy concerning Soviet expansionism; the US provided hundreds of millions of dollars via Pakistani intelligence to finance anti-Soviet *mujahideen* in Afghanistan, some of whom would later coalesce into the Taliban (Price, 2012, p. 55) after prevailing in the conflict that spawned al-Qaeda (BBC, 2004/7/20).

Imperial Realism is Real Imperialism: Good Guys, Bad Guys, Our Guys, Dead Guys

American rhetoric concerning the terrorism, tyranny, and thuggery of other states is rooted in an imperial realpolitik and reflects specific foreign policy goals. Thus states can be divided into four hierarchically ranked categories according to their discursive treatment by American power. Liberal, industrialized NATO and allied states with US-aligned interests making up the imperial core constitute the first category (good guys), followed by non-core states friendly to American interests (our guys). Non-core states more or less hostile to American interests make up the third (bad guys), and states targeted for intervention the fourth (dead guys). Membership in these categories can shift over time and can sometimes be ambiguous, as with Iraq under Saddam Hussein which at one point found itself partially aligned with US interests in its conflict with Iran, but soon found itself excluded again from the benefits of being on the right side of American realpolitik.

Good guys almost never find themselves at the pointed end of US catastrophizing rhetoric. One does not hear about the tyranny of France as it intervenes in former colonial possessions like Mali, nor do we hear US officials alleging that British intelligence may have provided support to terrorist organizations (Meacher, 2005/9/10); mass arrests and illegal searches in Toronto during 2010's G20 summit (Morrow, 2011/6/23) were not condemned as unacceptable thuggery blocking the legitimate aspirations of the Canadian people. These states are euphemistically termed the international community (Ching, 2012/9/12) and are effectively immune from humanitarian criticism. Their systems of government and economics are held to be self-evidently superior.

Official doctrines of liberal states emphasizing democratic and egalitarian principles might preclude some authoritarian states' entry into the good guys category, but friendly dictatorships with abysmal human rights records like Saudi Arabia or Turkmenistan need not fear hegemonic discourse from the White House proclaiming them to be the terror-states of ruthless tyrants. Instead we hear of US appreciation for "Saudi Arabia's leadership in working toward a peaceful and prosperous future," presumably being worked towards with the weapons and armour it has been sold by the US (Bureau of Near Eastern Affairs, 2013a), while pundits and "experts" agree that the absolute monarchy is the best option available (Hancock, 2004/4/20), or, in the case of the Central Asian dictatorships, mostly keep silent. Qatar, another absolute monarchy with no political parties (The Economist, 2013/6/8), recently sentenced a poet to life in prison (later reduced to 15 years) for insulting the leadership (BBC, 2013/10/21), but remains "a valuable partner to the United States" and NATO (Bureau of Near Eastern Affairs, 2013b).

States which defy US power or threaten US international hegemony, however, are treated discursively as agents of catastrophe. Attacks on humanitarian grounds are common as are criticisms of the lack of government transparency, the insufficient openness of markets and the supposedly questionable fairness of elections. Even democratically elected governments are accused of "undermining democracy" as with Venezuela (Bush, 2006, p. 15). A new-found appreciation for anarcha-feminist punk rock was apparently enlisted to express "serious concern" at Russia's sentencing of Pussy Riot members (Earnest, 2012). Iran, an Islamic state which nevertheless incorporates democratic elements such as elections (Parsi, 2013/6/13), and is "probably the most stable [state] in the Middle East outside of Israel, with the greatest degree of popular representation" (The Economist, 2013/9/23) remains the target of threats of war (Miryousefi, 2014/2/3) and accusations of human rights abuses (Bureau of Near Eastern Affairs, 2013c). These states openly espouse anti-US government positions, particularly criticizing US foreign policy, and the rhetoric leveled against them reflects a mutual animosity. Wieseltier writes in *The New Republic* of the leader of Iran, who is not a monarch,

> "This same mullah-king supports the murderer in Damascus and the murderers in Lebanon and Gaza, and remorselessly pursues a foreign policy animated by anti-Americanism and anti-Semitism and intra-Muslim hatred. We may have extended our hand, but the Supreme Leader — the title itself is repugnant to decent modern ears — has not unclenched his fist". (Wieseltier, 2014/1/25)

Unsurprisingly, no mention is made of American support for murderers in Riyadh or Jerusalem, nor of the repugnancy of the terms Supreme Court or Commander-in-Chief, nor that the term Supreme Leader is an English translation of a Farsi term of respect and does not appear in the Iranian constitution which simply refers to a Leader "equal with the rest of the people of the country in the eyes of law" (Islamic Republic of Iran, 1979).

States targeted for regime change experience a significant ramping up of apocalyptic rhetoric. Here catastrophization seeks "the anticipation and portrayal—realistic, exaggerated, or imaginary—of the imminent danger posed by an enemy whose intention and actions are not simply negative, but threaten the very existence of the group, the state, or the ruling power" (Ophir, 2010, p. 65). Where a state cannot be shown to directly threaten the American state or people, it is portrayed as threatening abstractions such as freedom and democracy upon which American "liberty" is purported to depend (Bush, 2006, p. 3); thus in Libya "protestors" were met with "an iron fist" wielded by a "brutal regime" which "chose the path of brutal suppression" and a "campaign of intimidation" and will no doubt "commit atrocities" after which a "humanitarian crisis would ensue" and the "region could be destabilized, endangering many of our allies and partners" (Obama, 2011/3/18). It is estimated that 152 civilians were killed by government forces during the initial protests (Uppsala Conflict Data Program, 2014). Compare this with rhetoric about Egypt, an American ally ruled since 1981 under a form of martial law (Shehata, 2004): upon Egyptian President Mubarak's removal from office after protests resulting in the deaths of 846 people (BBC, 2011/7/8), Obama said that Mubarak had "responded to the Egyptian people" and now it was up to the military who have "served patriotically and responsibly as a caretaker to the state" to institute democracy, while the US "will continue to be a friend and partner to Egypt" (Obama, 2011/2/11). The military has since deposed an elected government and sentenced 528 of its supporters to death (BBC, 2014/3/24); the US continues to regard its relationship with Egypt as important "for a variety of security, economic, regional reasons" though it has suspended "some" aid (Harf, 2014/3/25).

Words Matter:
US Media as Private Propaganda

Discourses surrounding war and intervention are not all created equal. Anti-war graffiti scrawled on an underpass does not carry the same authority and commonly ascribed legitimacy as an opinion piece in a national newspaper. Foucault, writing of medical professionals, argues that those agents judged to produce legitimate discourse benefit from a privileged status in relation to society including "criteria of competence and knowledge [and] legal conditions that give the right…to practice and extend one's knowledge" (Foucault, 1972, p. 50). Like medical professionals, those working in media enjoy conditions allowing them to *diagnose* problems with the appearance of scientific detachment, and their statements are imbued with a certain discursive authority.

Assertions appearing in privately-owned mainstream media are often assumed to stem from a professional competence unavailable to most others, and draw upon the privileged status of official sources to shore up their own legitimacy. One journalist who was covering the invasion of Iraq was asked by his Iraqi translator why he was quoting US officials when what they were saying was clearly misleading. He replied that a journalist must present both sides and let the reader draw their own conclusions: "I had to tell him I had no choice but to quote the American officials, even if I knew that by doing so I would give their half-truths a measure of credibility" (Fassihi, 2007, p. 171). In the same breath he writes that journalists who write "detailed contextual and emotional accounts of war" risk being accused of bias, after having written that "the US military has tried to manage the flow of information by expecting reporters to practice a sort of self-censorship" (Fassihi, 2007, pp. 169, 171). What is written between the lines but left unsaid is this: rather than simply giving a lying US official credibility by quoting him, an individual journalist risks losing credibility by refusing to quote a lying official or by frankly pointing out that he is lying. This is part of a sort of feedback loop of credibility in which the reader assumes that an official would not be quoted if he were not a credible source and that the journalist would not be writing if he were not a credible writer. Questioning the validity of either begins a chain reaction of deconstruction with no end in sight, for newspaper articles and government statements are not peer-reviewed and do not need to justify their assertions. Their claims to legitimacy are functions of their privileged discursive position in relation to society as a whole.

The philosopher Habermas writes that when speakers are engaged with one another there is an assumed "background consensus" wherein they recognize that four claims to validity are being fulfilled by the other speaker: that what the other is saying is intelligible; that its content is true; that it is appropriate for the speaker to be saying it; and that the speaker is being honest (Campbell, 1992, p. 341). The validity of any mainstream media's assertions likewise rests on these four propositions being unchallenged by the reader; further, it is in the nature of the news media format that they cannot actually be directly challenged by the reader in any way meaningful to the context of reading a newspaper. For this reason these assertions of validity are simply assumed to be legitimate, and most anything printed in a major newspaper becomes validated under the unquestionable background consensus of the press, even if it is not intelligible, true, appropriate or honest. A fine example is that of the phrase *war on terror*. Originating as a quotation from Bush administration officials, it became so widely used that eventually the quotation marks were dropped by major media and it began to be used as a stand-alone phrase to describe an aspect of US policy. The fact that the phrase is meaningless (that is, unintelligible: as with the war on drugs, one cannot fight a war against an entity that is not an army) was rendered moot by the press' permanent background consensus.

An attitude holding that the truth can be found between "both sides" of a story means that the truth can be *produced* by picking which two sides to present, and journalistic practice privileging the statements of powerful politicians means that they will always have an influence on this production. Their narratives are repeated thousands of times as dramatically divergent narratives become harder and harder to print while maintaining the illusion of objectivity. Their invective becomes normalized language. Their catchphrases become standard jargon. Their silences remain largely unnoticed.

A conservative pundit wrote in the Washington Post after the death of Hugo Chávez, one of the most outspoken anti-imperialist leaders in recent history, that he was a "dictator," "one of the most noxious figures in the hemisphere" who "denied basic civil liberties," tried to "destabilize democratic governments" and supported terrorist groups (Rubin, 2013/3/6). This echoes Bush-era rhetoric about Chávez's populism, though the pundit turned to more contemporary American conservatives, quoting a Republican congressman who hoped that "the oppressed people of Venezuela will be able to live in freedom, not under miserable tyranny". She scathingly contrasts this with Obama's less hysterical statement emphasizing the US' professed commitment to freedom and democracy. Two perspectives have been presented and journalistic principles have been preserved; what is lacking, one might note, is the perspective of any of the "oppressed people of Venezuela" getting ready to elect a new "dictator". Rhetoric about this democratically elected president being a dictator has been normalized in the western context; an example of this in practice can be found on the site About.com, whose overview of Chávez is entitled, "Hugo Chavez, Venezuela's Firebrand Dictator" (whereas Pinochet's is simply titled, "Biography"). On the other hand, one is hard pressed to find a news source openly referring to the Saudi regime as a thuggish oligarchy running a brutal dictatorship; instead the preferred term seems to be "deeply conservative" (eg. Elwazer & Quiano, 2014/4/3; Greene, 2014/1/10), the distinction being that one is an ally cooperating with Western capital and one is not.

Who gets labelled a terrorist group as opposed to freedom fighters is also a telling distinction and one largely made based on who the group opposes. As Yassir Arafat once put it, "the difference between the revolutionary and the terrorist lies in the reason for which each fights" (Arafat, 1974). Just as the leaders of most kinds of regimes will lay claim to some sort of democratic legitimacy, the detractors of most armed oppositions will portray them as terrorists. Thus militias and other armed subnational groups opposing the US and allied states are generally termed terrorists with little hesitation, or given the similarly loaded appellation insurgents. Similar groups fighting regimes unfriendly to American interests are generally called rebels or fighters, as in the ongoing Syrian debacle. Media are often more than willing to follow the lead of official word choice. As I am writing this, the government of Ukraine has inaugurated an "anti-terrorist operation" against pro-Russian separatists in the east of Ukraine whose actions have mostly consisted of occupying government buildings. Articles I found dealing with these events all used the term "anti-terrorist operation" but none questioned the use of the term (eg. Luhn, 2014/4/15; Carter, Smith-Spark & Black, 2014/4/15).

Conclusion

An accurate indicator of how foreign state or non-state actors will be rhetorically treated by US politicians can be found in their relationship to US interests. Systematic human rights violations by allies are glossed over, but similar violations by hostile actors are classified as being representative of imminent threats to be countered, perhaps by military intervention. The logic of neoliberal imperialism stresses the openness of markets to the penetration of US capital and the willingness of actors to facilitate US military objectives as being some of the most important elements of alliance, while the moral arguments of humanitarianism are employed to admonish and ultimately threaten those who fail to live up to these precepts.

As Mark Danner notes in his essay "Words in a Time of War": "truth is subservient to power. Power, rightly applied, *makes* truth" (Danner, 2007, p. 20). The enormous power of media-owning corporations allows them in many ways to control how truth is ascribed and to what. Interests closely aligned with neoliberal ideology more generally ensure that media narratives rarely differ substantially from official ones, and using sources such as government officials with obvious agendas and a great deal of motivation to utter mistruths being seen as a condition of respectable media objectivity compounds the near-unanimity of the discourses of media and government with regard to imperial practices. As a result, catastrophizing rhetoric is easily transplanted from official sources to the minds of the public, and mass media in the west often acts as a self-censoring conduit for official narratives. Public relations objectives of imperial planners, namely the dissemination of discursive processes that classify and identify threats and justify reactions to them, can be met with a minimum of difficulty. Anti-anti-imperialism becomes the default position in the minds of many, and as a result it becomes easier for NATO states to deploy violence in the furtherance of foreign policy objectives.

References

Arafat, Y. (1974). Yasser Arafat's 1974 General Assembly Speech. *Wikisource*.
    http://en.wikisource.org/wiki/Yasser_Arafat%27s_1974_UN_General_Ass
    embly_speech
BBC. (2004/7/20). Al-Qaeda's Origins and Links. *BBC*.
    http://news.bbc.co.uk/1/hi/world/middle_east/1670089.stm
————— . (2011/7/8). Egypt: Cairo's Tahrir Square Fills with Protesters. *BBC*.
    http://www.bbc.co.uk/news/world-middle-east-14075493
—————. (2013/10/21). Qatar Court Upholds Poet Mohammed al-Ajami's Sentence. *BBC*.

http://www.bbc.com/news/world-middle-east-24612650

———— . (2014/3/24). Egypt Court Sentences 528 Morsi Supporters to Death. *BBC*.
http://www.bbc.com/news/world-middle-east-26712124

Bremer, P. (1993). The West's Counter-Terrorism Strategy. In A. P. Schmid & R. D. Crelinsten (Eds.), *Western Responses to Terrorism* (pp. 255–262). London, UK: Frank Cass & Co.

Bureau of Near Eastern Affairs. (2012). US Relations with Algeria. Washington, DC: US Department of State.
http://www.state.gov/r/pa/ei/bgn/8005.htm

———— . (2013a). US Relations with Saudi Arabia. Washington, DC: US Department of State.
http://www.state.gov/r/pa/ei/bgn/3584.htm

———— . (2013b). US Relations with Qatar. Washington, DC: US Department of State.
http://www.state.gov/r/pa/ei/bgn/5437.htm

———— . (2013c). US Relations with Iran. Washington, DC: US Department of State.
http://www.state.gov/r/pa/ei/bgn/5314.htm

Bureau of South and Central Asian Affairs. (2013). US Relations with Turkmenistan. Washington, DC: US Department of State.
http://www.state.gov/r/pa/ei/bgn/35884.htm

Bush, G. W. (2001/11/8). Text: President Bush on Homeland Security. *The Washington Post*.
http://www.washingtonpost.com/wp-srv/nation/specials/attacked/transcripts/bushtext_110801.html

———— . (2002). President Delivers State of the Union Address. Washington, DC: Office of the Press Secretary.
http://georgewbush-whitehouse.archives.gov/news/releases/2002/01/20020129-11.html

———— . (2003/1/3). Remarks to the Troops at Fort Hood, Texas. Washington, DC: US Government Printing Office.
http://www.gpo.gov/fdsys/pkg/PPP-2003-book1/html/PPP-2003-book1-doc-pg20-2.htm

———— . (2003/9/12). Defeating Terrorists Must Be the Cause of Civilized World, Bush Says. Washington, DC: US Department of State.
http://iipdigital.usembassy.gov/st/english/texttrans/2003/09/200309121 54605hsans0.1757318.html

———— . (2006). National Security Strategy of the United States of America. Washington, DC: White House.
http://nssarchive.us/NSSR/2006.pdf

Byman, D. (2013/7/10). *Terrorism in North Africa: Before and After Benghazi*. Washington, DC: House Committee on Foreign Affairs.

http://www.brookings.edu/research/testimony/2013/07/10-terrorism-north-africa-before-after-benghazi-byman

Campbell, R. (1992). *Truth and Historicity*. Oxford, UK: Oxford University Press.

Carter, C.; Smith-Spark, L; & Black, P. (2014/4/15). Putin: Escalating Conflict Puts Ukraine on Brink of "Civil War". *CNN.*
http://www.cnn.com/2014/04/15/world/europe/ukraine-crisis/index.html?hpt=hp_t1

Ching, F. (2012/9/12). Who Defines the "International Community"? *The Diplomat.*
http://thediplomat.com/2012/09/who-defines-the-international-community/

Crawford, N. C. (2013). U.S. War Costs through 2013: $3.1 Trillion and Counting. *Costs of War.*
http://costsofwar.org/sites/default/files/articles/20/attachments/UScostsofwarsum_March2013.pdf

Danner, M. (2007). Words in a Time of War: On Rhetoric, Truth and Power. In A. Szántó & O. Schell (Eds.), *What Orwell Didn't Know: Propaganda and the New Face of American Politics* (pp. 16–36). New York, NY: Perseus.

Earnest, J. (2012). Press Briefing by Principal Deputy Press Secretary Josh Earnest, August 17. Washington, DC: Office of the Press Secretary.
http://www.whitehouse.gov/the-press-office/2012/08/18/press-briefing-principal-deputy-press-secretary-josh-earnest-8172012

The Economist. (2013/6/8). Democracy? That's For Other Arabs. *The Economist.*
http://www.economist.com/news/middle-east-and-africa/21579063-rumours-change-top-do-not-include-moves-democracy-democracy-thats

——— . (2013/9/23). Rebels and Tyrants. *The Economist.*
http://www.economist.com/blogs/democracyinamerica/2013/09/iran-and-syria

The Economist Intelligence Unit. (2013). Democracy Index 2012: Democracy at a Standstill. *The Economist.*
http://pages.eiu.com/rs/eiu2/images/Democracy-Index-2012.pdf

Elwazer, S. & Quiano, K. (2014/4/3). Indonesia Pays "Blood Money" to Save Maid from Execution in Saudi Arabia. *CNN.*
http://www.cnn.com/2014/04/03/world/meast/saudi-arabia-indonesia-maid/

Fassihi, F. (2007). Lessons from a War Zone. In A. Szántó & O. Schell (Eds.), *What Orwell Didn't Know: Propaganda and the New Face of American Politics* (pp. 166–173). New York, NY: Perseus.

Fassin, D. (2010). The Heart of Humaneness: The Moral Economy of Humanitarian Intervention. In D. Fassin & M. Pandolfi (Eds.), *Contemporary States of Emergency* (pp. 269–294). Cambridge, MA: The MIT Press.

Foucault, M. (1972). *The Archaeology of Knowledge.* New York, NY: Pantheon.

Government Accountability Office. (2011). *Climate Change: Improvements Needed to Clarify National Priorities and Better Align Them with Federal Funding Decisions.* Washington, DC: United States Government Accountability Office.
http://www.gao.gov/assets/320/318556.pdf

Greene, R. (2014/1/10). No Burqa Required: Muslim World Weighs in on Women's Dress. *CNN.*
http://www.cnn.com/2014/01/09/world/meast/religion-women-clothing/

Hancock, D. (2004/4/20). The Tangled Web of US-Saudi Ties. *CBS News.*
http://www.cbsnews.com/news/the-tangled-web-of-us-saudi-ties/

Hanieh, A. (2006). Praising Empire: Neoliberalism Under Pax Americana. In C. Mooers (Ed.), *The New Imperialism: Ideologies of Empire* (pp. 167–198). Oxford, UK: Oneworld Publications.

Harf, M. (2014/3/25). Daily Press Briefing. Washington, DC: Office of Press Briefings.
http://www.state.gov/r/pa/prs/dpb/2014/03/223927.htm#EGYPT

Hodges, A. (2011). *The "War on Terror" Narrative: Discourse and Intertextuality in the Construction and Contestation of Sociopolitical Reality.* New York, NY: Oxford University Press.

Islamic Republic of Iran. (1979). *Iranian Constitution.* Article 107, Section 2.
http://www.servat.unibe.ch/icl/ir00000_.html

Keenan, J. (2013). *The Dying Sahara: US Imperialism and Terror in Africa.* London, UK: Pluto Press.

Luhn, A. (2014/4/15). Ukrainian Troops Begin Military Operation to "Destroy Foreign Invader". *The Guardian.*
http://www.theguardian.com/world/2014/apr/15/ukrainian-troops-anti-terrorist-operation-kiev

Meacher, M. (2005/9/10). Britain Now Faces its Own Blowback. *The Guardian.*
http://www.theguardian.com/world/2005/sep/10/terrorism.politics

Miryousefi, A. (2014/2/3). Iran: Kerry, Obama Rhetoric Threatens to Derail Diplomacy. *The Christian Science Monitor.*
http://www.csmonitor.com/World/Security-Watch/Security-Voices/2014/0203/Iran-Kerry-Obama-rhetoric-threatens-to-derail-diplomacy

Morrow, A. (2011/6/23). Toronto Police Were Overwhelmed at G20, Review Reveals. *The Globe and Mail*.
http://www.theglobeandmail.com/news/toronto/toronto-police-were-overwhelmed-at-g20-review-reveals/article2073215/

Obama, B. H. (2011/2/11). Remarks by the President on Egypt. Washington, DC: Office of the Press Secretary.
http://www.whitehouse.gov/the-press-office/2011/02/11/remarks-president-egypt

————. (2011/3/3). Remarks by President Obama and President Calderón of Mexico at Joint Press Conference. Washington, DC: Office of the Press Secretary.
http://www.whitehouse.gov/the-press-office/2011/03/03/remarks-president-obama-and-president-calder-n-mexico-joint-press-confer

————. (2011/3/18). Remarks by the President on the Situation in Libya. Washington, DC: Office of the Press Secretary.
http://www.whitehouse.gov/the-press-office/2011/03/18/remarks-president-situation-libya

Office of the Coordinator of US Assistance to Europe and Eurasia. (2011). Foreign Operations Assistance: Turkmenistan. Washington, DC: US Department of State.
http://www.state.gov/p/eur/rls/fs/193723.htm

Ophir, A. (2010). The Politics of Catastrophization: Emergency and Exception. In D. Fassin & M. Pandolfi (Eds.), *Contemporary States of Emergency* (pp. 59–88). Cambridge, MA: The MIT Press.

Parsi, T. (2013/6/13). Iran's Election is Neither Free Nor Fair–But Its Outcome Matters. *The Globe and Mail*.
http://www.theglobeandmail.com/globe-debate/irans-election-neither-free-or-fair-but-it-still-matters/article12508248/

Powell, S. M. (2004). Swamp of Terror in the Sahara. *Air Force Magazine*, 87(11).
http://www.airforcemag.com/MagazineArchive/pages/2004/November%202004/1104sahara.aspx

Price, C. (2012). Pakistan: A Plethora of Problems. *Global Security Studies*, 3(1), 53–62.
http://globalsecuritystudies.com/Price%20Pakistan.pdf

Rice, C. (2008/5/29). Payment of Navigation and Other Fees for US Military Aircraft in Turkmenistan [Diplomatic Cable, ID: 08STATE67468_a]. Washington, DC: US Department of State.
http://www.wikileaks.org/plusd/cables/08STATE67468_a.html

Rubin, J. (2013/3/6). Obama's Atrocious Statement on Chavez's Death. *Washington Post*.
http://www.washingtonpost.com/blogs/right-turn/wp/2013/03/06/obamas-atrocious-statement-on-tyrant-chavezs-death/

Shehata, S. (2004). Egypt after 9/11: Perceptions of the United States. *Social Science Research Council.*
http://conconflicts.ssrc.org/archives/mideast/shehata/

Uppsala Conflict Data Program. (2014). General One-sided Violence Information. *UCDP Conflict Encyclopedia.*
http://www.ucdp.uu.se/gpdatabase/printonesided.php?hsId=277

Wieseltier, L. (2014/1/25). Iran Is Not Our Friend. *The New Republic.*
http://www.newrepublic.com/article/116229/iran-not-our-friend-diplomacy-shouldnt-blind-us-human-rights

Wood, E. M. (2006). Democracy as Ideology of Empire. In C. Mooers (Ed.), *The New Imperialism: Ideologies of Empire* (pp. 9–24). Oxford, UK: Oneworld Publications.

CHAPTER 8

Glorification of the Military in Popular Culture and the Media

✯ ✯ ✯ ✯ ✯

Laura Powell

Every day, images of the military are seen, whether through television shows, movies, the news, or recruitment ads. The tendency to portray the military and its members as unstoppable forces is prevalent in all forms of media. Is this tendency based on an accurate representation? The Pentagon has been working with Hollywood film producers for decades, in what is considered to be a mutually beneficial relationship through which the Department of Defense gets professional filmmakers to portray the military in the best possible light. Hollywood producers, who agree to make the modifications necessary to their films in order to get the Pentagon's approval, are granted access to millions of dollars' worth of military personnel and equipment for use in their productions. This relationship perpetuates the pristine image of the military as seen by media audiences worldwide and thus attempts to block a view of the darker side of the armed forces.

This pristine image in turn reinforces the idea that "service" men and women are unstoppable heroes in camouflage. The men and women who lost their lives overseas are welcomed home as heroes, yet those who are injured, either physically or mentally, are not awarded that same honour. In reality, when those injured return, they are more likely to be seen as broken people, unlikely to be able to resume their normal work, and many get discharged.

While they may not perceive themselves as heroes, the knowledge that others expect them to be untouchable may deter service members from getting help if they are affected by Post-Traumatic Stress Disorder (PTSD), which in turn results in the misreporting of occurrences of the disorder. For those brave enough to attempt to take control of their lives and stop living with PTSD, there is another obstacle in the way—clinicians. In order to make themselves look good with fewer cases of PTSD, or to save money on treatment, the Department of Defense ordered clinicians to misdiagnose the disorder.

At every turn, military members are asked to live up to unreasonable expectations, and, when they cannot meet them, they are stigmatized because of mental health issues. Thinking of men and women in military uniform as heroes is more damaging than not thinking anything of them at all. It is time to acknowledge the dark side of military conflict and the potential dangers one may face if one chooses to enlist.

Media Portrayal of the Military

Technology plays an important role in the ways in which military conflicts have been covered. Media coverage of World War I occurred through print, such as text and photographs, and radio which could be rendered unusable as per former President Woodrow Wilson's 1917 Executive Order 2585 stating that "all radio stations not necessary to the Government of the United States for naval communications, may be closed for radio communication" (Wilson, 1917/4/6). During World War II, the first televisions began to appear in the US, but not in great enough numbers to become an important medium through which to share the events of war. Radio remained an important way to be connected to the ongoing conflict (Old Time Radio Catalog, 2014). The most important changes in media coverage were to come.

The coverage of the Gulf War in 1991, especially by CNN, marked a change in the way military conflict was reported to audiences, which brought conflict into people's homes, and portrayed war as being painless and bloodless (Thussu, 2007, p. 116). Starting with the Gulf War, US military intervention abroad was presented as a form of humanitarian aid, made deliverable thanks to the superiority of US arms (Thussu, 2007, p. 116). The US Department of Defense, after purchasing all satellite imagery of Afghanistan in 2001 to prevent its use by anyone else, became an important provider of visuals for news providers, who had no other access to satellite images (Thussu, 2007, p. 117).

With the increased war coverage that accompanied the Gulf War, the media portrayed conflicts involving America and the military as clean and not uselessly violent, offering "a 'bloodless' version of conflict, with death and destruction minimized by the apparent surgical precision of bombardments" (Thussu, 2007, p. 117). By minimizing the human loss of war, the media and the Department of Defense hid the reality of military conflict from the masses.

The Pentagon's Involvement in Hollywood Film Productions

US Military involvement in Hollywood can be traced back to World War I with the creation of the Committee on Public Information in 1917 (Klindo & Phillips, 2005/3/14; Thussu, 2007, p. 123), which released government news, sustained morale, and censored the press until it was abolished in 1919 (National Archives and Records Administration [NARA], 2014). By World War II, the US military and Hollywood worked together in producing propagandistic films and documentaries (Klindo & Phillips, 2005/3/14; Thussu, 2007, p. 123). The partnership between the military and Hollywood, dubbed "Operation Hollywood" (Robb, 2004), was cemented with the creation of a "special movie liaison office, as part of the Office of the Assistant

Secretary of Defense for Public Affairs" (Thussu, 2007, p. 123). This union was the foundation of a mutually beneficial relationship between arms and entertainment through which producers would have access to military personnel and equipment if they allowed their work to be examined and changed as the Pentagon saw fit (Thussu, 2007, p. 124). Every year, movies romanticizing the military and conflict are produced and released to captivated audiences, while other films offer more realistic views of the military as a form of entertainment. It is to be expected that films may not be entirely accurate, however they generally represent only one side of a conflict and glorify war as "righteous, [and] undertaken for moral purposes" (Thussu, 2007, p. 123). Which movie benefits from the support of the military is at the Pentagon's discretion and up to the producers' willingness to comply with its demands.

Acclaimed films such as *Top Gun* and *Black Hawk Down* were made possible only through the Pentagon-Hollywood union (Thussu, 2007, p. 124). Of course this does not mean that award-winning films with military themes cannot be made without the Pentagon's support. *The Hurt Locker*, an Academy Award winning film, and one acclaimed by a former Secretary of Defense for its authentic portrayal of life in Iraq, saw its Pentagon support revoked because of scenes deemed unflattering to the image of the military (Zakarin, 2012/2/21). The Pentagon does not stop the production of movies of which it does not approve, and so films showing a side which the military does not want seen continue to be produced. However, it is in the Pentagon's favour to make Hollywood producers a deal they cannot refuse, by granting them access to millions of dollars' worth of military personnel and equipment, so that they can control the movies made about the military.

The Pentagon reserves the right to ask for any changes its officials see fit in films sent to them seeking assistance, and to deny support to any film they deem inappropriate or inaccurate, even if those films are historical and the producers are certain of their accuracy. However, the Pentagon's selection of worthy projects is unconstitutional. The Department of Defense, as a component of the government, should abide by the Constitution which "does not allow for the government to bestow benefits on those whose speech it approves of, while refusing to grant the same benefits to those whose speech it disapproves of" (Robb, 2004, p. 26). Movies such as *In the Valley of Elah*, based on the murder of Specialist Richard Davis by fellow Iraq War veterans shortly upon the end of their deployment, are not the films the Pentagon would support because they do not portray the military favourably (Lee, 2007/10/5; Zakarin, 2012/2/21). However, when the production team of *Thirteen Days*, a film about the Cuban missile crisis, requested support from the Pentagon, they were asked to change their script, in spite of the historical accuracy of the project (Robb, 2004, p. 53). The main issues of contention for the Pentagon were the portrayal of the Joint Chiefs of Staff which, while accurate, was considered too aggressive (Klindo & Phillips, 2005/3/14; Robb, 2004, p. 53), and the script which the Pentagon considered "revisionist history" (Robb, 2004, p. 54).

Portrayal of the Military in Music and Television

"Operation Hollywood" does not only concern Hollywood productions. Robb (2004) discusses numerous Pentagon film interventions, as well as a number of television shows censored by the military. Not all television series produced with assistance from the Pentagon were meant for adults. As with movies, the Pentagon's influence on the production of children's television shows ensured that the military was positively portrayed. For example, the series *Steve Canyon*, as well as some episodes of the shows *Lassie* and *The Mickey Mouse Club*, were produced under the watchful eye of the Pentagon. By complying with Pentagon demands for changes in scripts, producers would have access to military equipment and footage, and would, in return, create shows for young audience members who could be easily influenced and potentially grow up to be become recruits.

The Pentagon also does not only interfere with productions portraying mainly the military. As per the producer's request, the Pentagon was involved in the production of two episodes of the show *Lassie*, in which the intervention ultimately took the focus away from the beloved dog in favour of the military (Robb, 2004, pp. 303–305). The military intervention in *The Mickey Mouse Club* was not as subtle as with *Lassie*. This show was a great vehicle for the Pentagon to propagate the idea that the military is the place to be. After all, *The Mickey Mouse Club* had a following of some estimated 15 million young, receptive, and malleable minds (Robb, 2004, p. 307). The Pentagon was mostly involved in the production of segments called "Mouse Reels," one of which featured the first nuclear submarine, the *USS Nautilus*, and attempted to attract young boys to the Navy by making the submarine a place with all the comforts of home — "good food, games to play, a jukebox that plays the 'Mickey Mouse Club March,' and warm comfortable beds" (Robb, 2004, p. 309).

Three channels are dedicated to the military — Discovery's Military Channel, the Pentagon Channel, and the Military History Channel (Takacs, 2012, p. 13; Thussu, 2007, p. 124). Non-fiction shows focus on the people and the latest technologies in arms, such as the shows *Delta Company* and *Future Weapons*, both featuring what are essentially "killing machines" (Thussu, 2007, pp. 124–125). Reality television is not off-limits for the Department of Defense either. The show *Profiles from the Front Line* features men getting ready for, and on deployment in Afghanistan, one writer calling it "propaganda hour" (Gallo, 2003/2/26). The six episodes of the show depict big boys with big guns, leaving the comfort of their homes to do what they must for the good of their country. As Gallo (2003/2/26) explains, the series is not about the explosions but the individuals behind them. Perhaps the series was an attempt at reintroducing humans into conflicts the news media have rendered bloodless and almost free of humans, as discussed shortly.

The home improvement show *Extreme Makeover: Home Edition* has dedicated a small number of its episodes to the makeover of the homes of injured or deceased Iraq War veterans. Takacs argues that these shows are meant to teach the lesson that the state will not take care of you when you lose a limb or a relative to war, and that you need to rely on yourself and those close to you for support (2012, pp. 212-213). Such episodes tell us we owe "sympathy and consumer therapy" to veterans (Takacs, 2012, p. 212), yet the help veterans may need cannot be replaced by a shopping spree or a newly furnished home.

Music on the other hand does not require the assistance of the Pentagon for the production of elaborate and costly movies, therefore musicians and songwriters need not be censored by the military, allowing them to be more critical. The song "Hero of War" (Rise Against, 2008), offers a quick look at what the future holds for a new army recruit enlisting after being told he will see the world and get paid for doing so. Everything is going well at first as he bonds with the other recruits, and he thinks of the future, of when he will come back from deployment and of how everyone will think of him as a hero, but of how, if he must, he will die for his country. Soon the reality of war sets in, as he sings of the military's treatment of those they held captive, resisting at first but eventually giving in and participating in the abuse. As the song progresses, the experiences begin to take their toll on the soldier, and eventually he questions why people view him as a hero when all he has left are medals and scars.

Productions for Recruitment Purposes

Generally, American recruitment videos attempt to make their audience feel that when they join they will finally feel accepted and respected, like they have found where they belong, that the sky is the limit and they will get to see the world, and that they will have the opportunity to reach their full potential, as well as be able to help others. They are seen jumping out of helicopters and airplanes and arriving in numbers in armoured vehicles, as well as sharing moments together such as the fleeting fist bump or handshake for a job well done, but never under fire or injured and awaiting help. Recruitment films are an art, as their makers have to find the right balance of adventure — without showing any situations considered dangerous — and of wellbeing and comfort, without looking like a boring or tedious job. Recruitment films lure individuals with promises of an exciting life without ever informing them of the other side of reality.

Not all recruitment videos are limited to a few minutes of inspirational and exciting footage of smiling men and women in uniform hinting at the joy and fulfilment they experienced from enlisting. *Act of Valor*, a feature-length Hollywood production was born within the walls of the Pentagon and was the first recruitment film of its kind in America, not only by attempting to recruit potential Navy SEALs but also by starring active members (Zakarin, 2012/2/21).

Zakarin (2012/2/21) explains that *Top Gun* was also born of the union between the Pentagon and Hollywood, and, through Pentagon-tinted lenses, the Air Force was portrayed as the place to be for nonstop excitement and beautiful women. The film was not a recruitment film like *Act of Valor*, but it did not stop the military from attempting to make the most of the movie by setting up recruiters outside movie theatres. As filmmaker Oliver Stone said, "most films about the military are recruitment posters" (Robb, 2004, p. 25), and while they may not have the same background as *Act of Valor*, film projects supported by the Pentagon will most likely make some individuals consider signing up for the military.

What the Media Are Not Telling Us: Discrepancies between the News and Reality

Following the attacks of September 11, 2001, then President George W. Bush declared a "War on Terror," and from then on the media fervently covered the progression of events. However, they only reported the events, without doing much independent research and thus regurgitating the White House's claims of Saddam Hussein's weapons of mass destruction (Moeller, 2004/4/14). The media acted as an amplifying force to President Bush's claims, instilling unnecessary fear within the American population about their vulnerability in the face of terrorism, and any voice expressing differing perspectives was hushed and effectively buried by the hegemonic Bush-dictated rhetoric on terror (Moeller, 2004/4/14). Media coverage of the "War on Terror" very much reflected the US government's views on the matter rather than offering a well-rounded and objective representation of the conflicts in Iraq and Afghanistan. As long as the White House had something to say about weapons of mass destruction and protecting America against terrorists, the journalistic convention of prioritizing "breaking news" from "important" sources, such as the government, meant that all other news and voices would be considered much less important or worthy of air-time and ink (Moeller, 2004/4/14).

When covering conflict in warzones, correspondents are generally reporting "live," however up-to-the-minute coverage of war can result in the misreporting of events as journalists may have little time to corroborate their stories, or to verify the validity of their sources (Thussu, 2007, p. 114). Various 24/7 news providers desire to be the first to offer the latest development in major stories, creating competition between the networks, and such was the case with the events of September 11, 2001. When new developments became scarce, journalists used any new information, regardless of its origins or validity as long as some link with the terrorist attacks could be made, and would

also resort to speculation to give the impression they were
the first to offer their audience breaking news (Thussu,
2007, p. 114). Fox News, an American news channel, goes
beyond selectivity with their stories or sources. The manner in which events are covered, and the language used by
Fox news hosts in discussing military conflict, may be better suited for a personal blog than a serious news channel.
Largely based on opinions and laced with xenophobic
comments, the journalism of Fox News reporters and an-
chors lacks objectivity, and can be seen as "aggressive
cheerleading for the U.S. armed forces and their allies"
(Naureckas, 2002/1/1). Prioritizing patriotism over fact,
for example, Fox News justified the invasion of Iraq by
propagating "unfounded allegations that Iraq was linked
to the 9/11 attacks; that it possessed vast 'weapons of mass
destruction', and was ready and willing to use them"
(Thussu, 2007, p. 120).

To accurately convey wartime information to their
audiences, news media should first and foremost attempt
to maintain impartiality and be critical of the information
they are given and are about to propagate. However, the
general public is misinformed, or at the very least under-
informed, because the media remain uncritical and readily
accept whatever information they receive from the most
important player, the government. Pat Tillman, American
footballer and soldier, died while deployed in what was
reported as a heroic act that saved the lives of a number of
other American soldiers (Astore, 2010/7/22; Holden,
2010/8/19), or at least that was the story being told. In
reality, Tillman was killed by friendly fire and people from
his unit were made to lie about what really happened and
Tillman would become the ideal poster boy for the war
(Astore, 2010/7/22; Holden, 2010/8/19).

The cover-up of Tillman's death was not the only thing
people were not allowed to discuss. The Pentagon managed the news, effectively forbidding the coverage of
events that could portray the military unfavourably, and
encouraged the production of shows that could help civilians identify with soldiers and humanize war, such as pro-

grams showing the lives of soldiers during their deployment (Thussu, 2007, p. 115), as previously discussed.

The human cost of the US wars with Afghanistan and Iraq is high, yet few in the media dare discuss it or to its full extent. As of February 2013, 6,656 American service members died in Iraq and Afghanistan; however the numbers from the Pentagon are lower as they do not account for suicides (Costs of War, 2013/3). In addition, at least 3,000 Department of Defense contractors in Iraq and Afghanistan have perished, but the official number of casualties is not known (Costs of War, 2013/3). The number of casualties becomes significantly larger when those wounded in action are considered. As of May 2014, the Department of Defense claims that 51,960 individuals were wounded in Iraq and Afghanistan in Operation Iraqi Freedom, Operation New Dawn, and Operation Enduring Freedom (US Department of Defense, 2014). These casualty numbers do not account for service members suffering from PTSD, or those who have taken their own lives.

Portrayal of Military Members as Heroes

"A snappy uniform—or even dented body armor—is not a magical shortcut to hero status" (Astore, 2010/7/22) could be something someone who never jumped on the "Support the Troops" bandwagon would say about the military and the popular opinion that all service members are heroes. In reality, those are the words of William Astore, a retired lieutenant colonel of the US Air Force, who challenges the ever so popular labelling of service members as heroes. Astore (2010/7/22) defines a hero as, "someone who behaves selflessly, usually at considerable personal risk and sacrifice, to comfort or empower others and to make the world a better place". While this definition was not taken from a dictionary, it offers a description of the kind of person likely to be called a hero. The teenage boys who rode their bicycles in pursuit of a vehicle in which they saw a young girl who had vanished from her home earlier that day could be labelled as heroes, at least according to Astore's definition. However, not everyone needs to save someone's life to be considered a hero, and men and women in military uniform are often freely labelled as such, without being required to perform any grand selfless act for the greater good of the world.

Astore (2010/7/22) argues that labelling of service members as heroes is really a disservice to them as it ultimately results in displacing the reality of war. He explains that when the population of a country views its military as a group of heroes, it is likely to overlook the less-than-heroic things service members can be involved in while deployed. Leaning to live with PTSD and the things he did and witnessed in Iraq, a veteran explains that most of the people deployed thought they would do good, that he didn't "think anyone joins an army or goes off to war thinking they are going to do evil" (Gutmann & Lutz, 2010, p. 5). Not everyone who wears a military uniform is a hero.

No one thinks of heroes as damaged individuals, and by assigning them the hero label, we deprive them of recognition of their suffering the effects of wartime experiences. In turn, the label could discourage them from admitting they may need help for mental health issues because while they may not consider themselves heroes, they are aware of the general population's perception of them. Not labelling military men and women as heroes could allow them to feel more at ease seeking help if they required it because they would possibly not feel the pressure to be stronger than everyone else.

PTSD and the Media

To maintain the appealing image of the military as an opportunity for adventure and heroism, some of the "side effects" of war are tucked away. Military personnel and civilians alike know of the possible imminent dangers associated with engaging in combat, but no one readily speaks about any of them. Men and women who lost their lives while deployed return home as heroes in caskets wrapped in their country's flag. The news media include footage of ramp ceremonies, showing the caskets of the fallen being unloaded from planes, in their broadcasts. The military personnel who are injured during their deployment return home and do not get the same media coverage as to those who lost their lives. Those soldiers not physically injured get to return home at the end of their deployment, their injuries not as easily visible. The absence of obvious physical injuries does not mean military members returned home unscathed. PTSD is "an anxiety disorder characterized by reliving a psychological traumatic situation, long after any physical danger involved has passed, through flashbacks and nightmares" and is frequently found in individuals whose life or wellbeing was in jeopardy, such as individuals engaged in military combat (Canadian Mental Health Association [CMHA], 2014).

In the US, estimates suggest that 11–20% of Iraq War and Afghanistan War veterans, upward to 10% of Gulf War veterans, and approximately 30% of Vietnam War veterans were affected by PTSD (US Department of Veterans Affairs, 2014). A study of individuals deployed in Operation Enduring Freedom (Afghanistan), Operation New Dawn (Iraq), and Operation Iraqi Freedom (Iraq) shows that for the period of 2002 to 2014 (as of January 10, 2014), there were 118,829 reported cases of PTSD (Fisher, 2014, p. 2). The number of individuals whose PTSD was reported is substantial and it must be kept in mind that this number is most likely not representative of the full number of individuals affected by PTSD. Even if there are over 100,000 American soldiers diagnosed with the disorder, there remains a stigma associated with mental health issues which may dissuade military members from seeking help, resulting in under-reported incidences of the disorder. Individuals who seek professional help for mental health issues are not guaranteed the care they require.

Lack of Coverage and Resources for Personnel with PTSD

The military is not free of the stigma associated with mental health issues. PTSD and other conditions linked to it, such as depression and substance abuse, challenge the image of the military, and its members, as an unstoppable force. PTSD can be debilitating, making day-to-day life an exercise in perseverance and resilience. The real number of service members affected by PTSD may never be known because of individuals not seeking help, and because mental health professionals working for the military are allegedly pressured to misdiagnose and misreport disorders.

Michael de Yoanna and Mark Benjamin (2009/4/8) shared the story of an American soldier who served in Iraq. The soldier, Sgt. X, met with Douglas McNinch, a civilian psychologist working for the US Army, and recorded their discussion. Dr. McNinch had reported to the evaluation boards charged with evaluating service members and the disability benefits to which they are entitled, that Sgt. X suffered from an anxiety disorder, with no mention of PTSD. Deliberately misdiagnosing Sgt. X's condition meant he would not receive the treatment he was seeking and needed, and that he would not receive the benefits to which he was entitled. Sgt. X recorded Dr. McNinch confessing that clinicians, including himself, were pressured by the army to not diagnose PTSD, effectively preventing the Department of Veterans Affairs from having to pay for expensive and lengthy treatment and benefits.

The media do not need to do make much of an effort to keep PTSD out of the spotlight as the military is doing it for them. By pressuring clinicians to misdiagnose and mis-report the state of the mental health of service members seeking help, the military is effectively depriving them of the treatment and resources they need to improve their mental health, in order to save money and the reputation of heroism. Rather than making more resources available, the military deals with the increasing number of veterans seeking benefits by diminishing the gravity of the disorder and offering a (mis)diagnosis of Adjustment Disorder (AD). As this disorder is considered temporary, veterans who receive a diagnosis of AD are typically not eligible for benefits they would have received with a diagnosis of PTSD (de Yoanna & Benjamin, 2009/4/8). Other ways to avoid diagnosing PTSD in veterans is to blame personality disorders, mental disorders associated with a "rigid and unhealthy pattern of thinking, functioning and behaving (Mayo Clinic, 2014) or childhood trauma as the cause of mental health issues (de Yoanna & Benjamin, 2009/4/8).

Sgt. X is not alone. There are thousands like him, left to deal with their problems alone because they would be too much of a financial burden for the military, as they would also diminish the hero mystique. In 2009, de Yoanna and Benjamin wrote a number of articles for their "Coming Home: The Army's Fatal Neglect" series pertaining to PTSD and the military. The majority of the articles made reference to veterans who either committed suicide or who were behind bars for homicide because they had been misdiagnosed or could not get help.

This time, it is not the media censoring reality, but the military and the mental health professionals on its payroll. Men and women are denied their realities by people who do not want to spend much money to fix what was broken in war, even when that involves fellow citizens.

Conclusions

When men and women go fight wars in other countries, those who remain home can easily feel as though they have no connections to the deployed military or to the on-going conflict. The media do nothing to engage their audiences to the events taking place by misreporting the information and by omitting to share the dirty side of war. Fallen soldiers return home as heroes who sacrificed their lives for democracy and for their country, but no one hears about those gravely injured by friendly fire, those whose lives are in shambles because of PTSD, or even of the innocent men, women and children who perished in air raids.

Only by censoring the reality of conflict and by hiding the true cost of war can the government maintain a romanticized image of the military. To ensure access to potential recruits, the military must make itself attractive and appear as a once in a lifetime opportunity, but it can only do so by concealing the harsh reality that by enlisting you may lose yourself to PTSD, or limbs or your life to an IED.

By hiding the human cost of war, either by censoring cinematographic or television productions or by misreporting and underreporting the news, the media trivialize the sacrifice of the men and women who are not welcomed as heroes upon their return. Those same individuals, whose injuries may not be visible at first glance, are the ones who experience the brutality of war even after they return. To allow the service members affected by PTSD to get the help they require, the military must to stop instructing doctors to misdiagnose their condition, and the military must no longer be seen as an unstoppable force. By thinking of the men and women in uniform as heroes, we take away their humanness, their right to be vulnerable, and their right to ask for help.

References

Astore, W. J. (2010/7/22). Every Soldier a Hero? Hardly. *Los Angeles Times*.
http://articles.latimes.com/2010/jul/22/opinion/la-oe-astore-heroes-20100722

Canadian Mental Health Association (CMHA). (2014). Post-Traumatic Stress Disorder (PTSD).
http://www.cmha.ca/mental_health/post-traumatic-stress-disorder/#.UxqISfmwLwk

Costs of War. (2013/3). US and Allied Killed.
http://costsofwar.org/article/us-killed-0

de Yoanna, M., & M. Benjamin. (2009/4/8). I Am Under a Lot of Pressure to Not Diagnose PTSD. *Salon*.

http://www.salon.com/2009/04/08/tape/

Fisher, H. (2014). *A Guide to U.S. Military Casualty Statistics: Operation New Dawn, Operation Iraqi Freedom, and Operation Enduring Freedom.* Washington, DC: Congressional Research Service.
http://www.fas.org/sgp/crs/natsec/RS22452.pdf

Gallo, P. (2003/2/26). Review: 'Profiles from the Front Line. *Variety*
http://variety.com/2003/tv/reviews/profiles-from-the-front-line-1200543085/

Gutmann, M. & C. Lutz. (2010). *Breaking Ranks: Iraq Veterans Speak Out Against the War.* Los Angeles, CA: University of California Press.

Holden, S. (2010/8/19). When Heroism Means Finding Truth. *The New York Times.*
http://www.nytimes.com/2010/08/20/movies/20tillman.html?_r=0

Klindo, M. & R. Phillips. (2005/3/14). Military Interference in American Film Production. *World Socialist Web Site.*
http://www.wsws.org/en/articles/2005/03/holl-m14.html

Lee, H. (2007/10/5). In the Valley of Elah: Reducing Colonial War to Personal Trauma. *World Socialist Web Site.*
http://www.wsws.org/en/articles/2007/10/elah-o05.html

Mayo Clinic. (2014). Personality Disorders.
http://www.mayoclinic.org/diseases-conditions/personality-disorders/basics/definition/con-20030111

Moeller, S. (2004/4/14). Weapons of Mass Destruction and the Media: Anatomy of a Failure. *YaleGlobal.*
http://yaleglobal.yale.edu/content/weapons-mass-destruction-and-media-anatomy-failure

National Archives and Records Administration (NARA). (2014). Records of the Committee on Public Information. College Park, MD: National Archives and Records Administration.
http://www.archives.gov/research/guide-fed-records/groups/063.html

Naureckas, J. (2002/1/1). Fox at the Front: Will Geraldo Set the Tone for Future War Coverage? *Extra!*
http://fair.org/extra-online-articles/fox-at-the-front/

Old Time Radio Catalog. (2014). *World War II on the Radio.*
http://www.otrcat.com/wwii-on-the-radio.html

Rise Against. (2008). *Appeal to Reason* [CD]. Fort Collins, CO: Interscope.

Robb, D. L. (2004). *Operation Hollywood: How the Pentagon Shapes and Censors the Movies.* Amherst, NY: Prometheus Books.

Takacs, S. (2012). *Terrorism TV: Popular Entertainment in Post-9/11 America.* Lawrence, KS: University Press of Kansas.

Thussu, D. K. (2007). *News as Entertainment: The Rise of Global Infotainment.* Thousand Oaks, CA: Sage Publications Inc.

US Department of Defense. (2014). U.S. Casualty Status. Washington, DC: US Department of Defense.
http://www.defense.gov/news/casualty.pdf

US Department of Veterans Affairs. (2014). How Common Is PTSD? Washington, DC: US Department of Veterans Affairs.
http://www.ptsd.va.gov/public/PTSD-overview/basics/how-common-is-ptsd.asp

Wilson, W. (1917/4/6). Executive Order 2585 – Taking over Necessary and Closing Unnecessary Radio Stations. *The American Presidency Project.*
http://www.presidency.ucsb.edu/ws/?pid=75407

Zakarin, J. (2012/2/21). "Act of Valor" and the Military's Long Hollywood Mission. *The Huffington Post.*
http://www.huffingtonpost.com/2012/02/17/act-of-valor-military-hollywood_n_1284338.html

A Flickr of Militarization: Photographic Regulation, Symbolic Consecration, and the Strategic Communication of "Good Intentions"

★ ★ ★ ★ ★

Maximilian C. Forte

"Wars are won as much by creating alliances, leveraging nonmilitary advantages, reading intentions, building trust, converting opinions, and managing perceptions — all tasks that demand an exceptional ability to understand people, their culture, and their motivation". — Major General Robert H. Scales, Jr. (2004)

"Every action that the United States Government takes sends a message". — The White House (2009, p. 3)

Picture-perfect good intentions: healing babies, helping mothers, playing ball with boys, laying bricks, parading, working out, loving dogs. If one were to take at face value the US Department of Defense's photographic self-representations (which is what the leaders of the institution explicitly prefer), then one could be forgiven for believing that US military training involves learning basic techniques for skipping rope, holding hands, delivering Christmas gifts, and of course polishing and maintaining daunting machinery. The US Department of Defense (DoD), has created a utopian virtual world through the use of "social media" such as Flickr (an interactive image-hosting website owned by Yahoo), portraying the US military as, effectively, the world's biggest charitable association if not the world's happiest, but more than that: as a representative of the shared interests and common values that bind diverse peoples to the US. Under the presidency of Barack Obama, the *intended* effects of communication and "engagement" could be summarized as creating an impression of the US as a force for global good, in the minds of people around the world. These intended effects on foreign audiences involved having them recognize areas of "mutual interest" with the US; believing that the US "plays a constructive role in global affairs"; and, seeing the US as a "respectful partner" in efforts to "meet complex global challenges" (White House, 2009, p. 6). This is one way to keep memories of anti-colonialism at bay (Mooers, 2006, p. 2).

This chapter is based on a study of the complete collection of photographs uploaded to Flickr by the DoD, totaling 9,963 images spanning the years from 2009 to 2014.[1] One should note that the DoD as such is just one institutional front in the US military's overall social media presence. Each of the US armed services—the Navy, Marine Corps, Air Force and Army—has its own individual Flickr account (in addition to many other social media accounts). The DoD was chosen as the focus here as its image database is meant to be comprehensive of all of the armed services, with some degree of overlap (the same image uploaded to different armed services' accounts) and yet somewhat more manageable in size than some of the others (and smaller than all of the others combined). The analysis presented herein is not a quantitative one, nor does it offer any assumptions about the nature of the "audience(s)" for these images. Instead, by keeping in mind that photographs are the "products of specific intentionality" (Banks, 2001, p. 7), what is offered is a reading of intent and thematic structure, both from the concatenation of images produced to uphold certain humanitarian and globalist narratives, and from a reading of a plethora of documents outlining the social media and general communication strategies of the foreign policy apparatus of the US government and the US military in particular. Over 40 such documents were studied, and two dozen of those are cited here. A sample of 57 photographs is also presented.

Keeping in mind the damaging media exposure of the Vietnam war years, military control over the images of war distributed to the public has gone a distant step beyond the practice of "embedding" journalists (as during the second Iraq war), to directly producing its own media materials. However, that control can never be total. As in the case of the Abu Ghraib torture photographs, or the "Collateral Murder" video published by WikiLeaks in 2010 (both of which have been featured and discussed in previous volumes in this series), reality as constructed through pictorial representation always necessitates a *strategy* on the part of the military. If the realities of US military power asserted around the globe had been as simple and uncontroversial as the DoD Flickr account would like to suggest, then there would be no need for a strategy, and indeed no need for this social media practice. It would all be a matter of unquestionable fact that requires no defence. If anything it seems that the US military's media strategists are still painfully aware of the impact of Abu Ghraib, to the point of producing the *exact opposite*. However, in producing the exact opposite in order to shore up the credibility of the institution's image, it thus strains it, thus inviting further critical scrutiny. Before one might interject that this argument renders Pentagon media practice as flawed regardless of what it does, that would be a mistaken interpretation. This chapter is not so much about what the US military achieves with photography, as much as it is about *how* it does it, *why*, what this reveals about the cultural practice of US military media, and what the US military clearly chooses *not* to do and how that reflects on the actuality of its role in a post-liberal political formation that nonetheless still proclaims its democratic credentials.

Photographs, *contra* US military strategizing, do not speak for themselves. The patterns to be found among these thousands of images are in fact quite regular (because they were meant to be), and make a series of clear points. These photographs tend to represent the US military as a humanitarian, charitable organization, working among many communities around the world that are populated, for example, by children who are only too happy to be vaccinated and to skip rope with US soldiers. Female US soldiers have smiling close encounters with little girls, or cradle babies. When not displaying the pure, motive-less good intentions of the US military as big brother/baby-sitter for the world, the photographs produce a celebration of the awesome power and sophistication of US military technology: jets flying in formation, shiny drones illuminated at night like alien UFOs, or lines of massive ships at sea like armoured knights heading out on a crusade. Deterrence and "counter-terrorism" are thus built-in, sometimes with a smile.

Yet, there are virtually no images of actual combat, that is, the intended purpose of US military personnel and weaponry. Indeed, the US military ordinarily uses cameras in combat situations producing the kind of "COMCAM" imagery that is useful for determining targets and doing battle damage assessments—but this is not the kind of imagery present in the Pentagon's Flickr portfolio. The photographs here instead collectively portray a world rendered frictionless by the speed and ubiquity of American power and technology—without showing the battle effects of that power. In addition, by being tenuously emptied of political overtones, the photographs produce a political effect, for political purposes—they do not tell the horror stories of war, of blood shed and lives lost, of destruction and grief, but rather portray something like a birthday party. Indeed, gift giving is a central feature of most of the photographs featuring US military personnel and citizens of other nations.

Rather than being accountable to the public which funds it, the US military instead refuses to tell the truth of war, and the truth of its actions, and this in itself is a lesson about an institution that is presumably under civilian control in a democracy. The military's devotion to its own "mission" is singular and exclusive. It also reveals a military institution that possesses its own sense of its *raison d'être*, one bent on determining what will be its public answerability (if any).

The argument presented here is *not* that the photographs are "fake," "staged," or altogether "unreal". The staging is quite real, but real in many subtle and somewhat abstract ways than are normally considered, and not always staged in a straightforward sense. They are selective, partial, and framed. The dominant cultural prejudice arising from positivist methodology, which treats photographs as objective and neutral documentary records, is thus not being endorsed here. Instead, the understanding here is that as products of a particular culture, photographs are only perceived as real thanks to the cultural conventions in which we have been trained: "they only appear realistic because we have been taught to see them as such" (Wright, 1999, p. 6). The question then becomes one of interpreting the photograph as a structured record, neither an impartial one, nor merely a record of "the Other," and yet not one whose meanings can be restricted by the authorizations and regulations of the Pentagon. The photograph is instead treated here as, "a document which often reveals as much (if not more) about the individuals and society which produced the image than it does about its subject(s)" (Wright, 1999, p. 4).

The analytical methodology applied here follows the basic outlines found in Wright's (1999) *The Photography Handbook*, also in the works of visual anthropologists such as Banks (2001) and Pink (2001), and it borrows some of the conceptual analyses of Bourdieu (1991, 1999) and Ortner (1973). Following Wright's combination of realism, formalism, and expressionism, we examine the aesthetic intentions of the Pentagon's photographs by respectively looking *through* photographs (the subjects that the photographer purports to record), looking *at* the photographs (the methods and forms of depicting the select contents), and looking *behind* the photographs to consider what motivated their taking and the viewpoints embedded in the photographic act (Wright, 1999, pp. 38–39). In particular, we consider both the "indexical" and "symbolic" facets of the photographic collection, that is to say, what is traced out by the photographs as documents of something, and what is the intended representation of what is selectively shown (Wright, 1999, pp. 71–72). We analyse both the internal and external narratives of the photographs, that is, both contents and contexts of production (Banks, 2001, pp. 11, 12). Slightly modifying Wombell (as quoted in Wright, 1999, p. 72), the methodology in this chapter holds that "each image is an interpretation of a situation," and is not *just* its "objective representation".

The National Strategy for Public Diplomacy and Strategic Communication

"The U.S. is engaged in an international struggle of ideas and ideologies, which requires a more extensive, sophisticated use of communications and public diplomacy programs to gain support for U.S. policies abroad. To effectively wage this struggle, public diplomacy must be treated—along with defense, homeland security and intelligence—as a national security priority in terms of resources".— US Under Secretary for Public Diplomacy and Public Affairs (US Department of State, 2007, p. 11)

Our first task is to understand how the Pentagon and other agencies of the US government think about information, communication, and the media. The presence of various branches of the US military in multiple in social network sites, such as Flickr, broadly falls under various established directives, which supply us with not just the procedures and bureaucracy responsible for this communication, but also the logic and strategy.

The first and most comprehensive mandate, post-9/11, came from the State Department during the last presidential term of George W. Bush in the form of the "U.S. National Strategy for Public Diplomacy and Strategic Communication" (US Department of State [DoS], 2007), and from the Department of Defense with its "Execution Roadmap for Strategic Communication" (DoD, 2006b).[2] The State Department's National Strategy began by framing itself in terms of the overall US National Security Strategy, comprising eight major goals:

> "➢ To champion human dignity;
> ➢ To strengthen alliances against terrorism;
> ➢ To defuse regional conflicts;
> ➢ To prevent threats from weapons of mass destruction;
> ➢ To encourage global economic growth;
> ➢ To expand the circle of development;
> ➢ To cooperate with other centers of global power; and
> ➢ To transform America's national security institutions to meet the challenges and opportunities of the twenty-first century". (DoS, 2007, p. 2)

Underneath these, "public diplomacy" and "strategic communication" (more on these in the next section) are mentioned as key programs, whose activities should,

> "➢ Underscore our commitment to freedom, human rights and the dignity and equality of every human being;
> ➢ Reach out to those who share our ideals;
> ➢ Support those who struggle for freedom and democracy; and
> ➢ Counter those who espouse ideologies of hate and oppression". (DoS, 2007, p. 2)

"We seek to be a partner for progress, prosperity and peace around the world," the document proudly declared, and presumably the strategy outlined therein was designed to showcase these self-proclaimed virtues (DoS,

2007, p. 3). Confusingly, the document then outlined three further strategic objectives—a profusion of lists, most of which tend to repeat key themes already presented but in different words. These strategic objectives can be summarized as: 1) projecting "American values" by offering a "positive vision of hope and opportunity"; 2) marginalizing "violent extremists" in order to defend the values cherished by the "civilized"; and, 3) working to "nurture common interests and values" between Americans and peoples around the globe (DoS, 2007, p. 3). Along with the three strategic objectives, three strategic audiences are specified in this strategic document: 1) "key influencers" — which simply means influential public figures who usually help to shape public opinion or some portion of it; 2) "vulnerable" groups, and here the document specifies youths, women and girls, and Indigenous Peoples or other ethnic minorities; and, 3) "mass audiences" (DoS, 2007, pp. 4–5). Even so, "counterterrorism communications" were still listed as the exclusive focus of a new "Policy Coordinating Committee (PCC) on Public Diplomacy and Strategic Communication" (DoS, 2007, p. 9).

The National Strategy for Public Diplomacy and Strategic Communication also devotes considerable attention to the use of images. Here the State Department called on all government agencies to gather "compelling stories (including pictures and videotape if possible) of how American programs are impacting people's lives," which is in fact a key theme in the sets of photographs analysed for this project. Those persons abroad receiving health care from the US was a specified focus, among others. The State Department also emphasized the need for "a database of digital images and videos" as well as videos that "represent mainstream Muslim views and rejection of terrorists/extremism". To aid all agencies of the government involved in such work, "best practices" would need to be identified and shared (DoS, 2007, p. 10).

"Use good pictures and images"—here the National Strategy goes a step further in specifying the kinds of images to be recorded, and providing details on how the images are to be produced, framed, and selected. What are the "good pictures and images"? These are, as the document explained: "Well-choreographed pictures and images [that] convey emotion and/or action as well as a convincing story" (DoS, 2007, p. 26) — hence, staged yet real. Then specific guidelines are offered on how to produce such images — and we can see a lasting imprint of this National Strategy in many of the Pentagon's Flickr photographs taken overseas:

"➤ Before any event, think through a desired picture that would best capture and tell the story of the event.
➤ Where should the photo be taken — what is the background? The background should help convey where you are — the country, the city, the building, the environment. Should there be a flag in the background? Is there a banner behind or in front of the podium? Is a recognizable part of the building visible? What part of the building is recognizable? E.g., capture I.M. Pei's Pyramid as your background for an event at the Louvre rather than an unrecognizable column inside.
➤ Who should be in the picture? The principal along with those who are the focus of the event should be in the picture to help convey the story. Musicians? Youth? Government officials? E.g., if the Ambassador and State Minister for Education are speaking at a Fulbright event, make sure to get shots not just of the officials speaking but with Fulbright grantees in the photo.
➤ What is the action or the emotion? Are they dancing? Talking? Listening? Learning? Enthusiastic? Include props if that helps convey the story. E.g., if the Ambassador is meeting with 4th graders to give out books, the photo should include students holding the books, youth reading, pointing to a picture in the book, etc.
➤ The photographer should think through the location for the photo with all of the technical considerations in mind — not shooting into the sun, not in front of reflective glass or a mirror, not in shade or shadows, etc. The key people who need to be included in the shot should be identified.

> Look for the action or emotion. For action shots, get a tight shot rather than wide. A tight shot will convey more emotion in addition to the story. E.g., for a U.S. military big band in town with swing dancers, rather than capturing the whole crowd, pick out one couple in full enthusiastic swing dancing in front of a large U.S. flag and banner of the event so the country and occasion are conveyed". (DoS, 2007, p. 26)

Already then, there can be no doubt that the photographs we will encounter are, by definition, staged: choreographed to produce a predetermined effect. To keep from reminding viewers that these photographs are an artistic production, the artist must be kept out of the scene—hence the injunction above against taking photographs in front of mirrors or reflective glass. This is not reflexive art; this is instead the eye of god.

The Internet is also featured in the National Strategy, especially as a way to reach "youth audiences" and in recognition of a "dramatically different media landscape" (DoS, 2007, p. 32). "Internet outreach," using all of the major available web-media, was to be embraced "to share U.S. foreign policy messages with audiences around the world" (DoS, 2007, p. 32). The Pentagon's Flickr use thus represents a convergence of various approaches outlined in this National Strategy, especially concerning photography and the Internet.

Similarly, with respect to the Pentagon's own plans for "strategic communication" (DoD, 2006b), the military reasoned that, "conflict takes place in a population's cognitive space, making sheer military might a lesser priority for victory in the Information Age" (Borg, 2008, p. vii). Communication thus became an explicit part of a global counter-insurgency strategy, as Borg further explains: "the public information environment is a key battleground" (2008, p. vii). This is how the military sees that battleground:

"Some military leaders have labeled the current operating conditions as Fourth Generation Warfare—a term that refers to an enemy that operates in a virtual realm and uses mass media cleverly, effectively making the media the terrain. Personal electronic devices such as cell phones, digital cameras, video recorders, and various kinds of computers have created a new intersection between the individual and the mass media. The public can no longer be viewed as passive information consumers: the public now more than ever actively contributes to the information environment via World Wide Web sites, blogs, and text messaging, to name only a few". (Borg, 2008, p. vii)

An interesting set of contradictions, gaps, and silences are present in the text of this National Strategy, around the basic question of *why* public diplomacy is even needed. On the one hand, the National Strategy repeatedly asserted that "diverse populations" of the world share "our common interests and values" (DoS, 2007, p. 12 also p. 3) — which, if true, raises the question of what makes them "diverse," among other questions raised below. Yet, there is also uncertainty: the same document asked for audience analysis, "so we can better understand how citizens of other countries view us and what values and interests we have in common," which suggests that the assertion of commonality came before the evidentiary substance that was needed to support it (DoS, 2007, p. 10). On the other hand, the National Strategy emphasized that, "public diplomacy is, at its core, about making America's diplomacy public and communicating America's views, values and policies in effective ways to audiences across the world" (DoS, 2007, p. 12). If there are common values and shared interests to begin with, then why is there a need for public diplomacy? The document implicitly responds by saying that the policy is about "reminding" different populations of the values they share with the US, values that at the outset the document listed as a belief that,

> "all individuals, men and women, are equal and entitled to basic human rights, including freedom of speech, worship and political participation....all people deserve

to live in just societies that protect individual and
common rights, fight corruption and are governed by
the rule of law". (DoS, 2007, pp. 2, 12)

Leaving aside the question about why these populations
need "reminding" (no evidence of their memory lapses is
provided), the next question is: if there is uncertainty, as
the document itself suggests, that these values are indeed
shared and held in common, then how would public
diplomacy *change* that difference? Also, if the "violent
extremists" are an *extreme*, and marginal, then why does
the US seem to feel such a need to prove its own value?

Pentagon Media Activity: Public Affairs and Strategic Communication

"The battle of the narrative is a full-blown battle in the
cognitive dimension of the information environment,
just as traditional warfare is fought in the physical
domains (air, land, sea, space, and cyberspace)....a key
component of the 'Battle of the Narrative' is to succeed
in establishing the reasons for and potential outcomes of
the conflict, on terms favorable to your efforts. Upon our
winning the battle of the narrative, the enemy narrative
doesn't just diminish in appeal or followership, it
becomes irrelevant. The entire struggle is completely
redefined in a different setting and purpose". – US Joint
Forces Command (2010, pp. xiii–xiv)

A key part of the broader bureaucratic organization
behind the communications strategies under consideration
involves the role of Public Affairs (PA) Operations,
responsible for "communicating information about
military activities to domestic, international, and internal
audiences," which the Pentagon also refers to as
"community engagement activities" (DoD, 2008, pp. 1, 9).
PA Operations also indicates that its efforts are designed,

"to assure the trust and confidence of [the] U.S.
population, friends and allies, deter and dissuade

adversaries, and counter misinformation and disinformation ensuring effective, culturally appropriate information delivery in regional languages". (DoD, 2008, p. 2)

PA Operations also work to support "civil-military operations" and what the Pentagon calls "public diplomacy" (which, confusingly, the Pentagon has subsumed under the definition of "public affairs" above). "Civil-military operations" are defined by the Pentagon as activities that "establish, maintain, influence, or exploit relations between military forces, indigenous populations, and institutions, by directly supporting the attainment of objectives relating to the reestablishment or maintenance of stability within a region or host nation" (DoD, 2010a, p. 37). "Public diplomacy" is officially defined as, first,

"those overt international public information activities of the United States Government designed to promote United States foreign policy objectives by seeking to understand, inform, and influence foreign audiences and opinion makers, and by broadening the dialogue between American citizens and institutions and their counterparts abroad,"

and second,

"civilian agency efforts to promote an understanding of the reconstruction efforts, rule of law, and civic responsibility through public affairs and international public diplomacy operations". (DoD, 2010a, pp. 214–215; DoD, 2012, p. xvi)

The US military also plays a supporting role to the State Department which leads the US government's "strategic communication" effort, and it does so through information operations (IO),[3] public affairs, and public diplomacy (US Joint Forces Command [JFC], 2010, p. xii):

"Strategic communication (SC) refers to focused USG efforts to understand and engage key audiences to create, strengthen, or preserve conditions favorable for the advancement of USG interests, policies, and objectives through the use of coordinated programs, plans, themes, messages, and products synchronized with and leveraging the actions of all instruments of national power. SC combines actions, words, and images to influence key audiences". (DoD, 2011, p. II-9).

"Synchronized" is a key term here, as it informs us that communication was to be conceived as an instrument of state power, alongside political, economic, and military power. The Pentagon came to see "strategic communication" as a process: "Strategic communication essentially means sharing meaning (i.e., communicating) in support of national objectives (i.e., strategically)" (DoD, 2009, p. 2). The overall purposes of "strategic communication" are listed as:

"• Improve U.S. credibility and legitimacy;
• Weaken an adversary's credibility and legitimacy;
• Convince selected audiences to take specific actions that support U.S. or international objectives;
• Cause a competitor or adversary to take (or refrain from taking) specific actions". (DoD, 2009, p. 2)

For its part, the White House under Barack Obama described "strategic communication" as "the synchronization of our words and deeds as well as deliberate efforts to communicate and engage with intended audiences" (White House, 2009, p. 1), thus some notion of "engagement" came to be built into the process.[4]

Anthropology and Sociology have also been identified as key areas of expertise needed for "mapping the cognitive dimension," in terms that echo the justifications for launching the U.S. Army's Human Terrain System. The Joint Forces Command articulated this "need" as follows: because "cognitive factors can vary significantly between locality, cultures, [and] operational circumstances," the military may need to "leverage outside experts" who possess "unique skill sets not normally found in a military organization". The military would then have these experts "support joint intelligence preparation of the operational

environment, planning, and assessment, either by deploying them forward or through 'reachback'" (JFC, 2010, pp.
xv–xvi).

In terms of the military bureaucracy charged with
provision and supervision of images, in 2007 the Defense
Media Activity (DMA) was created, working under the
Assistant Secretary of Defense for Public Affairs
(ASD[PA]) (DoD, 2007a). The DMA was charged with
developing, acquiring, managing, providing, and
archiving,

> "a wide variety of information products to the entire
> DoD family (Active, Guard, and Reserve Military
> Service members, dependents, retirees, DoD civilians,
> and contract employees) and external audiences through
> all available media, including: motion and still imagery;
> print; radio; television; Web and related emerging
> Internet, mobile, and other communication
> technologies". (DoD, 2007a, pp. 2, 3)

The DMA was thus also responsible for providing the US
public with, "high quality visual information products,
including Combat Camera imagery depicting U.S. military
activities and operations" (DoD, 2007a, p. 2). The DMA
would provide education for both civilian and military
personnel engaged in public affairs, broadcasting, and
"visual information career fields" (DoD, 2007a, pp. 2, 3), in
part through the Defense Information School — thus
ensuring that the standards established by the military
could have a long-term impact, extending beyond the
military once its trained personnel joined the civilian
workforce (see also DoD, 2004). Significantly, where the
Internet is concerned, the DMA was placed in charge of
coordinating and integrating,

> "the utilization of motion and still imagery, print, radio,
> television, Web and new technology products in a
> manner that most effectively relates and distributes DoD
> and Military Service themes and messages to their target
> audiences through conventional and new technology
> multi-platform distribution vehicles". (DoD, 2007a, p. 3)

With specific reference to the Internet, in 2007 the Deputy Secretary of Defense issued a policy on "Interactive Internet Activities," that described the purpose of such activities: "Interactive Internet activities are an essential part of DoD's responsibilities to provide information to the public, shape the security environment, and support military operations" (DoD, 2007b, p. 1). Public affairs activities and products, as described by the policy, are intended to, "shape emotions, motives, reasoning, and behaviors of selected foreign entities" (DoD, 2007b, p. 1) — which is almost identical to the military's definition of "psychological operations" (DoD, 2006a, p. 10).

A more recent document concerning online media communication was a memorandum issued in 2010 by the Deputy Secretary of Defense, titled, "Responsible and Effective Use of Internet-based Capabilities," that spoke specifically of "social networking services" as "integral to operations across the Department of Defense" (DoD, 2010b, p. 1). The official presence of the Pentagon as a whole, and its various armed services, were the focus of the directive. The Assistant Secretary of Defense for Public Affairs was charged with providing the policy for, "news, information, photographs, editorial, community relations activities, and other materials distributed via external official presences" (DoD, 2010b, p. 8). This directive itself followed from twelve previous directives on public communications, issued over a period of twenty-eight years, each of which refers to other sets of directives, memoranda, and handbooks. These directives, Internet-specific as they are, have to be understood within a broader framework of what the US government terms strategic communication, public affairs, public diplomacy, and information operations, all of which are ultimately designed to target foreign audiences in order to change their perceptions of the US and the presence of US agencies in their countries. To some extent, domestic audiences are also targeted. Again, the authority in providing guidance fell to Public Affairs.

Exemplifying some of the structure, planning, codification and regulation of the military's activity in social media is a document titled, "U.S. Army Social Media Strategy, February 4–10, 2012". It does not spell out broad strategy (which would be redundant) as much as it is a schedule of online activities to be undertaken in a given period across various Army websites (US Army, 2012), in line with what the Army calls "best practices" (US Army, 2009b). Each day has a designated theme: "Soldiers, Super Bowl 2012, Military Working Dogs, Military Occupational Speciality Feature, Equipment, Army Investment, Fill in the Blank Friday," and each theme involves a schedule of online actions to be performed at different hours throughout the day. There is little room here for individual improvisation. The "top-line army message," regardless of the day's theme, was constant for that period: "The strength of our Army is our Soldiers. The strength of our Soldiers is our families. This is what makes us Army Strong". What is also important to note is that it seems a large part of the intended audience for this particular schedule consisted of soldiers and their families on base. Nonetheless, some of this is also directed to a broader, unspecified public, with "engagement questions" such as: "What's the first thing that comes to mind when you see 'big guns'?" This is followed by a series of predetermined messages to be posted to Twitter, and the uploading of a photograph to Flickr. There are also particular stories to spotlight, and these are the same for each day of this period: "African-Americans in the Army, Stories of Valor, Warrior Care News, Year in Photos (2011)". Thus, for the online US Army activity scheduled for Sunday, February 5, 2012 (Super Bowl Sunday), and combining three spotlight messages (African-Americans, stories of valor, warrior care), we have the following photograph (Figure 9.1) in the US Army's Flickr account:

Figure 9.1: Super Bowl Meeting

Official caption: "Chief of Staff of the Army Gen. Raymond T. Odierno [right] meets with Col. Greg Gadson [centre] at the Super Bowl in Indianapolis, Feb. 5, 2012". (Photograph: US Army).

Thus the Army produced a feature photo to capitalize on a major sporting event, into which it inserted a General, while also spotlighting Colonel Gregory D. Gadson who was himself a football player, a decorated veteran, and a garrison commander, and who was also injured by a bomb in Iraq, thus losing both of his legs. He is also African-American. The photograph could not have been better planned and choreographed to meet all of the day's scheduled objectives (see Figure 9.2).

Figure 9.2: US Army Online Message Schedule

	Sunday, 5 February
Theme:	Super Bowl 2012
Top-Line Army Message:	The strength of our Army is our Soldiers. The strength of our Soldiers is our families. This is what makes us Army Strong.
Flickr:	Upload photos of U.S. Army missions from sources such as DVIDS and Defense Imagery.
Engagement Question:	N/A
Facebook:	**8AM:** Staff Sgt. Aaron Koehn with the 176th Engineer Company, Washington Army National Guard, does masonry work with his Thai counterpart at the Ban Wang Nam Khiao elementary school. Multi-national forces are working together to improve interoperability at six humanitarian, civic action sites throughout Thailand as part of Exercise Cobra Gold. **11AM:** Are you ready for some football?!?! LINK TO http://www.army.mil/article/73116/ **2PM:** Publish photo album featuring photos of Soldier athletes **5PM:** Unlike many NFL runner backs, the U.S. Army 2nd Cavalry Regiment "Never Drop the Ball." LINK TO http://bit.ly/sRoLd
Twitter: *Tweet links to stories from the Army.mil lineup. As appropriate, incorporate #USArmy, #military, #War, #Afghanistan, #Soldier, #milhealth, #SOT, #WoundedWarrior and #HonorTheFallen hashtags.*	Fort Stewart is saving money and reducing energy - one wood chip at a time. http://bit.ly/BRc29 #energy The @ProFootballHOF U.S. Army Award for Excellence nomination period starts TODAY! http://bit.ly/BNbvW It's @SuperBowl2012 time! Check out Chairman of @thejcintstaff, GEN @Martin_Dempsey's message to you! http://bit.ly/BKI9H Way to go! An #ArmyAviation crew recently won a Air/Sea Rescue award for a mission in #Afghanistan http://bit.ly/BKvuY Unlike many @NFL runner backs, the #USArmy @2dCavalryRegt "Never Drop the Ball" http://bit.ly/8RoLF @SuperBowl2012 Don't become a statistic during @SuperBowl2012 http://bit.ly/88vAU
Google+:	N/A
Blogosphere:	N/A
Army.mil Spotlight:	• African-Americans in The Army • Stories of Valor • Warrior Care News • Year in Photos (2011)
STAND-TO!:	STAND-TO will NOT be published
Goal:	To educate & engage with U.S. Army audiences

Measures of Performance

- *Army Live:* Site Visits, Page Views and Number of Blog Posts
- *Army.mil:* Page views, Facebook Likes, Referral Traffic
- *Facebook:* Feedback Percentage, Impressions, Likes, Comments, Shares, etc.
- *Flickr:* Photo views, Comments, Number of photos marked as a Favorite
- *Twitter:* Number of Followers, Retweets, Tweetreach, etc.
- *STAND-TO!:* Total Number of Subscribers & Click Through-Rate

The grid of scheduled US Army messages to go online for Super Bowl Sunday, February 5, 2012.

This particular document flows from how the US Army, in particular, thinks through and strategizes about communication involving photographs, in broad terms, which in turn flows from the other documents already discussed.

What it also reveals is the level of precise planning, linearity in structure, and programmed messaging. This could all be fed just as easily to a computer. Subjectivity simply does not exist here, except as a quality of the expected manipulability of audiences' emotional state of being. Otherwise, between the military's positivist approach to photography, and its expectation that audiences take images at face-value, subjectivity is clearly the Achilles Heel of military doctrine and practice.

Finally, most of the military documents consulted for this project tended to emphasize standardization and unity of effort, "interagency" collaboration, with "joint approaches," and so forth—the desire for a functioning monolith of total integration exists, however, because a deeper reality denies it. As Borg (2008, p. ix) observed:

> "At face value, the services' interdependence of roles and missions makes it easy for the individual military services to support the DoD's strategic mission goals: victory is a shared claim. However, at a deeper level, the services are in constant competition with each other for limited budgetary authority, recruits and development of roles, missions, and their associated weapons systems. To this end, the services must out-communicate one another—successfully telling their stories to Congress, the American people, and their own forces."

Words, Deeds, and Perceptions: The Pitfalls of Strategic Communication

"Don't leave false illusions behind
Don't cry cause I ain't changing my mind
So find another fool like before
Cause I ain't gonna live anymore believing
Some of the lies while all of the signs are deceiving".—Alan Parsons Project, "Eye in the Sky"

While the US Army may think that a picture is worth a thousand words (US Army, 2010b, p. 21), the reality of "strategic communication" is its quiet struggle with the fact that *anything* can produce a message, that any military action can be worth "a thousand" more words than any photograph chosen for display by the US Army. In a report produced by the US Government Accountability Office (GAO), there was recognition of this from the Pentagon itself:

> "The Department of Defense (DOD) recognizes that everything it does communicates a message, from having soldiers distribute soccer balls in conflict zones to scheduling joint exercises off the coasts of foreign nations. However, DOD officials stated that the department has struggled for several years to strategically align its actions with the messages it intends to communicate to foreign audiences — an effort that is also referred to as strategic communication". (GAO, 2012, p. 1)

In recognition of the limits of understanding "the message" purely in terms of an objectified piece of information, the Pentagon began to shift its emphasis, with a decreasing focus on "strictly 'informational' activities," while viewing strategic communication more as an, "adaptive, decentralized process of trying to understand selected audiences thoroughly, hypothesizing physical or informational signals that will have the desired cognitive effect on those audiences" (DoD, 2009, p. 3). Indeed, it recognized that, "all DoD activities have a communication and informational impact" (DoD, 2009, p. 3).

The White House in 2009 dictated that "active consideration of how our actions and policies will be interpreted by public audiences," should form "an organic part of decision-making" (White House, 2009, p. 2). Does the Pentagon leadership realistically think that the objectives of strategic communication are being achieved, especially in terms of integrating likely "perception effects" into planning? The answer is: "The strategic communication process is always a work in progress, one that is inherently aspirational in its goals" (DoD, 2009, p. 9). There could be a more blunt answer. From a certain standpoint, the entire strategic communication effort is inherently and ultimately doomed: it will likely only win the approval of those who already support US foreign policy and its military interventions. The Secretary of Defense, Robert Gates, wished to ensure that, "potential communication impacts of both kinetic and non-kinetic actions — their likely 'perception effects' — are assessed and planned for *before* the actions are taken," and to make sure that, "our words and our actions are consistent and mutually reinforcing (closing the 'say-do' gap)," while examining "soft power" as an equal priority in consideration with "hard power alternatives" (DoD, 2009, p. 3). Regarding the "synchronization of words and deeds," the Pentagon sets this as a goal: "to integrate foreign audience perceptions into policy making, planning, and operations at every level" (GAO, 2012, pp. 2, 9; also, DoD, 2010d; White House, 2009). However, if it sincerely and seriously wished to pursue this, what would happen if likely "foreign audience reactions" to the US attacking another nation turned out to be overwhelmingly negative? Would the US cease and desist, afraid that its actions could contradict its stated intentions? Instead, what the Pentagon immediately does is decontextualize and narrow "audience reactions," reducing the discussion to the audience reacting to a specific, intentional communication act from the US military — such as a photograph, thus reversing its own policy above. The Pentagon thus offers these steps (GAO, 2012, p. 2):

"1. Identify likely audiences and desired audience perceptions for DoD communication.
2. Identify the audiences' probable reactions to that DoD communication.
3. Identify and make plans to address the gap between what DoD wants to communicate and what the key audience is likely to perceive.
4. Implement, monitor, and assess; makes changes to the plan if needed".

However, even at the level of defining what strategic communication actually means, there is marked variation and disagreement among US military and diplomatic officials, often speaking past each other because they implicitly refer to different things (GAO, 2012, p. 12).

Realism or Iconography? The Pentagon's Implicit Theory of Visual Representation

US military documents make it quite clear that, for the military, a photograph is a straightforward, truthful, and impartial record of reality as it appeared in front of the camera. However, at the same time these documents suggest that some images might be used as "enemy propaganda" whereas other images are safe in that they "support the mission" of the US military. Here I wish to outline what the US military has made available for the public record about its social media strategies, and in particular about its "Flickr strategy".

Supporting the military's mission and telling a story are the dual themes of the Pentagon's visual media strategy. To begin, the Pentagon has a definition for "visual information," which consists of:

> "one or more of the various visual media, with or without sound, to include still photography, motion picture photography, video or audio recording, graphic arts, visual aids, models, display, visual presentation services, and the support processes". (DoD, 2008, p. 9)

Specific reference to a strategy pertaining to photography and the use of Flickr, comes from the Office of the Chief of Public Affairs Online and Social Media Division (US Army, 2010a). The audience is defined as a global one, in addition to soldiers and their families, and veterans (US Army 2010a, p. 1). While the proclaimed aim of the Flickr account is to provide "a visual story of the U.S. army," the more specific points in the document suggest a narrower objective. In particular the Chief of Public Affairs states:

"the Social Media Team will only post content that supports the Army mission and the Army themes" (US Army,
2010a, p. 2). The Army will *not* post photographs that, "do
not support the mission of the U.S. Army," or those that,
"violate U.S. Army Operational Security (OPSEC) guidelines," or, "images that could be used as propaganda by
enemies of the United States," or, "images that contain any
content that could be construed as racist, derogatory, or
otherwise offensive," or, "images that show military personnel or government/contracted employees acting in an
unprofessional manner or engaging in any act that would
damage the image or reputation of the Army" (US Army,
2010a, p. 3). The Chief of Public Affairs also states that the
way of "measuring success" of these photographs is to
count the number of "views" that they receive (US Army,
2010a, p. 3).

The combined effect of these restrictions is therefore
not one designed to simply tell a "visual story" of the US
Army, but to tell only some stories that have a prescribed
political motivation (along with an unspoken faith in the
capacity of images to tell such stories). If Army Public
Affairs positions itself against "enemy use" of its photos
for "propaganda," it then implies what its objectives are,
which also constitute propaganda. Indeed, the notion that
it would be "propaganda" to use US Army photographs in
a critique of the US Army's "mission," is such a broad
view of "propaganda" that its aim is to remove any
question about the military's role just as it labours to pry
its self-representation away from the realm of propaganda.
The US Army thus seems to declare: it's propaganda when
they criticize us, but it's not propaganda when we tell
them our glory stories. The thinking is thus structured in
terms of simple political absolutes, and the state of political
exception is the rule of representation.

The additional restriction under the umbrella of Operational Security is, as we have seen in the massive over-
classification of information that was leaked by Bradley
Manning, a particularly oppressive one. The caution about
racist images or displays of unprofessional behaviour is

only necessary if the US Army is aware of the existence of these facets of US Army life. The final point is about "reputation," and here we can recall the impact of Abu Ghraib.

What is also remarkable about the "Flickr strategy" above is the implicit understanding that images contain a single, direct message, and that what is photographed, and how it is photographed, will determine whether an image is "successful" in supporting the US Army "mission". In other words, photographs can only be understood in one manner: the intended manner. Once one counts up the "views," then one can know how many people have had their perceptions successfully shaped by the US Army. It is a bet, even if not understood as such by the US Army: that members of the viewing public have the same prerequisite cultural training and ideological orientation that allows them to see an image as it was intended to be seen. It is a bet that, as another Army social media guidebook states, "a picture really is worth a thousand words" (US Army, 2010b, p. 21) and that the US Army can predetermine those words. It is necessarily a bet that pictures speak for themselves. It is a bet that images lack plenitude of information that can be read in many different ways. Indeed, it is even a bet that a piece such as this will not be written.

In general, the Pentagon's approach to photography fits well in descriptions of "scientific-realist" approaches that seek to "regulate the context" in which photographs are produced in order to produce "reliable" visual "evidence" (Pink, 2001, p. 97). The assumption made in this approach is that the photograph itself, the content of the photograph, would be the focus of the viewer's analysis. However, as the numerous directives and manuals attest, along with their detailed instructions on how to make useful and good pictures, the Pentagon actively regulates context, and that can be made visible in a critical analysis of the photographs.

So assured are they by the power of photography, Pentagon strategists never raise the following questions in any of their manuals and handbooks: if the US military can tell a "visual story," what is there to stop viewers from recognizing that it is, indeed, *just a story*, a narrative play, where one can play with any other stories one likes? Moreover, how do they know that the story will be read and understood as intended? The belief that photographs will speak for themselves is never unpacked by the military strategists. On the one hand, what a viewer actually sees and comprehends, even if not consciously, is largely a matter of *training*: having learned the cultural patterns and conventions for telling/reading visual stories (see Banks, 2001, p. 10). Thus any photograph may have, "no fixed meaning at all and, although physically static, its message becomes subject to the fluctuations of shifting social patterns" (Wright, 1999, p. 6). This suggests a limitation, for photographs do not speak across cultures as easily as the Pentagon's strategists think. Indeed, even within similar cultural formations disagreements over what is shown and how it is seen run rife. One may be reminded here of the argument between the French literary critic and semiologist, Roland Barthes, and the American-born French photographer, William Klein. Barthes fixated on one child's "bad teeth" in one of Klein's photos of children in Little Italy, New York. Klein was indignant and responded:

> "He's more interested in what he sees than in what the photographer sees. I saw other things when I took the picture…but Barthes isn't all that interested in what I see or what I've done. He's not listening to me—only to himself". (Wright, 1999, p. 8)

The Pentagon is waiting to discover that it is William Klein.

Contrary to the kind of early positivist appreciations of photographic "records" that also appealed to the new discipline of Anthropology,[5] there is nothing objective, realistic, or neutral about photographs. As Marcus Banks explained, if photographs seem to bear a semblance of life and agency within them, it is at least in part because "humans frequently displace…conversations onto inanimate objects" (2001, p. 10). In line with numerous critiques of the supposed impartial realism of photography, Pierre Bourdieu explained:

> "photography captures an aspect of reality which is only ever the result of an arbitrary selection, and, consequently, of a transcription; among all the qualities of the object, the only ones retained are the visual qualities which appear for a moment and from one sole viewpoint". (1999, p. 162)

Extending this argument, Bourdieu adds, "that which is visible is only ever that which is legible" (1999, p. 163). If military photographers think their products tell a true visual story, it's because what they wanted to see, and how they choose to see, is what shaped their photographic practice to begin with. Their photographs, therefore, are neither "realistic" nor "staged," but both: they are stagings of realities as understood by military photographers, according to the instructions they have received. As Bourdieu put it more broadly: "it is natural that the imitation of art should appear to be the most natural imitation of nature" (1999, p. 164):

> "at a deeper level, only in the name of a naive realism can one see as realistic a representation of the real which owes its objective appearance not to its agreement with the very reality of things (since this is only ever conveyed through socially conditioned forms of perception) but rather to conformity with rules which define its syntax within its social use, to the social definition of the objective vision of the world; in conferring upon photography a guarantee of realism, society is merely confirming itself in the tautological certainty that an image of the real which is true to its representation of objectivity is really objective". (Bourdieu, 1999, p. 164)

Again, this requires that photographers and viewers implicitly share the same understandings of "the reality of things," the same or similar "socially conditioned forms of perception" and hold in common an understanding of the social rules that structure representations. Photographs then are not so much "objective" as they are an *objectification* of already inculcated values. Military images are thus, as Bourdieu might say, *regulated images* that impose the military's "rules of perception" (Bourdieu, 1999, p. 168). Thus when we read the directives, policies, and manuals referred to in this chapter, what we are reading are the rules for the proper production of what might be called images made according to military regulations. That is *their* truth, rather than *the* truth. The resulting photographs, produced by a system of rules within an institution charged with communication, distribution, and legitimation, thus attain the status of *consecrated works* (Bourdieu, 1999, p. 177).

On the other hand, while situated within a surrounding discourse (one understood by both photographer and viewer) photographs may convey the meanings that are intended, however, a difficulty that presents itself has to do with the nature of the photograph: "its apparent plenitude, which flooded the observer with concreteness and detail, yet revealed little in the absence of a surrounding discourse" (MacDougall, 1997, p. 289). As explained by visual anthropologist David MacDougall (1997, p. 289): "an uncaptioned photograph is full of undirected potential". Here we might expand the meaning of the "caption" beyond the immediate text presented next to or underneath a photograph, to include the set of established and regular meanings understood by photographer and viewer alike. In the absence of these surrounding discourses, however, a photograph may say nothing at all just as it may say *too much* more than the thousand words the Pentagon wants it to say. The consequences for the Pentagon, which it cannot measure because it does not ask these questions, is that its photographs may register strongly with the learned emotions of a domestic, militarized audience, but have little or nothing to say with any positive resonance to other and more distant audiences. The Pentagon's own photograph captions seem to take much for granted, relying on a presentation of the seemingly minimalist details of when the photograph was taken, where, and who is pictured — as if it is all a simple matter of *fact*.

The only reason that the Pentagon persists is due to the belief in the objective, mechanical/digital veracity of the photograph and the belief that a photograph tells the truth, which is possibly a belief that is reinforced by the Pentagon's reliance on COMCAM battle imagery, further strengthened by its current drone surveillance cameras. Yet this truth can sometimes be the same as illusion — the intention of the military's Flickr images is to, "produce a *trompe l'œil*, fooling the viewer into believing that they have access to unmediated perception of the scene" (Wright, 1999, p. 40). The Pentagon's approach is an objectifying one, that holds that it is possible to record "reality," and that whatever is (made) visible must therefore be true (see Pink, 2001, p. 23).

Aside from the discussion above, it should also be noted parenthetically that the Department of Defense not only requires that photographs follow authorized guidelines for how to depict its forces, but also on how to depict "others" (see DoD, 2010c). Under the heading of "tips on the photographing of people," the DoD states: "be aware of taking pictures of children," and, "ask permission of people you have photos of to take the photo, use the photo and identify them in the photo". In addition it cautions, "please be sensitive to local cultural issues surrounding the photographing of people and various locations" (DoD, 2010c, p. 41). The *public* emphasis here is on cultural sensitivity and erring on the side of not photographing children. On the other hand, the DoD's own Flickr account is filled with photographs of unaccompanied children in different countries in the context of various US military missions. In war zones, little sensitivity is shown when depicting villagers being interviewed by members of the US Army's Human Terrain System, even as the Pentagon fulminated against WikiLeaks' Afghan War Diary for revealing the identities of informants by name. Here the Pentagon has gone a big step beyond that: giving a face that can match the name. Also of interest is that while the US military claims to show sensitivity in how it pictures others, the question of how it pictures itself to cultural others is largely beyond its grasp — how, for example, scenes of massive, gleaming killing machines carefully attended to by support staff might not be impressive, or a deterrent, but rather a hideous sign of everything gone wrong with a violent culture that worships itself.

"Now Picture This": The Pentagon's Pictorial Propaganda and Symbolic Power

"The sun in your eyes
Made some of the lies
Worth believing". — Alan Parsons Project, "Eye in the Sky"

In "reading" the Pentagon's Flickr collection, some principles from the subfield of visual anthropology can be useful. For example, we clearly know something now about the "author" of the pictures, which is more than just a single individual in any given case: the author is an institution, a strategy, a directive, a set of instructions, even a schedule. We also have the pictures themselves, and precise ideas of what the Pentagon wants them to say. In fact, the Pentagon can be even more precise (below). We also know nothing about the viewers of these photographs, so we cannot offer any concrete details here. We do know something about the photographic conventions being used (thanks to the State Department's instructions on "use good pictures and images"), and we know something of the social contexts (military exercises, disaster relief, occupation), and the encompassing power relations behind the production of these photographs. The mistake we are thus avoiding is thinking of photographs "as objects whose meaning is intrinsic to them," when meanings are instead *assigned* to them (Ruby, 1995, p. 5). What are intrinsic to the photographs produced by the Pentagon are the political motivations, subjectivity, and ethos of the institution (see Pink, 2001, p. 55). This does not at all mean that the contents of the pictures do not matter — they do. What matters more is figuring out which contents we are meant to notice and how we are to put those contents together in a meaningful fashion — which means going outside of the pictures for clues, as done in this chapter by examining US diplomatic and military strategy documents.

In 2009 the Department of the Army produced a field manual titled, "Visual Information Operations" (US Army, 2009a). One of the significant features of this manual is that it provides a clear set of categories of photographs to be produced that are intended to positively showcase US military operations. *All* of these categories are vividly displayed in practice, with numerous examples of each to be found in the Pentagon's own Flickr account. (Here the reader should also quickly review "use good pictures and images" in the National Strategy for Public Diplomacy and Strategic Communication discussed above.) We thus find examples of:

a) "Readiness Posture Imagery" that simply "display a unit's readiness";

b) "Significant Operations Imagery" that "documents situations and supports public or community affairs programs," such as a soldier interacting with children receiving medical aid from US forces;

c) "Significant Programs and Projects Imagery," which can feature the celebration of achieving a milestone of some sort for a specific unit or program, with the typical photo being of a ribbon-cutting ceremony;

d) "Civil Military Involvement Imagery" is a broad category similar to (b), one that purportedly chronicles "participation in disaster relief, civil disturbances, and environmental protection," and involves imagery that can be used as part of a public affairs or public diplomacy program — the Army claims that such "imagery transcends the language barrier and allows better cooperation between the representatives of the military and local citizens, both American and foreign";

e) "Construction Imagery," which appears frequently, showing US forces constructing, repairing, or maintaining buildings and other public facilities;

f) "Significant Military Events Imagery," which is a very broad category but in practice most resembles (c) above as it can involve depicting the granting of medals, or it can feature the deployment of troops, thus resembling (a) above; and,

g) "Military Life Imagery" which is a selective portrait of "military life," narrowed down to examples "such as Soldiers at work, physical training, new equipment usage, and enjoyment of life as a military family" (US Army, 2009a, pp. 2-5 — 2-8).

This is by no means a complete list, since the categorization is itself an unstable product of intention and perception, official motivation and viewers' interpretation. There are also examples of numerous photographs, discussed below, that do not readily fit into any of the categorical areas above. However, what the list above does do is to provide a starting point, and some limited insight as to what a photographic collection is meant to accomplish, from the military's perspective. If we were to sum up all of the above into one single message, it might be this: *happy, healthy, helpful, strong, successful, and ready to go*. It is not such a far-fetched summation, in light of the above, and is one that corresponds well with recruitment advertising. It is also the intentional opposite of other realities of war and US military actions: *angry, menacing, abusive, destructive, traumatized, flawed, retreating*.

Many of the photographs in the Pentagon's Flickr stream *suggest* collaboration between "locals" and US forces. The photographs themselves, however, are not collaborative productions. There is never an indication that the "locals" in any way initiated, conceived, sought, or desired to be photographed. Some certainly "agreed" or acquiesced) to be photographed, and that is about as charitable as we can afford to be.

The choices manifested in the Pentagon's Flickr photographs represent what Bourdieu called "a choice that praises," one that reflects an ethos stemming from internalized objective and common regularities and collective rules, such that a photograph expresses, "the system of schemes of perception, thought and appreciation common to a whole group" (Bourdieu, 1991, p. 131). The "whole group" in question here is of course the US military. What is perhaps most different from the range of cases studied by Bourdieu, is that we are not really dealing here mostly with behaviour that is more inspired than controlled, more unselfconscious than intentional, without a call to order or formal education (see Bourdieu et al., 1990, p. 43). The point of these directives, manuals and handbooks is precisely to institute a regular, formal, conscious and intentional selection of subjects according to fairly strict instructions. (Of course it may well be that the photographers, once educated according to the military's regulations and well practiced, develop a habitual and seemingly intuitive mode of choosing and framing particular images.)

Another way to understand the character of the photographic communication categories listed above and their intended meanings is by way of Sherry Ortner's (1973) outline of a methodology for understanding symbolism and symbolic power. First, it seems fair to say that what we are dealing with in these pictures are forms of what Ortner calls "elaborating symbols": they provide means for "sorting out complex and undifferentiated feelings and ideas, making them comprehensible to oneself, communicable to others, and translatable into orderly action" (Ortner, 1973, p. 1340). Second, they express power as elaborating symbols, in two distinct ways: a) they have "conceptual elaborating power" in that they provide or convey, "categories for conceptualizing the order of the world" (the proper place of military power in assuring US global dominance); and, b) "action elaborating power," in that they imply mechanisms for successful action (Ortner, 1973, p. 1340). Third, a particular type of elaborating symbol, one that closely aligns with (b) above, is what Ortner calls the "key scenario": this implies "clear-cut modes of action" that in this case are appropriate to representing US military success and military indispensability, and the key scenario also postulates a "basic means-ends relationships in actable forms" and provides "strategies for organizing action experience" (Ortner, 1973, pp. 1341, 1342). It is important to understand that Ortner in no way intends to separate thought from action, in any of her conceptualizations of symbolism.

In the various scenarios depicted in the categorical areas outlined above and demonstrated below, the US military virtually represents itself as the world's new Great Chief — protector, guide, gift-giver, and war-maker — who overrules if not outlaws all other (lesser) chiefs. If the US military repairs your home, and makes your children smile, then what does that say about *you*, after all, as a father or as a chief of your tribe? The arid, pretend-neutrality of the US military's rhetoric employed to categorize the diverse imagery listed above, is meant to render scientific what is in fact overwhelming ambition and national narcissism.

Help, Health, Happiness, and Hellfire

Let us turn finally to a selection of what may well be photographs that are emblematic of the categories above, and some that exceed the boundaries of those categories. These images include the official captions, which then form part of the commentary in my critical reinterpretation of the photographs, based on their contents and contexts. The same is largely true of the titles for the figures, which I supply.

Readiness Posture Imagery

Figure 9.3: Lined Up and Ready to Go

This photograph, taken on May 13, 2014, was officially captioned as follows: "US Marines and Sailors with the 22nd Marine Expeditionary Unit (MEU) stand at attention during a formation aboard the amphibious assault ship USS Bataan (LHD 5) in the Gulf of Aden May 13, 2014. The 22nd MEU was deployed with the Bataan Amphibious Ready Group as a theater reserve and crisis response force throughout the US Central Command and U.S. 5th Fleet areas of responsibility". (DoD photograph by Sgt. Austin Hazard, US Marine Corps)

As mentioned in the previous section, photographs in this category are meant to display a unit's readiness. Figure 9.3 displays a recurring aesthetic principle that one finds in the Pentagon's Flickr collection on this theme, which is that of quantity and symmetry. The official caption omits key details of the context of this photograph: the USS Bataan was here en route to the coast of Libya as a new round of civil war erupted the day before, led by a general who lived in exile in the US and worked with the CIA. The photograph thus displays readiness but does not indicate purpose, which as a result does little to inform US viewers. It does, however, suggest a way of being *globally positioned* regardless of particular, local destinations.

Figure 9.4: Ready to Drop

Taken on February 9, 2011, this was officially captioned as follows: "US Army paratroopers with the 82nd Airborne Division sit in an Air Force C-17A Globemaster III before an airdrop during a joint operational access exercise (JOAX) at Pope Air Force Base, NC, Feb. 9, 2011. JOAX is a joint Army and Air Force training exercise held to practice large-scale personnel and equipment airdrop missions". (DoD photograph by Staff Sgt. Greg C. Biondo, US Air Force)

As with the one before, Figure 9.4 again shows symmetry, quantity, and one might say poise. Readiness is conveyed by the rows of waiting paratroopers. Note again the choice of angle: high above the men, emphasizing the number and geometry of the formation in a manner that North American media consumers would likely find to be visually pleasing. Indeed, many DoD photos seem to have been produced with significant artistry, and sometimes apparently produced to feature the artistry itself, such as images of smoke in all colours (green, pink, yellow, purple) engulfing dramatically posed soldiers.

Significant Operations Imagery

Figure 9.5: Skipping Rope with Cambodian Children

The official caption for this photograph, taken on June 16, 2010, was: "School in Sihanoukville, Cambodia, June 17, 2010. Mercy is deployed as part of Pacific Partnership 2010, the fifth in a series of annual US Pacific Fleet humanitarian and civic assistance endeavors to strengthen regional partnerships". (DoD photo by Mass Communication Specialist 2nd Class Jon Husman, US Navy)

The definition of "significant operations imagery" in the previous section was rather ambiguous, apart from an example being a soldier interacting with children receiving medical aid from US forces. In that vein, here we have an example of a recurring theme in the DoD's Flickr account in this category, featuring US troops playing with children as they skip rope. As in most of these photographs, produced in very vivid colour, the bare feet of the locals feature prominently, in contrast with the heavily booted feet of US troops. It is rare to see the parents, or other local adults, in such photographs, which can give the impression that the children's only guardians on hand are the US forces themselves. There is no explanation as to how this activity fits in with the stated US military expedition to the area. The next photographs present more examples of this theme.

Figure 9.6: Skipping Rope in the Aftermath of the Earthquake in Haiti

Taken on January 26, 2010, and officially captioned as follows: "Department of Defense and the US Agency for International Development are in the area conducting Operation Unified Response to provide aid and relief to Haitian citizens affected by the 7.0-magnitude earthquake that struck the region Jan. 12, 2010". (U.S. Air Force photo by Tech. Sgt. Prentice Colter)

Figure 9.6 is an unusual photograph in that no US forces are shown within it. There is an unidentified adult at left, not in any US military attire, though it's conceivable that she might be an employee of USAID or of an affiliated local NGO. Still, we have no idea whether the Air Force photographer simply stumbled on this scene of apparent joy in the midst of extreme ruin and despair following Haiti's devastating earthquake, or produced it as a sign of cheer following the arrival of US forces.

Figure 9.7: Teaching a Haitian Orphan How to Jump

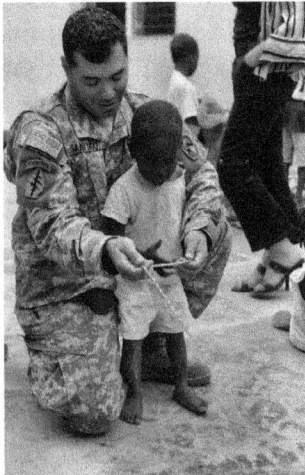

From March 7, 2010, the official caption for this photograph was: "US Army Sgt. 1st Class Arier Santiago teaches a Haitian child how to jump rope at the Solidante Fraternite orphanage in Port-au-Prince, Haiti, March 7, 2010. Santiago is in Haiti as part of Operation Unified Response". (DoD photo by Mass Communication Specialist 1st Class David A. French, U.S. Navy)

Again, the rope jumping motif appears, this time with a US soldier taking time out to show a Haitian child how it is done. Once again, we see a stark contrast between the well clothed, adult US soldier, and a local child, barefoot. In the background we can discern the presence of a white civilian, in high heels, whose presence is not commented upon in the caption. In this scene, as presented, no local guardians are shown at this orphanage site.

Apart from jumping rope, there are a great many more photographs of US forces interacting with children, with one of the more striking features of these kinds of photographs being the almost sudden appearance, and predominance, of female US forces ("sudden" if one views most of the DoD's collection of photographs in a continual stream). One example follows.

Figure 9.8: Encounter with a Little Girl in Afghanistan

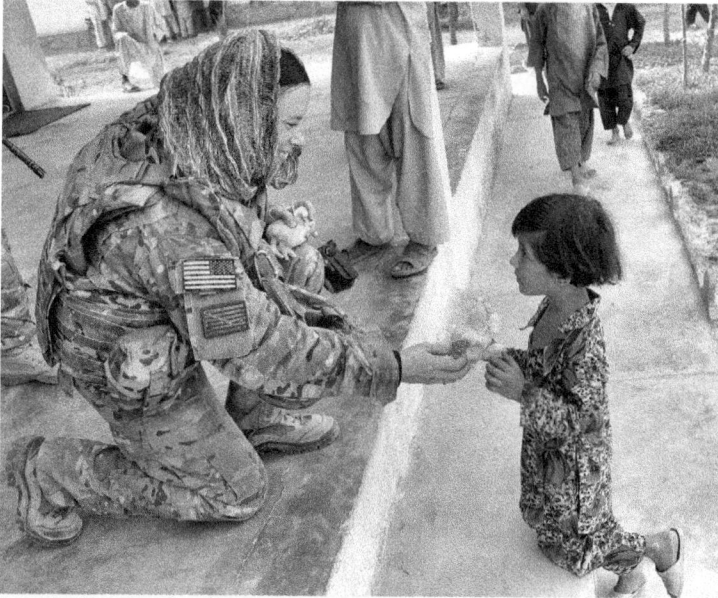

Though incorrectly dated as being taken on February 29, 2000, more than a year before the US invasion, the official caption for this photograph was: "U.S. Navy Lt. j.g. Meghan Burns, with Provincial Reconstruction Team (PRT) Farah, hands a stuffed animal to an Afghan orphan during a key leader engagement at the Farah Orphanage in Farah Province, Afghanistan, Aug. 4, 2013. PRT Farah's mission is to train, advise and assist Afghan government leaders at the municipal, district and provincial levels in Farah province, Afghanistan". (DoD photo illustration by Lt. Chad A. Dulac, U.S. Navy)

It's not clear how distributing toys to children either assists key Afghan leaders (not shown *contra* the caption), or is a part of "key leader engagement". Once again, however, *the orphanage* emerges as the preferred ground for such photographs—this is risky, especially as some well-informed and conscientious viewers might consider how US bombardments created a large number of Afghan orphans.

Figure 9.9 combines at least four common motifs: the American female presence, the child belonging to a different ethnicity and nationality, medical care, and play. The caption tells the familiar story of "humanitarian assistance," without any details as to who requested such assistance and why, why the US was willing to provide it, or how the child came to be in the photograph. Indeed, there even seems to be very little of what is needed for a routine medical exam, apart from a stethoscope. What is interesting about the caption, however, is the note about the US Navy having specialists in "mass communication". In addition, in the midst of all of this apparent gift-giving, the question must be asked: what is expected in return?

Figure 9.9: Care and Play

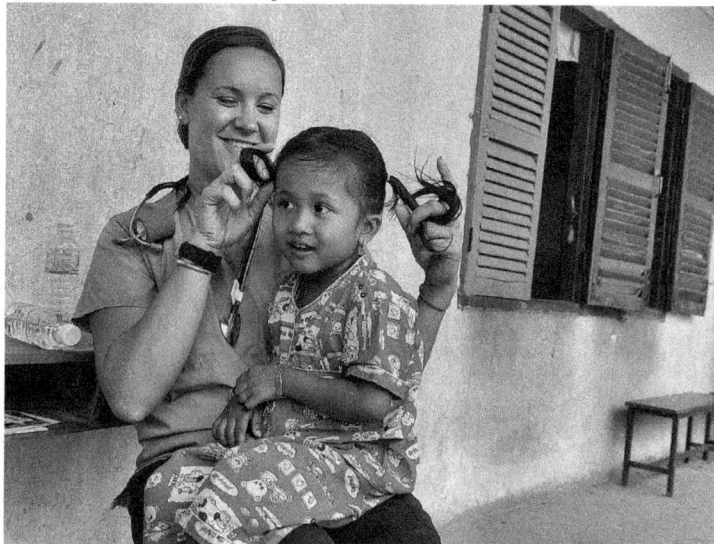

This photograph, taken on July 28, 2012, was captioned as follows: "Jacquelyn Bilbro, a registered nurse, entertains a child during a medical civic action project at Hun Sen Cheungkor Primary Elementary School, in Sihanoukville, Cambodia, July 29, 2012, during Pacific Partnership 2012. Pacific Partnership is an annual deployment of forces designed to strengthen maritime and humanitarian partnerships during disaster relief operations, while providing humanitarian, medical, dental and engineering assistance to nations of the Pacific". (DoD photograph by Mass Communication Specialist 2nd Class Roadell Hickman, US Navy)

Figure 9.10: Singing to Children

Taken on June 21, 2012: "US Navy Musician 2nd Class Kori Gillis, assigned to the US Naval Forces Europe Band ensemble Flagship, sings and dances with children at the Integracao Infantil Cristo Vida school in Nacala, Mozambique, June 21, 2012. Sailors and Marines embarked aboard high speed vessel Swift (HSV-2) visited the school during a community service project as part of Africa Partnership Station (APS) 2012. APS is an international security cooperation initiative facilitated by Commander, US Naval Forces Europe-Africa aimed at strengthening global maritime partnerships through training and collaborative activities in order to improve maritime safety and security in Africa". (DoD photo by Ensign Joe Keiley, U.S. Navy/Released)

In Figure 9.10, we learn about the US Navy also deploying its own musicians, seen here singing to children at a school, but as part of an unrelated effort concerning "maritime security". There is not even so much as a bottle of water in the photograph, let alone a significant body of water. The photograph, therefore, is not emblematic of the stated purpose of the military venture, but of something that covers over it: a professed liking for children around the globe, best shown by forces in uniform.

Figure 9.11: Piggybacking on US Troops

From April 12, 2013, this photograph had the following caption: "US Marine Corps Staff Sgt. Ruben Ramirez, left, a warehouseman, and Cpl. David Long, a packing specialist, both with Combat Logistics Regiment 35, 3rd Marine Logistics Group, III Marine Expeditionary Force, carry students at Maruglo Elementary School in Capas, Tarlac province, Philippines, April 12, 2013, during a community relations event as part of Balikatan 2013. Balikatan is an annual bilateral training exercise designed to increase interoperability between the Armed Forces of the Philippines and the US military when responding to future natural disasters". (DoD photo by Tech. Sgt. Jerome S. Tayborn, US Air Force)

Figure 9.11 again presents playing with little girls as if it were a requirement of military "interoperability". It is an interesting image for being so out of the ordinary: one would not expect to see (male) military personnel in our schoolyards in North America, playing with our little girls. Somehow, when displaced to the Philippines, this is made to stand as an altogether pleasant and normal way to pass time while adjusting to another society, as the US began its so-called military "pivot" to southeast Asia. It is as if the "strangeness" of the Asian context entitles US troops to behave in strange manners, but accepted as a normal display of good intentions. The photograph — whether or not the product of conscious intent is immaterial — is also important in projecting two contradictory positionings. On the one hand, there is the anti-anti-colonialist reversal, where now it is the native riding on the white man's back. This can also symbolize, however, a literal white man's burden, of "our" shouldering the responsibilities for "their" society's future. On the other hand, presenting others in the form of children, thus infantilizing the status of other societies subject to US action, is instead a rather undiluted message of classic colonial discourse. In line with the Pentagon's own cautions about photographing children (as we read in a previous section), it might have been strategically wiser not to take any such photographs, especially in a southeast Asian context where there have been numerous local complaints about US forces leaving their bases and sexually assaulting young women.

Figure 9.12: Military Madonna in Afghanistan

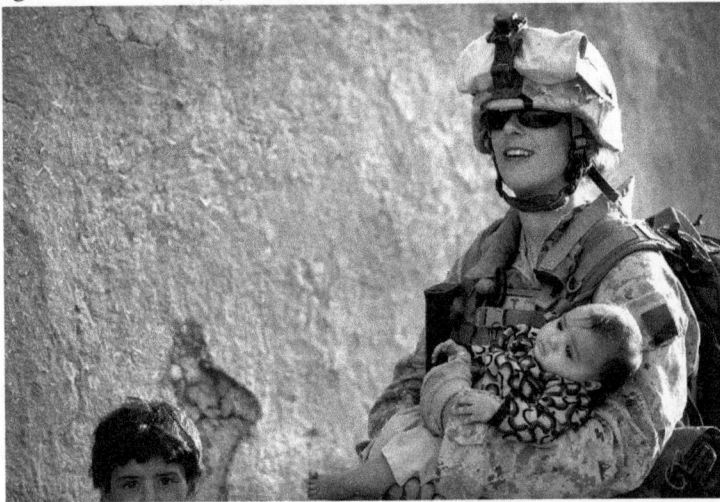

From August 3, 2010, this was captioned as follows: "US Navy Petty Officer 2nd Class Claire Ballante holds an Afghan child during a patrol with Marines from 1st Battalion, 2nd Marine Regiment in Musa Qa'leh, Afghanistan, Aug. 3, 2010. Ballante is part of a female engagement team that is patrolling local compounds to assess possible home damage caused by aircraft landing at Forward Operating Base Musa Qala". (DoD photo by Cpl. Lindsay L. Sayres, US Marine Corps)

Though strictly limited in visual contents, Figure 9.12 still provides ample room for interpretation, especially in light of the of the official caption. This is literally about putting a smile on a bad situation, as the caption suggests there are local complaints about damage caused by a nearby US landing strip. Here once again a female soldier is presented in a mothering role, as a proxy for the child's natural parent. The "naturalness" of the cradling is belied however by the woman looking up and away from the child, as if she had scooped up and held the child as a mere prop. The Naval petty officer is also heavily attired in combat gear, in stark contrast with the children. The other child in the bottom left, though almost cropped out of the photography entirely by the military, was clearly doing something of which we see little or nothing in these photographs: *returning the gaze*. Figure 9.13 is offered as a companion image, which repeats some of the key messages: female US troops playing mother to little Afghan girls. The title for this image is a line from the 1765 *Mother Goose's Melody*, "Pat a Cake".

Figure 9.13: So I Do, Master, As Fast As I Can

From October 31, 2011, the official caption for this photograph was: "US Army Sgt. Stephanie Tremmel, right, with the 86th Special Troops Battalion, 86th Infantry Brigade Combat Team, interacts with an Afghan child while visiting Durani, Afghanistan, Nov. 1, 2010. Soldiers visited the village to dismantle an old Russian tank, which the villagers will sell for scrap metal to buy food to get through the winter". (DoD photo by Spc. Kristina L. Gupton, US Army)

Figure 9.14: Reading to Students

Taken on October 2, 2013, the original caption for this photograph read: "US Navy Lt. Shayna Rivard, left foreground, a battalion surgeon attached to Combat Logistics Battalion 13, 13th Marine Expeditionary Unit, reads to students of the Bal Bhavan School in Panaji, Goa, India, Oct. 1, 2013, during a volunteer outreach as part of exercise Shatrujeet 2013. Shatrujeet is an annual training exercise conducted by US and Indian service members to share knowledge and build interoperability skills. (DoD photo by Sgt. Christopher O'Quin, US Marine Corps)

Figure 9.14 differs in some respects, though repeating the theme of female US forces coupled with children, in exercises that seem to bear little relevance to the stated military mission. Here a military surgeon is neither in uniform, nor offering medical care, but seemingly reading to students from one of their own books. The action seems to be staged for the camera, even more than in other cases. This also appears to be conducted not in a regular classroom; given the presence of the pupils' sandwiches, this possibly happened during a lunch break which, if correct, would suggest a short photo-op type of event. The children's teachers do not appear in the photograph, apparently so that the place of the adult can be monopolized by US military personnel.

In the case of Figure 9.15, which again features the recurring theme of native children interacting with US soldiers, one more feature is made apparent. While all of these photographs invite us to share the US military's gaze, in this instance we see that gaze in direct operation as one of the soldiers (at right) is himself taking a photo within this photograph. The event thus appears like a form of military tourism, held under the auspices of humanitarianism. Interestingly, the caption omits any mention of whether these soldiers were responsible for building the new school.

Figure 9.15: Sharing the Gaze

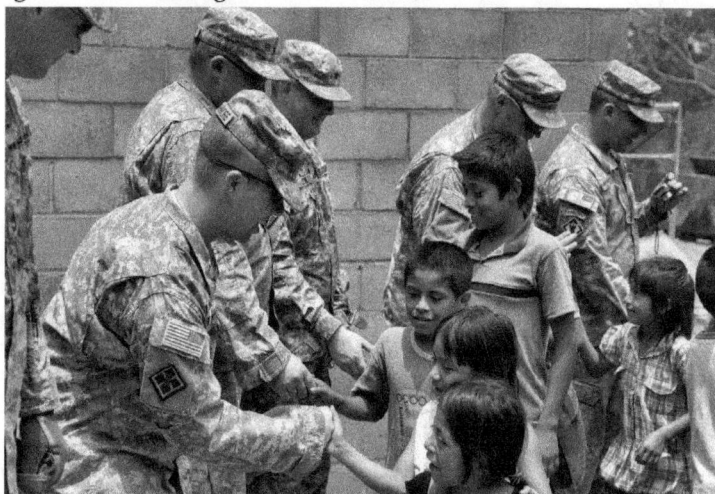

This photograph, taken on May 8, 2014, was captioned as follows: "US Soldiers assigned to the 1430th Engineer Company, Michigan Army National Guard shake hands with Guatemalan school children after touring their new school in Chiquimula, Guatemala, May 8, 2014, during Beyond the Horizon (BTH) 2014. BTH is a recurring chairman of the Joint Chiefs of Staff-directed, US Southern Command-sponsored joint and combined humanitarian exercise in which troops provide services to communities in need while receiving deployment training and building important relationships with partner nations". (DoD photo by Sgt. Austin Berner, US Army)

In addition to photographs featuring native children in various interactions with a variety of US military forces, there is another major theme under the heading of "significant operations imagery" that involves the provision of medical treatment. One such example, that clearly maximizes the leitmotif of bare feet, is shown in Figure 9.16.

Figure 9.16: The Foot Doctor

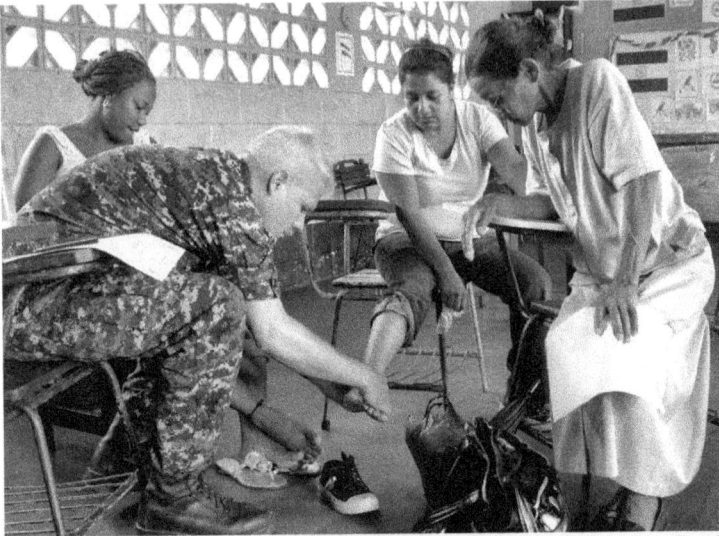

From September 17, 2010, the caption read as follows: "US Navy Cmdr. Tim Burgis, embarked aboard the multipurpose amphibious assault ship USS Iwo Jima (LHD 7), looks at a patient's foot at a medical site in Bluefields, Nicaragua, Sept. 17, 2010. Iwo Jima is anchored off the coast of Nicaragua in support of the Continuing Promise 2010 humanitarian civic assistance mission. (DoD photo by Mass Communication Specialist 1st Class Eric J. Rowley, US Navy)

Figures 9.17 and 9.18 below, in addition to Figure 9.10 above, were chosen to magnify the spread of US military operations across Africa. The active engagement in combat in Africa, from Libya to Somalia, are not featured in the collection—instead we have a large array of "humanitarian" events presented. This is part of the US military's massively increased presence across the broad centre of the African continent, spearheaded by its new combatant command, AFRICOM. Also, we may note the tendency in the photographs to have African-American troops at the forefront of these photographed interactions with African civilians, just as women troops are at the forefront of interactions with children. It is presented enough times that it cannot be mere "tokenism," but it may nonetheless be an effort to camouflage the strange foreignness of the US military presence.

Figure 9.17: A MEDCAP in Djibouti

This photograph, taken on May 4, 2011, was captioned as follows: "US Army Capt. Vincent Fry performs a check on a child from Obock, Djibouti, during a recent medical capacity program (MEDCAP) mission May 5, 2011. Fry and other medical experts from Combined Joint Task Force - Horn of Africa treated more than 1,800 patients for a variety of ailments during the two-day MEDCAP". (DoD photo by Lt. Col. Leslie Pratt, U.S. Air Force)

Figure 9.18: AFRICOM Brings You This New School

From August 20, 2013, the official caption for this photograph was: "US Secretary of the Navy Ray Mabus talks with villagers in Grumesa, Ghana, before a ribbon-cutting ceremony for a new school Aug. 20, 2013. Construction of the school was a US Africa Command-sponsored project that resulted from a trip Mabus took to the region two years earlier, when he was briefed about a lack of schools in the area. Ghana was one of several countries Mabus visited in Africa to meet with US Sailors and Marines, discuss security issues with military and civilian officials and reinforce partnerships with African nations". (DoD photo by Mass Communication Specialist 1st Class Arif Patani, US Navy photo)

There are numerous DoD photographs with a sports theme, showing US forces playing with locals, whether children or adults. Examples are shown in Figures 9.19 and 9.20. The core message seems to be joy, good health, and camaraderie. It also appears as if "interoperability" was not just about developing further ties to local military and security apparatuses, but also penetrating the wider society. Next to medical care (offered for free, without any of the debates about free healthcare that rage on in the US itself), giving toys, skipping rope, cradling, and reading stories, this completes the overall picture presented herein of a US military that persistently thrives to project an image of itself as a leading humanitarian organization. The balancing act is more than a little unsteady, as it involves momentary demilitarization (through a suspension of disbelief) of the image of the military, while clearly portraying the militarization of civilian action such as humanitarian aid.

Figure 9.19: Volleyball in Cambodia

From December 24, 2009, the caption was: "A US Sailor with the mine countermeasures ship USS Avenger (MCM 1) jumps to block a shot during a volleyball game with members of the Royal Cambodian Armed Forces in Sihanoukville, Cambodia, June 15, 2011. The Avenger was in Cambodia as part of a Western Pacific deployment". (DoD photo by US Navy)

Figure 9.20: Militarizing Community Relations in the Philippines

Taken on May 9, 2014, the original caption was: "US Marine Corps Lance Cpl. David B. Doran, left, an administrator with the 9th Engineer Support Battalion, plays basketball with Filipino residents during a community relations project as part of Balikatan 2014 at Air Force City High School in Mabalacat, Philippines, May 9, 2014. Balikatan is an annual bilateral training exercise designed to increase interoperability between the Armed Forces of the Philippines and the US military when responding to natural disasters". (DoD photo by Lance Cpl. Allison DeVries, US Marine Corps)

Finally for this subsection, there is Figure 9.21, still on a sports theme, but a bit of an outlier compared to other photographs in the collection, and one with an ambiguous visual message that it could destabilize the political purposes of such media efforts. Not only is this an unusual image for having been recorded in a domestic context, in New York City, but it might disquiet some viewers to see troops arrayed in front of the New York Stock Exchange, as if underscoring what some astute observers have historically seen as the role of the US military in protecting Wall Street and US-led transnational capitalism. The reviewers who processed and posted this photograph were either unaware of the potentially contradictory messages this image could open up, or they were (hence a question as the title of the image). The photograph thus carries undertones of Smedley Butler (see Appendix B in Volume 2 of this series). On the other hand, and this accounts for some of the ambiguity, it could have been approved because it features military participation in a major annual event in New York, as well as a landmark building in the city, and of course the gigantic US flag, which serves as the essential "summarizing symbol," condensing powerful sentiments of what the system means to an ideal-typical, patriotic American citizen (Ortner, 1973, pp. 1339–1340).

Figure 9.21: A Radical in Our Midst?

This photograph, taken on May 21, 2011, was officially captioned as follows: "US Marines with the 24th Marine Expeditionary Unit lead a run to ground zero in New York City May 31, 2011, as part of Fleet Week New York 2011. More than 3,000 Marines, Sailors and Coast Guardsmen participated in community outreach events and equipment demonstrations in the New York City area for Fleet Week. The week's activities marked the 27th year that the city has hosted the sea services for the celebration". (DoD photo by Sgt. Randall A. Clinton, US Marine Corps)

Significant Programs and Projects Imagery

This category of photographs is described by the US Army as involving events such as the celebration of achieving a milestone of some sort for a specific unit or program, with a typical photo being of a ribbon-cutting ceremony. Figure 9.22 clearly involves the celebration of achieving a milestone, one in particular that often eludes most media and public commentaries on the identity of "our troops," who in the US case consist of a great many non-nationals. This is a group of transnational or migrant soldiers, as they achieve recognition as US citizens. Figure 9.23 continues the theme of the US military spread under the pretext of fighting "terrorism," but without the humanitarian gloss we saw in the previous subsection. It also serves to highlight a military-to-military relationship, conveyed in person. Figure 9.24 is certainly representative of a significant milestone: a rare image of the last unit to leave Iraq. Interesting, apart from the artistry of the photographer, is the otherwise sombre and subdued atmosphere, as if the troops were leaving as quietly as possible, without any fanfare. In colour, with its heavy sand and clay tones blanketing the image, one might think of China's "Terracotta Army": funerary figures buried with the first emperor of China, Qin Shi Huang, in his necropolis.

Figure 9.22: Migrant Soldiers

From February 10, 2012, the official caption for this photograph was as follows: "US Soldiers, Marines and Airmen raise their right hands and swear the oath of citizenship during a naturalization ceremony at Kandahar Airfield in Afghanistan Feb. 10, 2012. The Service members were granted citizenship after receiving their certificates and viewing a congratulatory video message from President Barack Obama". (DoD photo by Sgt. Amanda Hils, US Army)

Figure 9.23: Greeting the "War on Terror" in Tonga

The official caption for this November 9, 2010, photograph was: "Chairman of the Joint Chiefs of Staff Navy Adm. Mike Mullen greets Tonga Defense Service honor guardsmen in Nuku'alofa, Tonga, Nov. 9, 2010. Mullen visited Tonga on the second stop of a Pacific tour to thank the Tongan people for their support of the war on terrorism". (DoD photo by Mass Communication Specialist 1st Class Chad J. McNeeley, U.S. Navy)

Figure 9.24: The Last Unit to Leave Iraq

This photograph was taken on September 28, 2008, was officially captioned as follows: "US Soldiers with Fox Company, 52nd Infantry Regiment, 2nd Battalion, 12th Field Artillery Regiment, 4th Stryker Brigade Combat Team (SBCT), 2nd Infantry Division, United States Division-Center, listen to a convoy brief Aug. 16, 2010, at Contingency Operating

Base Adder, Iraq, during their final convoy out of theater. The 4th SBCT is the last combat brigade to leave Iraq". (DoD photo by Sgt. Kimberly Johnson, U.S. Army/Released)

Civil Military Involvement Imagery

As we know from the category descriptions provided by the US Army, photographs in this range will tend to feature "participation in disaster relief, civil disturbances, and environmental protection". Given the degree of US intervention in Haiti immediately following its earthquake in 2010, numerous photographs express this theme, of which a very small sampling is provided here. In Figure 9.25, we can spot a couple of powerful summarizing symbols, defined by Ortner as symbols "which are seen as summing up, expressing, representing for the participants in an emotionally powerful and relatively undifferentiated way, what the system means to them" (1973, p. 1339). A symbol, such as the US flag, is the centrepiece of Ortner's explanation of what summarizing symbols do. As she elaborated, summarizing symbols constitute a "category of sacred symbols in the broadest sense, and includes all those items which are objects of reverence and/or catalysts of emotion," such as the US flag (prominent in Figure 9.25), or the cross (also in Figure 9.24) (Ortner, 1973, p. 1340). In particular,

> "the American flag…for certain Americans, stands for something called 'the American way,' a conglomerate of ideas and feelings including (theoretically) democracy, free enterprise, hard work, competition, progress, national superiority, freedom, etc. And it stands for them all at once. It does not encourage reflection on the logical relations among these ideas, nor on the logical consequences of them as they are played out in social actuality, over time and history. On the contrary, the flag encourages a sort of all-or-nothing allegiance to the whole package, best summed up on a billboard I saw recently: 'Our flag, love it or leave.' And this is the point about summarizing symbols in general — they operate to compound and synthesize a complex system of ideas, to

'summarize' them under a unitary form which, in an old-fashioned way, 'stands for' the system as a whole". (Ortner, 1973, p. 1340)

Aside from the flag, the cross is the *red cross*, which has become the internationally recognizable symbol of neutral and impartial emergency medical care—except that in this case, it is on a US military vessel. Moreover, the dominant position of ships in Figures 9.25 and 9.26 may evoke a myriad of deep historical associations involving deliverance, rescue, migration, importation, invasion and, in sum, the international reach of power. The ship is the first mass medium of border crossing, and a symbol of globalization that emerged centuries before the first satellite transmission.

The US government is impressed enough with the visual power of these images that Figure 9.26 now appears as the headlining image on the US Agency for International Development's (USAID) site for the Office of US Foreign Disaster Assistance (OFDA).[6] Figure 9.26 also mentions the presence of a Disaster Assistance Response Team (DART)—not to be confused with Canadian teams, which perform the same functions and have the same name—and one can see the acronym on the back of the man's baseball cap, which itself is a recognizable symbol of American identity.

Figure 9.25: From Over the Horizon

The official caption for this September 2, 2011, photograph was: "Family and friends watch as hospital ship USNS Comfort (T-AH 20) docks at Naval Station Norfolk, Va., Sept. 2, 2011, after returning from a five-month deployment in support of Continuing Promise 2011. Continuing Promise is a regularly scheduled mission to countries in Central and South America and the Caribbean, where the US Navy and its partnering nations work with host nations and a variety of governmental and nongovernmental agencies to train in civil-military operations". (DoD photo by Mass Communication Specialist 2nd Class Rafael Martie, US Navy)

Figure 9.26: An AID DART into Haiti

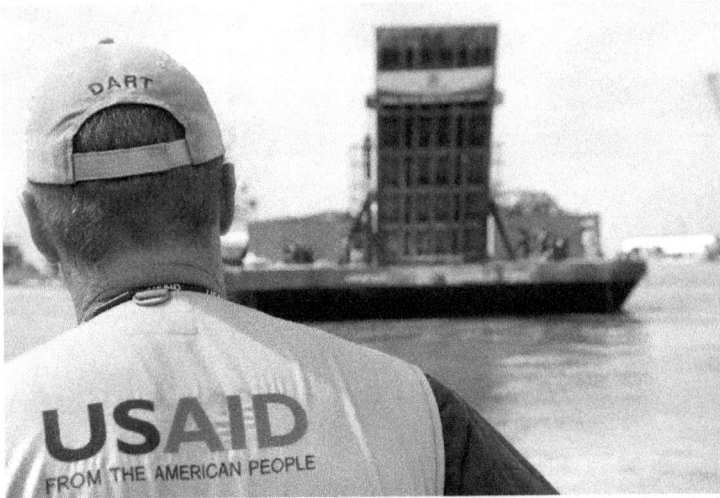

From January 26, 2010, the official caption was: "A member of the United States Agency for International Development's (USAID) Disaster Assistance Response Team looks on as humanitarian relief supplies from Puerto Rico arrive in Port-au-Prince, Haiti, Jan. 26, 2010, as part of Operation Unified Response". (DoD photo by Mass Communication Specialist 2nd Class Chris Lussie, US Navy)

The dramatic shift over the past decade that witnessed the militarization of US foreign aid, is represented in Figures 9.27 and 9.28. The photographs show far more artistry, or artifice, than a mere ethnographic documentary record—emphasizing angle of vision especially. In Figure 9.27, the US military officer is strategically placed beneath "Hope for Haiti"—he is the prime actor here, leaning forward with determination, and the Haitian man is the recipient. In Figure 9.28, more of a portrait than an objective recording, there is a play with light and shadow: a large mass of bags of aid delivered, and outside the door in the light, the military instrument that delivered the bounty. These are efforts to incessantly remind Americans and the rest of the world: *we* help *them*, *they* depend on *us*. Even just visually/symbolically (let alone practically), the US is thus still the primary beneficiary of its aid program.

Figure 9.27: Hope for Haiti

This was photograph was taken on November 8, 2010. Its official caption was as follows: "US Navy Cmdr. Mark Becker, left, the mission commander of Southern Partnership Station (SPS), greets Robenson Lucceus, a public relations coordinator for International Child Care, prior to turning over a mobile medical clinic to the organization in Port-au-Prince, Haiti, Nov. 8, 2010. The clinic, donated as part of Project Handclasp, was delivered by high speed vessel Swift (HSV-2) as part of the SPS mission. Project Handclasp transports educational, humanitarian and goodwill materials on a space-available basis aboard US Navy ships. SPS is a deployment of various specialty platforms to the US Southern Command area of responsibility". (DoD photo by Mass Communication Specialist 2nd Class Ricardo J. Reyes, US Army)

Figure 9.28: This Food Aid was Brought to You by...

From August 7, 2010, this photograph's official caption read as follows: "A CH-47 Chinook helicopter carrying disaster relief supplies is shown prior to a humanitarian mission in Khyber Pakhtunkhwa, Pakistan, Aug. 7, 2010. Humanitarian relief and evacuation missions are being conducted as part of the disaster relief efforts to assist Pakistanis in flood-stricken regions of the nation". (DoD photo by Staff Sgt. Horace Murray, US Army)

Construction Imagery

Given that the stated aim of this category of photographs is to represent US forces constructing, repairing, or maintaining buildings and other public facilities, this would seem to be motivated to produce images that are the opposite of the US' once noteworthy COMCAM recordings of buildings being bombed or struck by missiles. Rather than destruction then, the US military here reaches for the opposite: construction. In fact, there is no single image in the DoD Flickr account of any target destroyed in combat. It is this direct and obvious avoidance of the very realities created by the US military itself, which recommends use of the term "propaganda" for these images, in the popularly understood sense of the term propaganda. While Figure 9.15 might have also come under the heading of construction imagery, a more common example would be what we see in Figure 9.29. (On a technical note, there is an unusual line around each person shown in Figure 9.29, either a black line around the entire contour of the body, or a white line. This is present in the original, and is not a product of editing for reproduction here.)

Figure 9.29: Painting Walls in Vietnam

From June 9, 2010, the caption for this photograph was: "US Sailors embarked aboard the Military Sealift Command hospital ship USNS Mercy (T-AH 19) paint the living facilities at the Binh Dinh Leprosy Hospital in Quy Nhon, Vietnam, June 10, 2010, during Pacific Partnership 2010. Mercy is in Vietnam conducting the fifth in a series of annual US Pacific Fleet humanitarian and civic assistance endeavors to strengthen regional partnerships". (DoD photo by Mass Communication Specialist 3rd Class Matthew Jackson, US Navy)

Significant Military Events Imagery

This category is somewhat mixed in terms of how its contents are described by the US Army, which can range from the granting of medals to the deployment of troops. Given the degree to which the "support the troops" mantra has been institutionalized in US popular consciousness, it is interesting to note the *relative* scarcity of images such as Figure 9.30 in the DoD's collection, which involve granting medals for heroic action. I can offer no explanation for this, apart from the speculation that other objectives (such as those above) are more urgent representational priorities, especially for an international audience.

Figure 9.30: President Obama Presents a Medal of Honour

Taken on May 13, 2014, this photograph's official caption was: "President Barack Obama presents the Medal of Honor to former US Army Sgt. Kyle J. White during a ceremony May 13, 2014, at the White House in Washington, DC. White was recognized for exposing himself to enemy fire to save the lives of coalition troops during an attack in Aranas, Afghanistan, Nov. 9, 2007. White had been assigned to Chosen Company, 2nd Battalion, 503rd Infantry Regiment, 173rd Airborne Brigade Combat Team at the time of the battle". (DoD photo by Sgt. Mikki L. Sprenkle, US Army)

Military Life Imagery

The final category of photographs, following the US Army's guide in the last section, is a general one, not very well marked off from the others, but that includes within it examples such as soldiers at work, physical training (or exercise), the use of new equipment, and enjoyment of "life as a military family". Arguably, the images presented below would sit well within this category. It is a reasonable assumption that the purpose of this category is to spotlight persuasive images that will boost recruitment and retention. Whereas families grieve, this particular "family" (as photographed) has known very few instances of witnessing the return of caskets with troops killed in action, few funerals, and only occasional graveside visits. Indeed, such images are very late additions to this collection. Instead, families tend to be shown as always in the process of being reunited, forever coming home, yet somehow never leaving.

Figure 9.31 is the paradigmatic, traditional American representation of this reuniting, worthy of comparison with *Life* magazine's now iconic photo from New York's Times Square on V-J Day (August 27, 1945), of a sailor kissing a nurse. It is by no means far-fetched to expect today's military photographers to be steeped in the dominant visual and symbolic norms of their culture and to be trained in a practice that builds on "what works" — and again, whether they do so consciously or not does not matter. The blue sky (in the original), added to the bright white dress and the wife's red shoes, is a composition that only accentuates the colours of the small American flag she is waving with her right hand, as if to double the flag.

Figure 9.31: Reunited

This photograph, from July 29, 2009, was captioned as follows: "US Navy Lt. j.g. Peter Goodman greets his wife during a homecoming

ceremony for the guided-missile frigate USS Klakring (FFG 42) in May-
port, Fla., July 29, 2009. Klakring is returning from a deployment conducting theater security cooperation engagements with regional nations
in the US 6th Fleet area of responsibility". (DoD photo by Mass Communication Specialist 2nd Class Gary B. Granger Jr., US Navy)

Of course, families must also eat together. There are a
few such photographs of meals shared collectively, in the
DoD's collection. Figure 9.32, when viewed together with
its original caption, conveys a number of strong,
controversial messages. One is the traditional image of the
African-American man serving meals — possibly not
intentional, but likely to conjure up such associations
among at least some viewers nevertheless. The other is that
it is Thanksgiving Day, and traditional US fare is being
served to US troops *and* their Honduran counterparts. This
form of culinary colonization is, at least in the Central
American context, a known method for resocializing local
troops to eat like Americans and less like the peasant
families they came from, in order to break cultural bonds
of familial identification. A classic telling of this comes
from the Salvadoran writer, Manlio Argueta, in his 1980
novel, *One Day of Life*. In that novel, a newly recruited
member of El Salvador's US-trained Special Forces
describes the meals served by their *gringo* trainers:

> "Imagine, take mashed potatoes, for example, which I
> didn't know shit about. I'll explain it to you: it's
> something like mashed corn but it's potatoes, all beaten
> up or ground up, you wouldn't believe it....I don't even
> know why they call it purée. Look, I'll tell you
> something to be frank, and pardon my language, purée
> looks like shit except it smells like semen. Can you
> imagine being forced to eat it?...Mornings, we have
> orange juice and a kind of milk called yogurt. Well, the
> little juice is all right, but the yogurt, what the fuck is
> that? Pardon my expression; well, so you'll know, if the
> purée smells like semen, yogurt is almost semen itself".
> (Argueta, 1991 [1980], pp. 91–92)

Figure 9.32: American Thanksgiving in Honduras

Taken on November 27, 2013: "US Army Command Sgt. Maj. Norriel Fahie, assigned to the Army Support Activity, serves Thanksgiving dinner to a member of Joint Task Force-Bravo in the dining facility at Soto Cano Air Base, Honduras, Nov. 28, 2013. Members of Joint Task Force-Bravo and their Honduran counterparts were treated to a Thanksgiving Day meal with all the trimmings in celebration of the holiday. Joint Task Force-Bravo leadership, as well as leaders from the Army Support Activity, Army Forces Battalion, Joint Security Forces, 612th Air Base Squadron, 1-228th Aviation Regiment, and Medical Element wore their dress uniforms and served the members of the task force". (DoD photo by Capt. Zach Anderson US Air Force)

Military personnel "at work" are also a key element of this category, and here we may find an almost countless number of images depending on how one defines "at work". For the sake of simplification and efficiency, I have narrowed this down to a particular subset of images involving routine, everyday maintenance work and other basic chores that stand apart from everything shown thus far. For example, as in Figure 9.33, there are many photographs of US military personnel in very tight places: inside engines and inside tubes, intakes, and shafts of various sorts, performing maintenance tasks. These contrast strikingly with the everyday maintenance tasks that many Americans would be familiar with, such as changing their engine oil or installing a new blade on the lawnmower.

These images instead boast of complex and possibly risky technical challenges in maintaining complex military machines of daunting size. The images are thus a celebration of both modernization and American "can do". Other images, such as Figures 9.34 and 9.35, represent a common visual motif of the collection, showing military personnel as tiny beings visible through small openings in colossal, titanic walls of steel or aluminum. The contrast appears to be a boast of technological monumentality, of imposing weight, of the gargantuan constructions of the US military, one whose very blueprints seem to mandate global rule.

Figure 9.33: Tube City

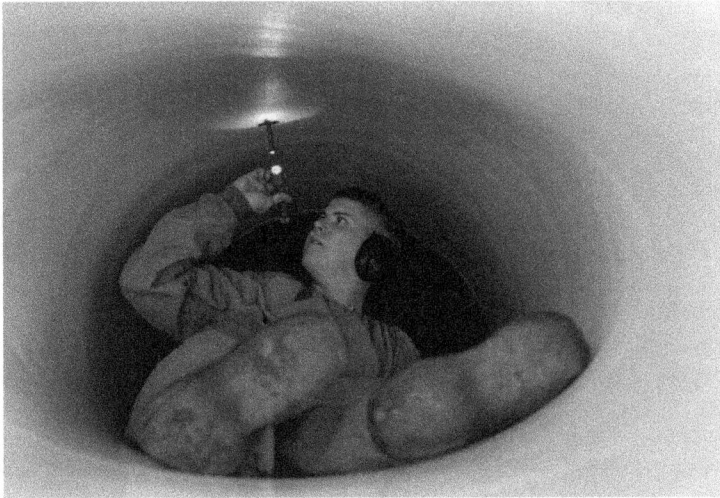

April 12, 2013: "US Air Force Senior Airman Logan Sponsel, a crew chief assigned to the 169th Aircraft Maintenance Squadron, South Carolina Air National Guard, inspects the intake of an F-16 Fighting Falcon aircraft during a phase II readiness exercise April 12, 2013, at McEntire Joint National Guard Base, SC. The exercise was intended to evaluate the 169th Fighter Wing's ability to operate in a chemical warfare environment". (DoD photo by Staff Sgt. Jorge Intriago, US Air National Guard)

Figure 9.34: Mooring a Giant

April 15, 2014: "US Sailors observe the mooring process aboard the amphibious assault ship USS Boxer (LHD 4) after the ship arrived April 15,
2014, at Joint Base Pearl Harbor-Hickam, Hawaii. The Boxer conducted
a deployment in the US 5th Fleet and 7th Fleet areas of responsibility and
participated in Ssang Yong 14 during Marine Expeditionary Force Exercise (MEFEX) 2014. MEFEX 2014 was a US Marine Corps Forces Pacific-
sponsored series of exercises between the US Navy and Marine Corps
and South Korean forces. Among the exercises were the Korean Marine
Exchange Program, Freedom Banner 14, Ssang Yong 14, Key Resolve 14
and the Combined Marine Component Command 14 command post
exercise. (DoD by Mass Communication Specialist 3rd Class Diana Quinlan, US Navy photo)

Figure 9.35: A Wall of Metal

April 21, 2013: "A US Sailor aboard the aircraft carrier USS John C. Stennis (CVN 74) issues directions to line handlers pierside upon arrival to Joint Base Pearl Harbor-Hickam, Hawaii, April 21, 2013. The John C. Stennis Carrier Strike Group was returning from an eight-month deployment to the US 5th Fleet and US 7th Fleet areas of responsibility". (DoD photo by Mass Communication Specialist 3rd Class Diana Quinlan, US Navy)

Physical training and trying equipment are also entered as elements of this category. Not infrequently, these images take on a bit of a "sci-fi" lustre that would appeal to the mainstream of western popular culture. Here one can see everything from men launching mysterious hand-held drones (Figure 9.36), to joggers with gas masks (Figure 9.37), to a rare admission of a "posed" photograph in the case of a radar screen's projection on a man's face (Figure 9.38), with electrical blue, green and yellow colours in the original. Elements of power that are highlighted here range from the muscular to the robotic to the cybernetic.

Figure 9.36: Hand Launching a Mini Drone in Iraq

October 9, 2009: "US Army 1st Lt. Steven Rose launches an RQ-11 Raven unmanned aerial vehicle near a new highway bridge project along the Euphrates River north of Al Taqqadum, Iraq, Oct. 9, 2009. Rose is assigned to Charlie Company, 1st Battalion, 504th Parachute Infantry Regiment, 1st Brigade Combat Team, 82nd Airborne Division, which is assisting Iraqi police in providing security for the work site". (DoD photo by Spc. Michael J. MacLeod, US Army)

Figure 9.37: Jogging through Chemical Warfare

February 21, 2010: "Embarked Marines assigned to the 31st Marine Expeditionary Unit (MEU) run, wearing gas masks on the flight deck for an early morning physical exercise aboard amphibious dock landing ship the USS Harpers Ferry (LSD 49). Harpers Ferry is a part of the forward-deployed Essex Amphibious Ready Group (ARG) and is conducting Spring Patrol to the Western Pacific Ocean". (US Navy photo by Gas Turbine System Technician Mechanical Chief Joel Monsalud)

Figure 9.38: I, Robot

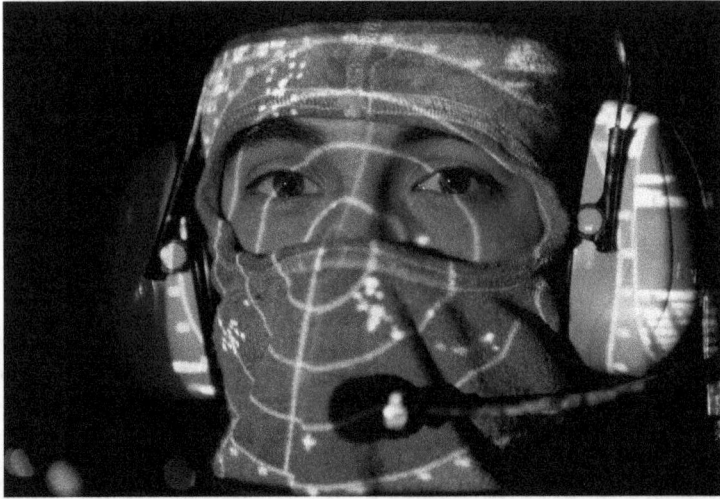

May 19, 2013: "A US Sailor portrays combat readiness in a posed photo aboard the amphibious transport dock ship USS San Antonio (LPD 17) during International Mine Countermeasures Exercise (IMCMEX) 13 in Bahrain May 19, 2013. IMCMEX is an international symposium and exercise designed to enhance cooperation, mutual maritime capabilities and long-term regional stability between the US and its international partners". (DoD photo by Mass Communication Specialist 3rd Class Lacordrick Wilson, US Navy)

Finally, another aspect of collective "military life" that features enjoyment and entertainment are the not uncommon performances by major pop music acts that star in concerts for the troops in locations distant from the US. It is perhaps thanks to the scenes of surreal vulgarity and out-of-place rock concerts in the film *Apocalypse Now*, that we do not see more images such as Figure 9.39 in the DoD collection. The collection in fact barely contains even a minimal sampling of the wide range of star performances by major names in the US music industry that have taken place far and wide across US military deployments overseas.

Figure 9.39: Ashanti for War

July 4, 2013: "The singer Ashanti performs during a concert for Service members at the Transit Center at Manas, Kyrgyzstan, July 4, 2013". (DoD photo by Staff Sgt. Krystie Martinez, US Air Force)

Beyond Realism, Beneath Good Intentions

The final set of images in the DoD collection exceed the boundaries of the stated categories and their typical examples. Here we see the US military as an almost independent actor on an equal footing with the civilian political administration of the US, one well known to be capable of outshining and outmanoeuvring civilian agencies of government in terms of funding, political clout, and public visibility. Though comparatively minimal in number, in light of the many other photographs in its collection, the DoD itself produces images attesting to the fruition of the military-industrial complex in the arenas of mainstream mass media and in the conduct of foreign policy. For example, in Figures 9.40, 9.41, 9.42, 9.43, and 9.44, Admiral Mike Mullen's appearances on *The Daily Show* with Jon Stewart are featured, along with an intimate scene of backstage banter; a meeting with a bejewelled Katie Couric at a gala event; and, appearances that show an altogether cozy relationship between the media and the military. (It also appears that Mullen had a photographer dedicated to him, as all of the photographs in which he appears were taken by the same individual, over a period of two years at least.) We see media celebrities, euphemistically referred to as journalists, present at elite events where they are united with the military and corporate executives for shared causes that revolve around military needs. The images show the range of stances of media personalities: deference, proud association, and familial amicability. It would be a reasonable reaction to see this as more fashionable-looking form of Soviet media; these few images bear traces of relationships that have reduced journalists to private information contractors of the state or, in other words, regime media.

Figure 9.40: Military-Media Friendship

June 16, 2011: "Chairman of the Joint Chiefs of Staff Navy Adm. Mike Mullen, left, speaks with TV host Jon Stewart June 16, 2011, at the Stand Up for Heroes dinner in Washington, DC. The event, sponsored by the Bob Woodruff Foundation, gathered more than 800 people including military officials, corporate executives, media members and congressional leaders to increase awareness and raise funds to assist injured Service members, veterans and their families". (DoD photo by Mass Communication Specialist 1st Class Chad J. McNeeley)

Figure 9.41: Admiral Mullen on The Daily Show

January 6, 2010: "Jon Stewart interviews Chairman of the Joint Chiefs of Staff Adm. Mike Mullen, US Navy, during an airing of the Daily Show with Jon Stewart in New York City on Jan. 6, 2010". (DoD photo by Petty Officer 1st Class Chad J. McNeeley, US Navy)

Figure 9.42: Admiral Mullen on CBS' Face the Nation

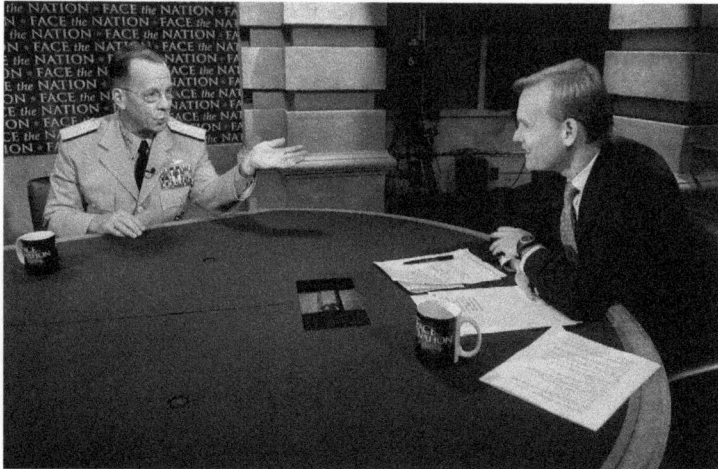

July 5, 2009: "Chairman of the Joint Chiefs of Staff Navy Adm. Mike Mullen gives an interview to John Dickerson during the CBS news program Face the Nation in Washington, DC, July 5, 2009. During the interview, Mullen discussed the wars in Iraq and Afghanistan, North Korea's recent missile tests and his recent visit to Russia. (DoD photo by Mass Communication Specialist 1st Class Chad J. McNeeley, US Navy)

Figure 9.43: Katie Couric and Admiral Mullen

October 15, 2009: "CBS Evening News anchor Katie Couric greets Chairman of the Joint Chiefs of Staff Navy Adm. Mike Mullen and his wife Deborah during the Alfred E. Smith Memorial Foundation Dinner at the Waldorf-Astoria Hotel in New York City, NY, Oct. 15, 2009". (DoD photo by Mass Communication Specialist 1st Class Chad J. McNeeley, US Navy)

Figure 9.44: The Military-Media-Academia Complex

October 5, 2009: "From left, Chairman of the George Washington University (GWU) Board of Trustees Russell Ramsey, CNN Chief International Correspondent Christiane Amanpour, Secretary of State Hillary

Rodham Clinton, Secretary of Defense Robert M. Gates, Director of GWU School of Media and Public Affairs Frank Sesno and President of GWU Steven Knapp pose for a photograph before the start of an interview at the university in Washington, DC, Oct. 5, 2009. (DoD photo by Master Sgt. Jerry Morrison, US Air Force)

Continuing from Figure 9.44, we rarely get glimpses in the DoD collection of the renewed ties between the military and academia and the US and the increased militarization of US university campuses since September 11, 2001. Figure 9.45 provides some small visual testament to that fact, in an otherwise unremarkable photograph that is easy to miss. The caption is of greater interest, as it points to the creation of special programs that raise students with military ties to a privileged place of greater attention and care on campus.

Figure 9.45: The Militarized Campus

October 3, 2012: "Jill Biden, the wife of Vice President Joe Biden, speaks about being a military mother as US Army Gen. Raymond T. Odierno, the chief of staff of the Army, looks on during an event for Operation Educate the Educators, a Joining Forces initiative, Oct. 3, 2012, at George Mason University in Fairfax, Va. During the event, it was announced that more than 100 colleges and universities had signed the Joining Forces commitment to help prepare educators to lead classrooms that are more responsive to the social, emotional and academic needs of military children". (US Army photo by Staff Sgt. Teddy Wade)

There are also a few photographs, such as 9.46 and 9.47, showing the military branch of government directly engaged in the conduct of foreign policy. These can include images of military officers, who though they may not be of the highest rank are nonetheless meeting with heads of state or government. There are also images of the civilian Defense Secretary meeting with counterparts abroad. It is interesting to note the absence of US civilian diplomatic staff from these photographs, which privilege the US military relationship with foreign leaders. In a limited manner then, we are presented with traces of some of the major changes in the international profile of the US since its self-declared "war on terror" began, that boosts the military face of the US abroad. It is limited in extent in the DoD collection, primarily because the collection does not exist to serve the purposes of deeper discussion and debate, but to recruit, win hearts and minds, boast, and bolster ideological agendas such as "humanitarian intervention" and the "war on terror".

Figure 9.46: US Navy Office Meets Liberia's President Ellen Johnson-Sirleaf

September 15, 2009: "Liberian President Ellen Johnson-Sirleaf greets US Navy Chief Boatswain's Mate Timothy Kelker in Monrovia, Liberia, Sept. 15, 2009, during the closing reception for a two-week medical civil action project (MEDCAP) in support of Africa Partnership Station (APS). During the MEDCAP, medical teams attached to HSV-2 Swift provided medicine, examinations and treatment to more than 2000 residents. APS is an international initiative under US Naval Forces Europe/Africa that brings together US, European and African partners to enhance maritime safety and security on the African continent. (DoD photo by Mass Communication Specialist 1st Class Dan Meaney, US Navy)

Figure 9.47: Meeting with Saudi Arabia's Defence Minister

December 9, 2013: "US Secretary of Defense Chuck Hagel, right, greets Saudi Arabian Minister of Defense Crown Prince Salman bin Abdulaziz Al Saud in Riyadh, Saudi Arabia, Dec. 9, 2013. Hagel met with various leaders to discuss issues of mutual importance". (DoD photo by Erin A. Kirk-Cuomo)

Other photographs whose contents either exceed the boundaries of the categories we have covered, or that justifiably belong in categories of their own, concern the technological instruments of war themselves. Various weapons systems are imbued with a kind of agency in a variety of artistically conceived images; gone is any pretence of scientific-realism and objective recording. Instead, what appears to take over is *love*. These are adoring views of hardware and its prowess. For example, in the stylistically identical cases of Figures 9.48 and 9.49, that share the same colouration in the originals as well, we are presented with what look like gleaming alien vessels, the first is a Global Hawk drone, and the second a Globemaster air freighter—attending the Globemaster is a "loadmaster," and those supervising paratroopers who will jump from the plane are "jumpmasters". The prevalence of the words *globe*, *global*, and *master* is noteworthy, as these are the new symbols of US supremacy posed as globalization.

In Figures 9.50 and 9.51 we instead go back in time, in symbolic terms, to the cowboy romance of the dusty plains in the Old West. This is quite an established genre of photography, and even now the Internet contains mountains of photographs of cowboys and horses at sunset. It would be impossible for the military photographers to have remained immune to these cultural codes. Rather than the lone cowboy or gun-slinging hero riding off into the sunset, however, we encounter very many images of a helicopter or a transport plane set against a giant sun in a marvellous sunset. Surely such images cannot be reduced or framed as mere "documentary records": the artifice is too imposing, too structured and respectful of American lore and cultural convention, that they are meant to produce and reinforce a message and not simply "record" one impartially. The captioning, in these cases, is meant as a superficial formality, a control mechanism that suggests that there really was no emotional or artistic point to these images, which stand as stunning advertising for the private corporations which produced these machines under contract with the Pentagon. Note also that these images are not isolated incidents: this style has been produced, from what I have seen, over a period of at least four years in the DoD collection, by different photographers. This suggests schooling and a set of guidelines unlike the ones shared with the public.

Figure 9.48: Global Hawk

November 25, 2010: "US Air Force maintenance technicians conduct preflight checks on an RQ-4 Global Hawk unmanned aerial vehicle assigned to the 380th Expeditionary Operations Group at an undisclosed location in Southwest Asia Nov. 23, 2010". (DoD photo by Staff Sgt. Andy M. Kin, US Air Force)

Figure 9.49: Globemaster

December 11, 2010: "US Air Force Senior Airman Raheem Crockett, a loadmaster with the 17th Airlift Squadron, inspects the engines of a C-17A Globemaster III as the aircrew conducts pre-flight checks before a mission in support of Operation Toy Drop at Joint Base Charleston, SC, Dec. 11, 2010. Operation Toy Drop is an annual combined service philanthropic project where, in exchange for a donated toy, thousands of paratroopers receive a lottery ticket for the chance to jump with international jumpmasters and earn foreign jump wings". (DoD photo by Tech Sgt. Manuel J. Martinez, US Air Force)

Figure 9.50: Hercules Rides Off into the Sunset

May 2, 2014: "A US Air Force C-130E Hercules aircraft takes off during Emerald Warrior 14 at the Stennis International Airport in Kiln, Miss., May 2, 2014. Emerald Warrior is a US Special Operations Command-sponsored two-week joint/combined tactical exercise designed to provide realistic military training in an urban setting". (DoD photo by Senior Airman Colville McFee, US Air Force)

Figure 9.51: Seahawks Flying into the Setting Sun

October 9, 2013: "A US Navy MH-60S Seahawk helicopter, bottom, assigned to Helicopter Sea Combat Squadron (HSC) 7 and an MH-60R Seahawk helicopter assigned to Helicopter Maritime Strike Squadron (HSM) 74 patrol near the aircraft carrier USS Harry S. Truman (CVN 75) in the Gulf of Oman Oct. 3, 2013. The Harry S. Truman, the flagship for the Harry S. Truman Carrier Strike Group, was deployed to the US 5th Fleet area of responsibility conducting maritime security operations and theater security cooperation efforts in support of Operation Enduring Freedom". (DoD photo by Mass Communication Specialist Seaman Karl Anderson, US Navy)

Figure 9.52: Seahawk Sunset in the Persian Gulf

March 26, 2011: "A US Navy HH-60H Seahawk helicopter assigned to Helicopter Anti-Submarine Squadron (HS) 15 conducts plane guard duties for the aircraft carrier USS Carl Vinson (CVN 70) at sunset March 26, 2011, in the Persian Gulf. The Carl Vinson Carrier Strike Group is deployed supporting maritime security operations and theater security cooperation efforts in the US 5th Fleet area of responsibility". (DoD photo by Mass Communication Specialist Seaman Timothy A. Hazel, US Navy)

In a further twist on the humanitarian gloss, there is a strikingly significant number of photographs in the DoD collection that feature troops dressed as Santa Claus, even in warzones. The more common application is to feature Santa Claus or Santa's Little Helper figures handing out gifts — these may be gifts to troops, or gifts to local villagers in an effort to win hearts and minds. Again, these are not isolated occurrences: they are an established visual theme across all of the armed services' Flickr accounts, stretching back at least five years. Seemingly everything in the US has gone to war, resulting in the production of a counterinsurgent Santa Claus — see Figures 9.53, 9.54, and 9.55.

Figure 9.53: Santa Claus and a Little Helper Perform a Cargo Airdrop

December 24, 2013: "US Soldiers assigned to Combined Joint Special Operations Task Force-Afghanistan look out over the Afghan countryside from the rear of an aircraft Dec. 24, 2013, after dropping bundles containing care packages, Christmas stockings and mail to Soldiers stationed at a remote base in eastern Afghanistan". (DoD photo by Capt. Thomas Cieslak, US Army)

Figure 9.54: Santa Claus in Helmand province, Afghanistan

December 24, 2012: "US Marine Corps Gen. James F. Amos, left, the commandant of the Marine Corps, speaks to Service members during a Christmas Eve show at Camp Leatherneck, Helmand province, Afghanistan, Dec. 24, 2012." (DoD photo by Staff Sgt. Ezekiel R. Kitandwe, US Marine Corps)

Figure 9.55: Santa Claus and Operation Goodwill

December 16, 2009: "U.S. Marine Corps Master Gunnery Sgt. Joseph Haggins, dressed as Santa Claus, presents a gift to a Filipino child during Operation Goodwill at the Manila Day Care Center in Manila, Philippines, Dec. 16, 2009. The operation gives US Marines and their families stationed in Okinawa, Japan, an opportunity to spread goodwill in the region during the holiday season". (DoD photo by Sgt. Leon M. Branchaud, US Marine Corps)

Finally: women and girls (Figures 9.56 and 9.57). In a regime of global military dominance that proclaims the salvation of oppressed women in target nations, it is not surprising to find the occasional iconic photographic of the veiled woman or little girl in the DoD's Flickr collection. Thus in Figure 9.56 we have a Salvadoran girl, positioned next to a map of Central America, as if she were the part that represents the whole. Figure 9.57 presents a veiled woman—*any will do*, the only significant detail that this photograph seeks to draw attention to is her dress. However the captions, as is often the case, fail to explain or candidly admit why these photographs were taken. These images stand out from others in that women and girls are alone in these photographs, without US forces present within the image frame. They thus take on the status of a target, the object that awaits liberation by the US, the purported raison d'être for its "humanitarian" missions and its strident defence of "human rights," abroad. In many ways, as described by Pas (2013), gender has become an instrument of US imperialism, ever in search of a damsel in distress to liberate from a male adversary.

Figure 9.56: Central America as a Little Girl

May 29, 2013: "A girl watches as US Soldiers assigned to Joint Task Force Jaguar work on a new school in support of Beyond the Horizon (BTH) 2013 in Sonsonate, El Salvador, May 29, 2013. BTH is a Chairman of the Joint Chiefs of Staff-directed, US Southern Command-sponsored joint and combined field training humanitarian exercise in which troops specializing in engineering, construction and health care provide much-needed services to communities in need while receiving valuable deployment training and building important relationships with partner nations". (DoD photo by Spc. Aaron Smith, US Army)

Figure 9.57: The Veiled Woman

January 6, 2013: "A woman walks down a sidewalk in Farah City, Afghanistan, Jan. 6, 2012". (DoD photo by Lt. j.g. Matthew Stroup, US Navy)

What is Missing?

What is not shown in the DoD collection, that instead are established facts of US military intervention abroad (such as torture, bombardment of civilians, drone strikes, etc.) could occupy volumes. However, what is important to note here is what could have been shown that would *not* have greatly disturbed the propaganda intent of the DoD's collection, and could even have served it, but was left out nonetheless out of an apparent fear of any chance of political contamination. For example, of the 9,963 photos examined for this project, only 73 showed Barack Obama, the official Commander-in-Chief, and the only such Commander since the Flickr account was instituted. Michelle Obama herself is shown nearly half as many times. Accounting for this minimization is difficult; one might speculate that it is part of an attempt to create a neutral, de-politicized veneer for the collection. This would complement the de-militarized glaze, that is, where there are no photographs of actual warfare, and no scene where anyone is bleeding. In Flickr, the Pentagon has achieved zero-casualty warfare, which is why I argued at the outset that what is presented is a utopian, virtual world. Israel, a major partner of the US in the Middle East is not ignored, but in light of the collection as a whole it would be easy to forget seeing any photographs involving Israeli figures, having been kept at a minimum.

Aside from this, among the gaps in our knowledge that the Pentagon documents do not address, is how these photographs are accessed by "the public". Are the "views" entirely the product of the US military pushing links to those photographs in social media? Are the photographs reproduced by mainstream media? Do "viewers" find the photographs accidentally, through more or less related Internet searches? Do viewers who go to the Pentagon's Flickr site view discrete images, one by one, or do they use the "play" function and view them all as part of a continuous sequence? If the photographs are meant to tell a "visual story" about the US military, are they each meant to tell this story individually, or are they meant to do so collectively? I have addressed these questions to the Department of Defense and at the time of writing, months later, still did not receive a reply.

Conclusion: The Visual Imperium

"I am the eye in the sky
Looking at you
I can read your mind.
I am the maker of rules
Dealing with fools
I can cheat you blind.
And I don't need to see any more
To know that
I can read your mind." — Alan Parsons Project, "Eye in the Sky"

One of the possibly more fruitful areas of inquiry to come out of studies of contemporary imperialism could be one that looks at imperialism's multi-sensory lines of attack, especially when it hooks into domains of consumption and entertainment. This is clearly what the US military is doing by entering Flickr—it does not need Flickr to host its photographs, after all, just like most western defence ministries do not use Flickr and instead rely on their own government's websites to host images. Social media, however, is where the "mass audiences" allegedly are, and that is where the Pentagon thus wants to be too. This project thus had to do with the seeding of social media by the US military, a topic which has interested me for several years now. But what is the importance of the photograph?

In answering this last question, I will reprise some of what we know about the status of the photograph in western societies such as the US. Photographic images have enjoyed virtually unlimited authority in modern society, furnishing a sense of knowledge gained yet dissociated from personal experience. In this sense, the image-world has increasingly come to substitute for the concrete world of actuality. People in our society have been trained to experience reality as a set of images, as a reflection of appearances. Popular commentary on momentous events, such as 9/11, will frequently resort to this sort of reflection: "it happened like in a movie". The modern, western image consumer may thus feel that reality can be possessed through images of reality, especially when images are believed to be realistic records. Some have argued that images have become the dominant language of the modern world. As Susan Sontag argued,

> "a society becomes 'modern' when one of its chief activities is producing and consuming images, when images that have extraordinary powers to determine our demands upon reality and are themselves coveted substitutes for firsthand experience become indispensable to the health of the economy, the stability of the polity, and the pursuit of private happiness". (Sontag, 2005 [1973], p. 119)

Images also enlarge realities, by eliminating the physical distance that separates the viewer from the viewed. Photography has thus played a fundamental role in the westernized globalization of the world, as a technology of *capture*, at the heart of what I referred to as *abduction* in the introductory chapter to this volume. It is thus an excellent complement to globalized military capture. It is a useful technology too, coming as it does with a boast of realism that is preserved even now, though not without challenge. In light of the geopolitical facts of US dominance, the Pentagon turns to photography understanding "the power of photographs to legitimize" those facts (Banks, 2001, p. 47). What the Pentagon thus also achieves is a continued Euro-American positioning of sight as primary among the human senses, thus fortifying the imperium of vision — now all the Pentagon has to do is establish the primacy of *its* vision.

The Pentagon's photographs appropriate other people's realities and reframe them to suit the US' strategic objectives, thus photography acts as a device that controls and instructs. The photographs are part of a pictorial propaganda system — propaganda not because they are "false" in any simple and naïve sense, but because they are primarily conceived as part of a global public relations campaign to sway minds.

But do they sway minds? These photographic media campaigns, such as the Pentagon's, represent a virtual conquest, but there is little actual danger of these images acting on anyone, and no evidence that anything in the "real world" has been altered by this campaign. At worst, they legitimize and reinforce what has long been established by colonialism, in broad terms, since the US' own westward expansion, its wars against Indians, and its annexationist ventures in the Caribbean and Pacific. Flickr then simply becomes the newest means of encoding what has long been coded: the civilization-barbarism dichotomy, the focus on women in other societies, the public health campaigns, schooling, contrasts in clothing, gazing at cultural others, the bare feet, the Old West, Thanksgiving,

Santa Claus, technological supremacy, and US empire as a gift to humanity. If there is one achievement that US military photographers can properly boast about, it is that they have gained expertise in the visual conventions that have become hegemonic in their culture and national ideology.

However, those photographers and the ones who direct them can also claim to have added or fortified some newer conventions, associated with the more recent ideology of globalization as progressive Americanization. The photographs can thus be "read" as depicting a world rendered frictionless by US movement. Speed is implied by the kinds of vehicles that are featured, while ubiquity is read in the numerous geographic locations of the various exercises and campaigns shown. *Technology is the ultimate solution* — that is what these images collectively promote. Yet, there is another reality to this US-dominated, globalist imagery — the lack of depth. There is a socio-cultural *thinness* about these photographs: multiple, discrete pictures, offered in rapid succession and abundant amounts, extricated from local contexts, which can produce an effect of *range without depth*. Range without depth is akin to the experience of *flight*. It's not surprising that a military that relies so heavily on aerial dominance (because life on the ground gets too messy for US forces), should have a supersonic, aerial-experiential view of the world.

Added to the above, there is the paradoxical move of demilitarizing the military's "militaryness" even as the military militarizes areas that were previously the preserve of civilian agencies (such as foreign aid and diplomacy). The additional paradox is that of the Pentagon pretending to produce depoliticized records of what is a political process of intervention and global dominance, while failing to serve the public by being fully accountable to it and showing the full range of truths of US military action abroad.

Yet, there may be a disquieting reality that is faithfully represented by at least some of these photographs. Even if we were to be uncharitable, and assert that only one per-

cent of what is shown about peoples around the world col-
laborating with US forces, and enjoying if not welcoming
their presence, is true, then that should give us some
pause. If many individuals and sectors of diverse societies
around the world are only glad to receive, participate and
interact with US military forces, then it should also rede-
fine what is understood by anti-imperialist praxis — that it
too, like imperialism, starts at home, and it starts with us.

Notes

1   The US Department of Defense's Flickr "photostream" is ac-
     cessible at
     https://www.flickr.com/photos/39955793@N07/. The re-
     view of photographs on which this chapter is based was
     concluded on February 18, 2014. Periodic subsequent visits
     were designed to take further samples of images on themes
     already covered in this chapter.
2   The State Department distinguishes between "public affairs"
     and "public diplomacy". "Public affairs" refers to communi-
     cation with a domestic, US audience. "Public diplomacy" in-
     volves communicating to foreign audiences (White House,
     2009, p. 7).
3   Information Operations have more to do with communica-
     tion during combat, and can involve military deception, elec-
     tronic warfare, and psychological operations. They are very
     much related to "strategic communication," but this chap-
     ter's focus is on the more ostensibly "benign" modes of mili-
     tary media activity that are practiced on an everyday basis
     and involve mostly civilian audiences worldwide.
4   Between the State Department, Pentagon, and intelligence
     apparatus, there has been a growing proliferation of pro-
     grams, concepts and terms relating to spreading information
     designed to (win) support for US foreign policy, that even
     attempts at charts tend to look like spaghetti, an almost in-
     comprehensible nesting of loops and circles (see for example
     JFC, 2010, pp. II-4, II-7).
5   Photography was invented at roughly the same time as
     Euro-American Anthropology began to take a more formal
     shape, and at the same time as a new phase of western colo-
     nial expansion was underway. It is interesting to see a simi-

lar set of convergences at work in the Pentagon's attraction to visual media today, reproducing many of the same flawed and now outmoded assumptions.

6   The website for USAID's Office of US Foreign Disaster Assistance can be accessed at http://www.usaid.gov/who-we-are/organization/bureaus/bureau-democracy-conflict-and-humanitarian-assistance/office-us. A DART is simply a rapid deployment team available for disaster recovery.

References

Argueta, M. (1991 [1980]). *One Day of Life*. New York, NY: Vintage Books.

Banks, M. (2001). *Visual Methods in Social Research*. London, UK: Sage.

Borg, L. J. (2008). Communicating with Intent: The Department of Defense and Strategic Communication. Cambridge, MA: Program on Information Resources Policy, Center for Information Policy Research, Harvard University. http://pirp.harvard.edu/pubs_pdf/borg/borg-i08-1.pdf

Bourdieu, P. (1991). Towards a Sociology of Photography. *Visual Anthropology Review*, 7(1), 129–133.

————. (1999). The Social Definition of Photography. In J. Evans & S. Hall (Eds.), *Visual Culture: The Reader* (pp. 162–180). London, UK: Sage.

Bourdieu, P., with Boltanski, L.; Castel, R.; Chamboredon, J-C; & Schnapper, D. (1990). *Photography: A Middle-Brow Art*. Cambridge, UK: Polity Press.

MacDougall, D. (1997). The Visual in Anthropology. In M. Banks & H. Morphy (Eds.), *Rethinking Visual Anthropology* (pp. 276–194). New Haven, CT: Yale University Press.

Mooers, C. (2006). Introduction: The New Watchdogs. In C. Mooers (Ed.), *The New Imperialists: Ideologies of Empire* (pp. 1–8). Oxford, UK: Oneworld Publications.

Ortner, S. B. (1973). On Key Symbols. *American Anthropologist*, 75(5), 1338–1346.

Pas, N. (2013). The Masculine Empire: A Gendered Analysis of Modern American Imperialism. In M. C. Forte (Ed.), *Emergency as Security: Liberal Empire at Home and Abroad* (pp. 43–71). Montreal, QC: Alert Press.

Pink, S. (2001). *Doing Visual Ethnography: Images, Media and Representation in Research*. London, UK: Sage.

Ruby, J. (1995). *Secure the Shadow: Death and Photography in America*. Cambridge, MA: MIT Press.

Scales, Jr., R. H. (2004). Culture-Centric Warfare. *U.S. Naval Institute Proceedings*, (130)10, 32–36.

Sontag, S. (2005 [1973]). *On Photography*. New York, NY: Rosetta Books.

US Army. (2009a). *FM 6-02.40, Visual Information Operations*. Washington, DC: Headquarters, Department of the Army.
https://ia600801.us.archive.org/11/items/ost-military-doctrine-fm6_02x40/fm6_02x40.pdf

————— . (2009b). Social Media Best Practices (Tactics, Techniques, Procedures). US Army: Online and Social Media Division.
http://web.archive.org/web/20110813093603/http://www.au.af.mil/pace/documents/army_soc_media_best_practices_jun09.pdf

————— . (2010a). Flickr Strategy. Office of the Chief of Public Affairs Online and Social Media Division.
http://www.slideshare.net/USArmySocialMedia/us-army-flickr-strategy

————— . (2010b). Army Social Media: Optimizing Online Engagement.
http://www.slideshare.net/USArmySocialMedia/2010-army-social-media-book

————— . (2012). U.S. Army Social Media Strategy, February 4-10, 2012.
http://openanthropology.files.wordpress.com/2014/05/social_media_strategy4-10feb2012.pdf

US Department of Defense (DoD). (2004). Department of Defense Directive Number 5160.48, July 2—DoD Public Affairs and Visual Information (PA&VI) Education and Training (E&T). Washington, DC: Department of Defense.
http://webcache.googleusercontent.com/search?q=cache:gB-4CiuEvVQJ:www.au.af.mil/pace/epubs/516048p.pdf+&cd=1&hl=en&ct=clnk&gl=ca

————— . (2006a). Department of Defense Directive Number O-3600.01, August 14—Information Operations (IO). Washington, DC: Department of Defense.
https://www.fas.org/irp/doddir/dod/info_ops.pdf

————— . (2006b). QDR Execution Roadmap for Strategic Communication. Washington, DC: Office of the Under Secretary of Defense.
http://www.defense.gov/pubs/pdfs/QDRRoadmap20060925a.pdf

————— . (2007a). Department of Defense Directive Number 5105.74, December 18—Defense Media Activity (DMA). Washington, DC: Department of Defense.
http://www.dtic.mil/whs/directives/corres/pdf/510574p.pdf

————— . (2007b). Policy for Department of Defense (DoD) Interactive Internet Activities, June 8. Washington, DC: Office of the Deputy Secretary, Department of Defense.
https://www.fas.org/sgp/othergov/dod/dod060807.pdf

————— . (2008). Department of Defense Instruction Number 5400.13, October 15 – Public Affairs (PA) Operations. Washington, DC: Department of Defense.
http://www.dtic.mil/whs/directives/corres/pdf/540013p.pdf

————— . (2009). Department of Defense Report on Strategic Communication. Washington, DC: Office of the Secretary of Defense.
http://www.au.af.mil/au/awc/awcgate/dod/dod_report_strategic_com munication_11feb10.pdf

————— . (2010a). Department of Defense Dictionary of Military and Associated Terms (as amended through 15 March 2014). Washington, DC: Department of Defense.
http://www.dtic.mil/doctrine/new_pubs/jp1_02.pdf

————— . (2010b). Directive-Type Memorandum (DTM) 09-026 – Responsible and Effective Use of Internet-based Capabilities. Washington, DC: Office of the Deputy Secretary, Department of Defense.
http://www.defense.gov/news/dtm%2009-026.pdf

————— . (2010c). Getting Started with Flickr. [PowerPoint presentation].
http://www.slideshare.net/DepartmentofDefense/getting-started-with-flickr-4746458

————— . (2010d). Quadrennial Defense Review Report. Washington, DC: Department of Defense.
http://www.defense.gov/qdr/qdr%20as%20of%2029jan10%201600.pdf

————— . (2011). Joint Operation Planning (Joint Publication 5-0). Washington, DC: Joint Chiefs of Staff, Department of Defense.
http://www.dtic.mil/doctrine/new_pubs/jp5_0.pdf

————— . (2012). Peace Operations (Joint Publication 3-07.3). Washington, DC: Joint Chiefs of Staff, Department of Defense.
https://www.fas.org/irp/doddir/dod/jp3-07-3.pdf

US Department of State (DoS). (2007). U.S. National Strategy for Public Diplomacy and Strategic Communication. Washington, DC: Under Secretary for Public Diplomacy and Public Affairs.
http://www.nyu.edu/brademas/pdf/publications-moving-forward-strategic-communication-public-diplomacy.pdf

US Government Accountability Office (GAO). (2012). DOD Strategic Communication: Integrating Foreign Audience Percep-

tions into Policy Making, Plans, and Operations. Washington, DC: United States Government Accountability Office.
http://gao.gov/assets/600/591123.pdf

US Joint Forces Command (JFC). (2010). Commander's Handbook for Strategic Communication and Communication Strategy (Version 3.0). Washington, DC: US Joint Forces Command Joint Warfighting Center.
http://www.dtic.mil/doctrine/doctrine/jwfc/sc_hbk10.pdf

White House. (2009). National Framework for Strategic Communication. Washington, DC: The White House.
https://www.fas.org/man/eprint/pubdip.pdf

Wright, T. (1999). *The Photography Handbook*. London, UK: Routledge.

CONTRIBUTORS

Tristan Biehn is working toward her Honours in Anthropology at Concordia University in Montreal. She hails from St. John's, Newfoundland, yet has spent almost half of her life in the US, primarily in Pennsylvania. Her current research focuses on the infrastructure(s) and interactions of native land claims, the Canadian government, and mining interests. She has also studied erotic agency among the performers of Montreal's burlesque community.

Keir Forgie holds a BSc Hons Neuroscience degree from Dalhousie University in Halifax, and is enrolled in a BA Hons Anthropology at Concordia University in Montreal. He is originally from Regina, Saskatchewan. His primary research and study interests have been in the areas of neural plasticity, synaptogenesis, neuropathic pain following spinal cord injury, global health, and the global obesity epidemic. In September, he will begin his first semester of medical school at Dalhousie University, class of 2018.

Maximilian C. Forte is the director of the New Imperialism seminar from which this volume emerged. He is a professor in the Department of Sociology and Anthropology at Concordia University in Montreal. His research focuses on "humanitarian" imperialism, the corporatization and militarization of academia, neoliberalism and plural understandings of democracy. He also teaches courses in Political Anthropology, Indigenous Resurgence, Globalization, and on imperialism in the history of Anthropology.

Mathieu Guerin is completing a BA Honours in Anthropology at Concordia University in Montreal. While originally from Québec City, Mathieu grew up and spent most of his life in Calgary, Alberta. His primary research and study interests have been in the areas of science and technology studies, posthumanism, and Political Anthropology.

Hilary King is graduating from Concordia University with a BA Major in Sociology and a Minor in Women's Studies. She is originally from Vancouver, BC. Her primary research and study interests have been in the areas of homonormativity, whiteness, and Canadian settler colonialism.

John Manicom is specializing in Anthropology with a minor in Mandarin Chinese at Concordia University in Montréal. He is originally from Gatineau, Québec. His primary research and study interests have been in the areas of youth homelessness, gender and sexuality, and the dynamics of power.

Karine Perron is graduating with a BA Specialization in Anthropology and Minor in Sociology at Concordia University in Montreal. She is originally from Drummondville, Quebec. Her primary research and study interests have been in the areas of political and economic anthropology, media studies, and social movements.

Laura Powell is completing her BA in Anthropology at Concordia University in Montreal, with a minor in Canadian Irish Studies. She is originally from Sainte-Agathe-de-Lotbinière, Quebec. Her study interests have been in the areas of Irish studies, and armed conflicts.

Émile St-Pierre is completing a BA Honours in Anthropology at Concordia University in Montreal. He has an interest in medical anthropology, and more specifically in the use and circulation of pharmaceuticals as well as biomedical knowledge and technologies.

INDEX

www.ingramcontent.com/pod-product-compliance
Lightning Source LLC
Chambersburg PA
CBHW031217290326
41931CB00034B/182